FROM THE APPLE ORCHARD TO KAPYONG

3 RAR IN KOREA, SEPTEMBER 1950 – APRIL 1951

AUSTRALIAN ARMY CAMPAIGN SERIES / 34

FROM THE APPLE ORCHARD TO KAPYONG

3 RAR IN KOREA, SEPTEMBER 1950 – APRIL 1951

Hardie Grant
CUSTOM

BOB BREEN

Published in 2026 by Hardie Grant Custom, an imprint of Hardie Grant Publishing, on behalf of the Australian Army History Unit.

Hardie Grant Custom (Melbourne)
Level 11, 36 Wellington Street
Collingwood VIC 3066, Australia
www.hardiegrant.com.au

Hardie Grant acknowledges the Traditional Owners of the Country on which we work, the Wurundjeri People of the Kulin Nation and the Gadigal People of the Eora Nation, and recognises their continuing connection to the land, waters and culture. We pay our respects to their Elders past and present.

A catalogue record for this book is available from the National Library of Australia

From the Apple Orchard to Kapyong: 3 RAR in Korea, September 1950 – April 1951
ISBN 9781761452956
Publishing Director: Courtney Nichols
Project Editor: Shahirah Hambali
Series Editor: Garth Pratten
Editor: Courtney Page-Allen
Art Director: Dallas Budde
Cover Design: Blue Cork
Typesetter: Patrick Cannon
Cartographer: Catherine McCulloch
Printed in Malaysia by 1010 Printing Asia Limited

SERIES EDITOR FOREWORD

From the Apple Orchard to Kapyong is the 34th title published in the Australian Army Campaign Series. Commencing in 2006 and spanning over a century of Australian Army operations, the Campaign Series is one of the most sustained endeavours in Australian military history publishing. It is also the third series of books produced by the Australian Army specifically for the purposes of professional military education.

The Army's first professional education series consisted of six volumes written by Colonel Eustace Keogh between 1954 and 1965 to assist officers preparing for the military history examinations that were then required for promotion. The second series was instigated in 1990 by then Chief of the General Staff, Lieutenant General John Coates, as the basis of an Army-wide history education program for Army officers; four volumes were published by Training Command between 1991 and 1995. The current Campaign Series similarly resulted from an initiative by the Strategic Advisory Group to the Chief of Army, Lieutenant General Peter Leahy, to promote an understanding of military history among the Army's future generation of commissioned and non-commissioned leaders. These three series are united not only by a recognition of the value of the study of history to the military profession but by the imperative to provide clear, concise accounts of the Australian Army's operations accompanied by a wealth of supporting illustrations, organisational charts and maps.

The Campaign Series does not seek to derive explicit lessons from history but rather to explore the factors shaping the outcomes of military operations: tactics, techniques and procedures, weapons and other technology, logistics, command and leadership. History does not repeat but it does rhyme. As Paul K Van Riper, one-time Commander of the US Marine Corps Combat Development Command, observed, 'The vicarious experiences provided through study of the past enable practioners of war to see familiar patterns of activity and to develop more quickly potential solutions to tactical and operational problems'. Context is critical to forming judgments – there are no single factor explanations. The Campaign Series thus also encompasses the political aims, national strategy and campaign objectives of the operations it examines alongside the characteristics of the operational environment.

Unlike a lot of Australian military history, the Campaign Series does not beat a nationalist drum. As Keogh once noted, 'our history is full of great military myths, most of which we thoughtlessly accept at their face value'. If we reduce history to a set of shallow cliches we deny ourselves both an insight into the true complexity of war and military operations, and the chance to profit from that experience. The Campaign Series questions decisions, outcomes and established narratives, and embraces the perspectives of allies and adversaries alike.

Above all, the Campaign Series is grounded in the human experience of war. As Keogh observed, 'the basic material which the soldier uses in ... [their] ... profession is human nature – men and women. They must know how people react to the stresses of war, and how they react to danger and adversity, to triumph and disaster'.

Although intended for a military readership, the accessible style and attractive presentation of the Campaign Series has made it popular with a more general readership. I am delighted the partnership between the Australian Army History Unit and Hardie Grant is enabling the Campaign Series to continue to educate Australia's soldiers and encourage a more sophisticated understanding of the Army's history in the wider community.

Associate Professor Garth Pratten SFHEA FRHistS
Series Editor

CONTENTS

MAPS

Location and geographical feature names used in this book are contemporary common/local usage in 1951. Modern names may vary from the names used here.

FIGURES

MAP SYMBOLOGY LEGEND

MILITARY

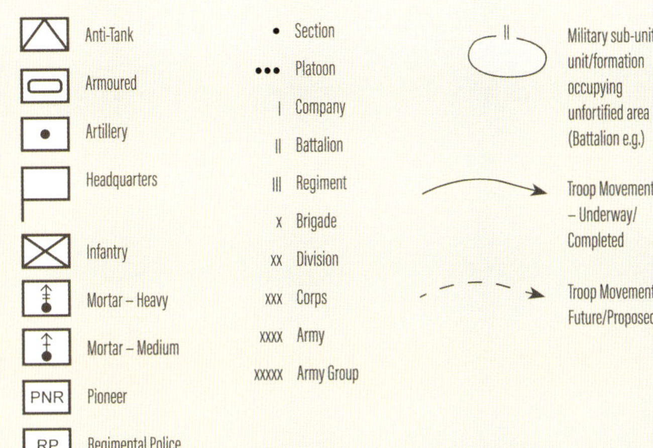

CIVILIAN

Note on map colours: Contour colours represent terrain, not necessarily specific heights.

PREFACE

IN JUNE 1950, the Australian Army was just under three years old and comprised three infantry battalions: the 1st, 2nd and 3rd Battalions of the Royal Australian Regiment (1 RAR, 2 RAR and 3 RAR). That month in North Asia, the communist Democratic People's Republic of Korea (North Korea) invaded its US-backed southern neighbour, the Republic of Korea (South Korea). The war between the two Koreas pitted a 22-nation United Nations (UN) force against North Korea and its allies: China and the Soviet Union. For the newest incarnation of the Australian Army, Korea was the first test.

Once again, Australia was sending soldiers into battle on foreign soil – this time to support the US-led Western alliance against communism during the Cold War and uphold the fledgling United Nations Charter. Australia's involvement was also a practical example of alliance politics. The negotiations that ultimately led to the establishment of the Australia, New Zealand, United States (ANZUS) Treaty, committing the signatories to mutual defence if any one of them was attacked, were in progress when the Korean War began. The Korean War renewed collaboration between Australian and British allies when 3 RAR joined two British battalions to form the 27th British Commonwealth Brigade (27 BCB).

The Army's participation in the Korean War included several remarkable unit actions. In 1950–51, 3 RAR excelled during both offensive and defensive operations. At Kapyong in April 1951, the battalion executed an exemplary rapid defensive manoeuvre, which, along with other Korean War battles, was pivotal in shaping the Army, particularly the Royal Australian Regiment. Korean War veterans influenced the Army's ethos and training practices, serving as role models for leadership, and personal and professional behaviour, during the Regiment's involvement in the Malayan Emergency, the Indonesian Confrontation and the Vietnam War. Several subalterns who served in Korea with 3 RAR went on to command battalions in Vietnam and achieved general officer rank in the 1980s. Although different wartime experiences moulded them in a different era, the individual and collective behaviour of those who fought in Korea, especially from September 1950 and at Kapyong in April 1951, should inform the contemporary Army.

Kapyong represented a moment of great peril for the UN forces involved. On the evening of 23 April 1951, Chinese formations advancing along the Kapyong Valley at the spearhead of an offensive aimed at South Korea's capital, Seoul, forced a Republic of Korea (ROK) infantry division into a chaotic southwards retreat. Thousands of South Korean soldiers and panic-stricken refugees streamed past 3 RAR's blocking positions, as well as those of the 2nd Battalion, Princess Patricia's Canadian Light Infantry (2 PPCLI). The US 72nd Heavy Tank Battalion's A Company, situated on the valley floor adjacent to and forward of the Australian positions, was also caught in the chaos. The 16th Field Regiment, Royal New Zealand Artillery, had to 'leapfrog' its 25-pounder field gun batteries amidst the withdrawal to resume and then maintain support to 27 BCB. The Australians, Canadians, New Zealanders and Americans were ordered to deny advancing Chinese formations a route down the valley for as long as possible – a task that required immense bravery and resilience.

In answering the question 'Why Kapyong in April 1951?', I will consider the battle's context and how events and decisions made in the preceding months shaped the fighting and its outcome. Within that broader context, I look at the more challenging and significant question: 'Who fought at Kapyong, and how and why did they fight the way they did?' This book begins with 3 RAR's time on garrison duties in Japan in 1950, and its hasty reinforcement and deployment to Korea that September. It follows the battalion's spirited northward advance and subsequent withdrawal, the debacle at Pakchon in November, and several other operations in the lead-up to April 1951.

Including the battles of Pakchon and Kapyong in a single volume acknowledges Pakchon – a largely forgotten battle with only a page in the Official History. Pakchon was an unintended, chaotic rehearsal for Kapyong. The Australians, who conducted a frontal attack, followed by a hasty defence and premature withdrawal, at Pakchon, knew the price to be paid if orders were unclear and withdrawal was not supported by artillery fire. It was not executed with well-practised drills and tight coordination.

While Australian, Canadian, US, New Zealand and British forces were engaged at Kapyong on 25 April 1951, another battle was being fought forty kilometres to the west on the Imjin River. To demonstrate how things can go wrong, as well as how challenges can be met, I have also included the defeat of the 1st Battalion, the Gloucestershire Regiment (hereafter referred to as the Glosters), at the Imjin River. Their fate highlights the risks of deploying battalions forward in isolated locations. The Battle of the Imjin River demonstrated the cost when a defensive layout is dispersed, high ground is conceded early, supply lines are cut and reinforcements are cancelled.

The lessons from the Pakchon and Imjin debacles, as well as the Kapyong triumph, are not merely historical anecdotes. They are relevant to today's Australian Army and its future, particularly in the event of a short-notice overseas deployment to conduct combat operations under foreign command against a near-peer opponent, or even the less dangerous but often more complicated and politically sensitive overseas campaigns associated with armed peace support operations.

The actions of those who fought at Kapyong in April 1951 are worthy of commemoration, reflection and emulation. I have included recollections from Australian Korean War veterans, most of whom fought at Kapyong, and draw on interviews which I recorded in the early 1990s with a cross-section of veterans. I also consulted writer Kit Denton's and veteran Jack Gallaway's interviews and correspondence with veterans, as well as interviews conducted by Dennis Smith for the documentary *Heroes of the Forgotten War: The Battle of Kapyong*. At times, I infer, based on the available evidence, the thinking that influenced commanders' and their subordinates' decisions and actions.

This book builds on my 1992 account of Kapyong. My challenge was, as it remains nearly thirty-three years later in 2025, that accounts of the battle differ, and in some instances, veterans disagree about what occurred. Animosities and personal and professional differences of opinion might also have coloured recollections. I have attempted to fill most of the knowledge gaps regarding the activities of key individuals during the battle. The resultant narrative, while it may still be ripe for controversy, is presented with the utmost care and attention to detail, aiming to provide the most accurate and impartial history possible to educate, commemorate, and inspire today's Australian Army.

Bob Breen
Woolgoolga, NSW
September 2025

ACKNOWLEDGEMENTS

CORRESPONDENCE, WRITINGS AND INTERVIEWS of veterans from the battles of Pakchon and Kapyong informed this volume of the Campaign Series. This legacy not only 'voiced' the narrative with recollections but also enabled me to compare eyewitness accounts in my quest for accuracy. In 1992, I received full access to as many veterans as circumstances allowed, though there were still gaps. I am indebted to those who have helped cover some of these omissions. These enhancements included books and accounts written by Ben O'Dowd, a key company commander during the battle; and 3 RAR veteran Jack Gallaway, who was not at the battle; as well as chapters for 'Fight Leaders', written by Alf Argent, 3 RAR's Intelligence Officer and a key participant at Kapyong; and David Butler, a 3 RAR veteran in 1950. A draft manuscript by CO 3 RAR at Kapyong, Lieutenant Colonel Ian 'Bruce' Ferguson, passed on to me by Kit Denton, provided insight into his rationalisation of events and decisions.

Jack Gallaway, the 3 RAR Signals Sergeant in 1950–51, granted me access to all his research material when he and I donated documents and interview recordings to the 3 RAR Museum in 1992. I am grateful to Bob Bakkers and Bob Dabinett, a former RSM of the Army, both volunteers at the 3 RAR Museum, who assisted me with accessing all these records and other material on Kapyong Day and Anzac Day 2021. Over the years, an increasing number of veterans have contributed their recollections to the Australian War Memorial and the Australians at War Film Archive. I am grateful to them all for filling in the gaps and enabling a more thorough analysis.

The team at the Australian Army History Unit, led by Head Tim Gellel, Series Editor Associate Professor Garth Pratten, historian Dr Ian Hodges, Publications Manager Dr Jason Smeaton and researcher Bruce Ferguson, has bolstered my efforts with their professional advice and careful editing. The Australian War Memorial provided photographs, and Catherine McCulloch was responsible for the maps. I accept full responsibility for the content and opinions expressed, acknowledging that my interpretations do not necessarily reflect the views of the Australian Army or the Army History Unit.

ABBREVIATIONS

1 MX	1st Battalion, the Middlesex Regiment
1 RAR	1st Battalion, the Royal Australian Regiment
2IC	Second in Command
2 RAR	2nd Battalion, the Royal Australian Regiment
3 RAR	3rd Battalion, the Royal Australian Regiment
2 PPCLI	2nd Battalion, Princess Patricia's Canadian Light Infantry
27 BCB	27th British Commonwealth Brigade
29 BCB	29th British Commonwealth Brigade
AIF	Australian Imperial Force
ANZUS	Australia, New Zealand, United States security treaty
BCB	British Commonwealth Brigade
BCOF	British Commonwealth Occupation Force
BHQ	Battalion Headquarters
CAPT	Captain
CGS	Chief of the General Staff [later Chief of Army]
CHQ	Company Headquarters
CMF	Citizen Military Forces
Coy	company
CO	Commanding Officer
CSM	Company Sergeant Major
DCM	Distinguished Conduct Medal
DMA	Director of Military Art
DSO	Distinguished Service Order
GSO	General Service Officer
HMAS	Her Majesty's Australian Ship (until September 2022)
HE	High explosive
HQ	Headquarters
IO	Intelligence Officer

K Force	Korea Force
KIA	Killed in Action
LT	Lieutenant
LTCOL	Lieutenant Colonel
MBE	Member of the British Empire
MC	Military Cross
MM	Military Medal
MMG	Medium Machine Gun
MX	Middlesex
NCO	Non-Commissioned Officer
NSW	New South Wales
OC	Officer Commanding
O Group	Orders Group
Pl	platoon
POW	Prisoner of War
RAAF	Royal Australian Air Force
RAR	Royal Australian Regiment
RMC	Royal Military College
RMO	Regimental Medical Officer
RNZA	Royal New Zealand Artillery
ROK	Republic of Korea
SAS	Special Air Service
SP	Self-Propelled
UN	United Nations
US	United States
WIA	Wounded in Action
WO2	Warrant Officer Class Two

CHAPTER 1

ORIGINS OF A FIGHTING INFANTRY BATTALION

IT IS ESSENTIAL TO set the scene for the battle of Kapyong with 3 RAR's back story. Of particular importance are the events leading up to the battalion's short-notice deployment, from garrison duties in the post-Second World War British Commonwealth Occupation Force (BCOF) in Japan, to combat operations on the Korean Peninsula. The central contemporary lesson from 3 RAR's deployment experience is that the Army must maintain units at high readiness lest sudden strategic developments prompt the government to deploy land forces overseas at short notice. Those units, especially when put under time pressures, require external support for their pre-deployment preparations, including reinforcement, administrative tasks, mission rehearsals and addressing any deficiencies in weapons, equipment and stores.

At the end of the Second World War, the need for Allied troops to occupy Japan created the impetus to form a regular Australian Army infantry force.[1] The Government had already begun demobilising its military forces and was raising a smaller volunteer force to form Australia's Interim Army. On 21 August 1945, Australia's Minister for the Army announced that volunteers for the occupation of Japan would be sought from formations dispersed throughout the South West Pacific theatre. They were formed into the three battalions of a newly designated 34th Infantry Brigade. The 7th Division, based at Balikpapan, provided personnel for the 65th Australian Infantry Battalion. The 66th Battalion swelled with volunteers from the 9th Division (North Borneo and Tarakan) and Australian Corps troops, and the 67th Battalion comprised men from the 3rd (Bougainville), 6th (Wewak) and 11th (Rabaul) Divisions.[2] The average age of officers was 26, and that of other ranks was 23; they had an average of three years and five months of war service. Only 3 per cent were married. The battalions thus comprised young, highly motivated, seasoned troops. Though many had enlisted voluntarily 'for the duration', they differed little from experienced 'regulars'.[3] The 34th Brigade assembled on the island of Morotai in the Netherlands East Indies for training. Its members signed up for at least twelve months and sailed for Japan in February 1946.[4]

There were two proposals for naming the 34th Brigade battalions. They reflected the Army's fondness for its British connections. In anticipation of a Royal visit in 1949, the fledgling Directorate of Infantry proposed that the 65th Battalion become the 1st Battalion, King George VI's Australian Rifle Regiment; the 66th Battalion become the 1st Battalion, Queen Elizabeth's Australian Footguards; and the 67th Battalion become the 1st Battalion, Princess Margaret's Australian Infantry Regiment. In 1948, another proposal designated the 65th Battalion, the 1st Battalion, City of Sydney's Own Regiment; the 66th Battalion, the 1st Battalion, Royal Melbourne Regiment; and the 67th Battalion, the 1st Infantry Battalion, the Oxley Regiment.[5]

On 23 November 1948, the Federal Government permitted the brigade's battalions to be designated the 1st (formerly the 65th), 2nd (previously the 66th) and 3rd (formerly the 67th) Battalions, and renamed the brigade the Australian Regiment. Four months later, His Majesty King George VI granted the title 'Royal', creating the Royal Australian Regiment. Aside from the British Crown at the top, the RAR badge reflected Australian fauna, flora and First Nations heritage. It featured the kangaroo and a wattle wreath, supported by a boomerang inscribed with the title 'Royal Australian Regiment', and a banner with the motto 'Duty First'.

Concurrent with the establishment of the RAR, the government decided to withdraw two infantry battalions from the British Commonwealth Occupation Force (BCOF) that had been deployed to Japan in 1946. 1 RAR and 2 RAR sailed for Australia at the end of 1948, leaving 3 RAR to maintain Australia's BCOF representation.[6]

By May 1950, 3 RAR was under-strength, having been in Japan for several years. The irregular arrival of officers and NCOs into key roles, along with the departure of those who had 'done their time', made the battalion's rebuilding and training that year quite challenging. The battalion consisted of inexperienced soldiers and young officers, and recent Duntroon graduates from the classes of 1947 and 1948, supported by a core of experienced Second World War veterans.[7]

Alf Argent, 3 RAR's Intelligence Officer, remembered that in mid-1950, battalion life comprised guard duty in Tokyo, on the Kure docks or at some BCOF buildings. In the warmer months, companies rotated through a training camp at Hara-mura without ever getting much beyond platoon exercises. Argent also thought morale was surprisingly high considering the battalion's short history and high turnover of personnel. Newcomers, he said, accepted this camaraderie as the normal thing.[8] Over the coming months, though, rivalries within the battalion between veterans and newcomers became more pronounced.

On 11 June 1950, the Australian Government announced that 3 RAR would leave Japan at the end of the year. Preparations began immediately. Australian BCOF units repatriated personnel, spare parts and equipment.[9] The battalion's members looked forward to occupying the battalion's first Australian home in the newly completed Enoggera Barracks in Brisbane.[10] Many experienced officers, NCOs and soldiers returned to Australia to prepare for the battalion's arrival. There would be no reinforcement from Australia before the remainder of 3 RAR embarked. Two weeks after re-deployment preparations began, the Korean War broke out. Official Historian Robert O'Neill wrote, '... nothing could have been more remote from the minds of Australian servicemen in Japan than that they would be involved in a major war'.[11]

A vast body of literature exists on the origins of the Korean War. For this book, suffice it to say that the communist North Korean government aimed to reunify the divided Korean Peninsula under communist rule by force. When North Korea's Korean People's Army units crossed the 38th parallel – the border between North and South Korea – into South Korea on 25 June 1950, the United States pressed the United Nations (UN) to intervene. Urging a ceasefire, the UN called upon member nations to assist South Korea.

Seventy-two hours after launching their invasion, the North Koreans captured the southern capital, Seoul, and continued their southward march. The rapid North Korean advance and South Korean collapse prompted the United States, with UN backing, to enter the war in force.[12] United States naval vessels and aircraft were committed within a week. In early July 1950, as North Korean forces continued their southward advance, US Marines began landing on the Korean Peninsula's southern tip.[13]

The United States and its allies were mobilised under Chapter 7 of the UN Charter to preserve South Korea's territorial integrity. Still, the defence of South Korea also put the commitment and effectiveness of the newly established United Nations to the test. The Korean Peninsula was the first significant Cold War battleground in a contest of ideologies, political systems and military might. Robert O'Neill's Official History analysed the Australian Government's immediate and reflexive decision to commit Australian forces to the UN intervention.[14] Australian Prime Minister Robert Menzies, persuaded by Deputy Prime Minister Arthur Fadden, Foreign Minister Richard Casey and members of his Cabinet, was quick to commit the Mustangs of No. 77 Squadron, RAAF, located in Japan, and the frigate HMAS *Shoalhaven* and destroyer HMAS *Bataan*, already in North Asian waters. Within a week, No. 77 Squadron was operating with allied aircraft in Korean airspace, and Australian naval vessels were patrolling Korean waters with British and US ships.[15]

Any further Australian military commitments would be more complex, amidst negotiations between Australia, Britain and the United States over Cold War security arrangements. British and Australian Commonwealth defence planning had not envisaged deploying significant land forces to the Korean Peninsula. While the government considered its commitment to Korea, other significant issues continued to occupy senior political and military figures. Australia was concluding a peace treaty with Japan, considering the possibility of committing forces to the Middle East, confronting a rise in insurgencies in Southeast Asia and negotiating over what would become the ANZUS Treaty. At the same time, Australia's armed forces were grappling with a lack of manpower and equipment, limiting the Army's ability to rapidly deploy combat forces.[16] United States pressure for its allies to commit ground forces nevertheless increased in July.[17] For the Menzies Government, the dilemma was how to meet the expectations of its two major allies, Britain and the United States.[18]

Rumours that 3 RAR was deploying to Korea started soon after hostilities began in June, but in Japan, preparations for the redeployment to Enoggera continued throughout late June and July. On 4 July, Lieutenant General Sir Horace 'Red Robbie' Robertson, the Australian BCOF Commander-in-Chief, strenuously denied the rumours and media speculation.[19] On 11 July, 3 RAR's CO, Lieutenant Colonel Floyd 'Stan' Walsh, attended an HQ BCOF conference at Kure to discuss accommodation arrangements at Enoggera.[20]

Soldiers of C Company, 3 RAR, march to field exercises in Hara-mura, Japan, before embarkation for Korea, 10 August 1950. (PHOTOGRAPHER: PHILLIP HOBSON, AWM HOBJ1045)

Political expediency changed 3 RAR's destiny. Britain and New Zealand were about to commit ground troops to Korea. Seeking political and diplomatic advantage, the Acting Australian Prime Minister, Arthur Fadden, unexpectedly announced during an evening radio interview on 25 July that 3 RAR would deploy immediately to Korea under the command of US General Douglas MacArthur's UN forces. He wanted to be the first to announce it, ensuring the maximum political benefit for Australia in the United States amidst the ANZUS Treaty negotiations.[21] Fadden succeeded. A few hours after his sudden, opportune announcement, Britain and New Zealand announced their troop commitments.[22]

3 RAR was warned to prepare for active service on 26 July. Few in the battalion's ranks, nor the Australian public, could have known that it was being committed to war as much to meet the needs of Australian–US diplomacy as to defend South Korea.[23] At the time the announcement was made, 3 RAR comprised 20 officers and 530 soldiers. The challenge was to build it to a strength of 39 officers and 971 soldiers, raise a support company with mortars and heavy machine guns, and 'top-up' weapons, equipment and stocks from Australia.[24]

Coincidentally, Robert Menzies arrived in the United States the following day. He asked for, and received, permission to address a joint sitting of the Senate and the Congress on 1 August. Menzies spoke expansively about Australia's military contributions to, and diplomatic support for, the US position on the Korean Peninsula, promising that Australian troops would be deployed to Korea in a few weeks and suggesting that Australians, New Zealanders and British soldiers would eventually form a Commonwealth Division. Prompted by Menzies' fulsome support, albeit accompanied by a modest military contribution, President Truman awarded him the insignia of the Chief Commander of the Legion of Merit and promised his support for a $AUD 250 million World Bank loan to Australia.[25]

The rush to Korea

For the third time in less than four decades, Australia was assembling an expeditionary force for overseas deployment. 3 RAR was far from ready for war. Alf Argent remembered the expediency of the times: 'With the stroke of a pen, A Company was redesignated Support Company, a sub-unit we had all read about in the training pamphlets, but which many of us had not seen in khaki, as it were'. Training began to raise support weapons platoons armed with 3-inch mortars, Vickers heavy machine guns and anti-armour weapons.[26]

In Japan, 3 RAR relied on BCOF for preparation resources and a 'top-up' of weapons, equipment and stores. In Korea, 3 RAR would depend on the US supply chain for vehicles, ammunition, rations, water, additional weapons, communications equipment, and other essential items, such as winter clothing. While this level of Australian dependence on major allies was the norm in the 1950s, it left Australian troops vulnerable to the priorities of their allies for firepower, casualty evacuation and logistic support when these systems were under pressure.

Additional manpower for 3 RAR would have to come from Australia. Volunteers were sought from 1 RAR and 2 RAR. The government also launched a campaign to recruit 1,000 men with Second World War experience to serve in the Army for three years, including one year in Korea. These recruits became known as Korea, or simply 'K', Force and underwent training in Australia before sailing for Japan to join 3 RAR. Among the volunteers were men who had chafed at being too young to serve in the Second World War. Others enlisted to escape their civilian circumstances – perhaps creditors, a wife or girlfriend, or the law. Captain Don Beard, a 25-year-old Australian volunteer medical officer serving with BCOF and later with 3 RAR in 1950–51, described K Force as a 'motley crew'.[27]

Not everyone viewed the new force in quite this way. Captain Bernard 'Ben' O'Dowd, MBE, a 32-year-old ex-AIF officer commissioned from the ranks, appreciated the calibre of K Force reinforcements. He had been with 3 RAR since it was raised as the 67th Battalion in Morotai and observed that the veterans dispatched from Australia infused technical skills and combat experience into a soft, under-strength, inexperienced battalion. He said later that 87 per cent of his own company at Kapyong were ex-AIF men.

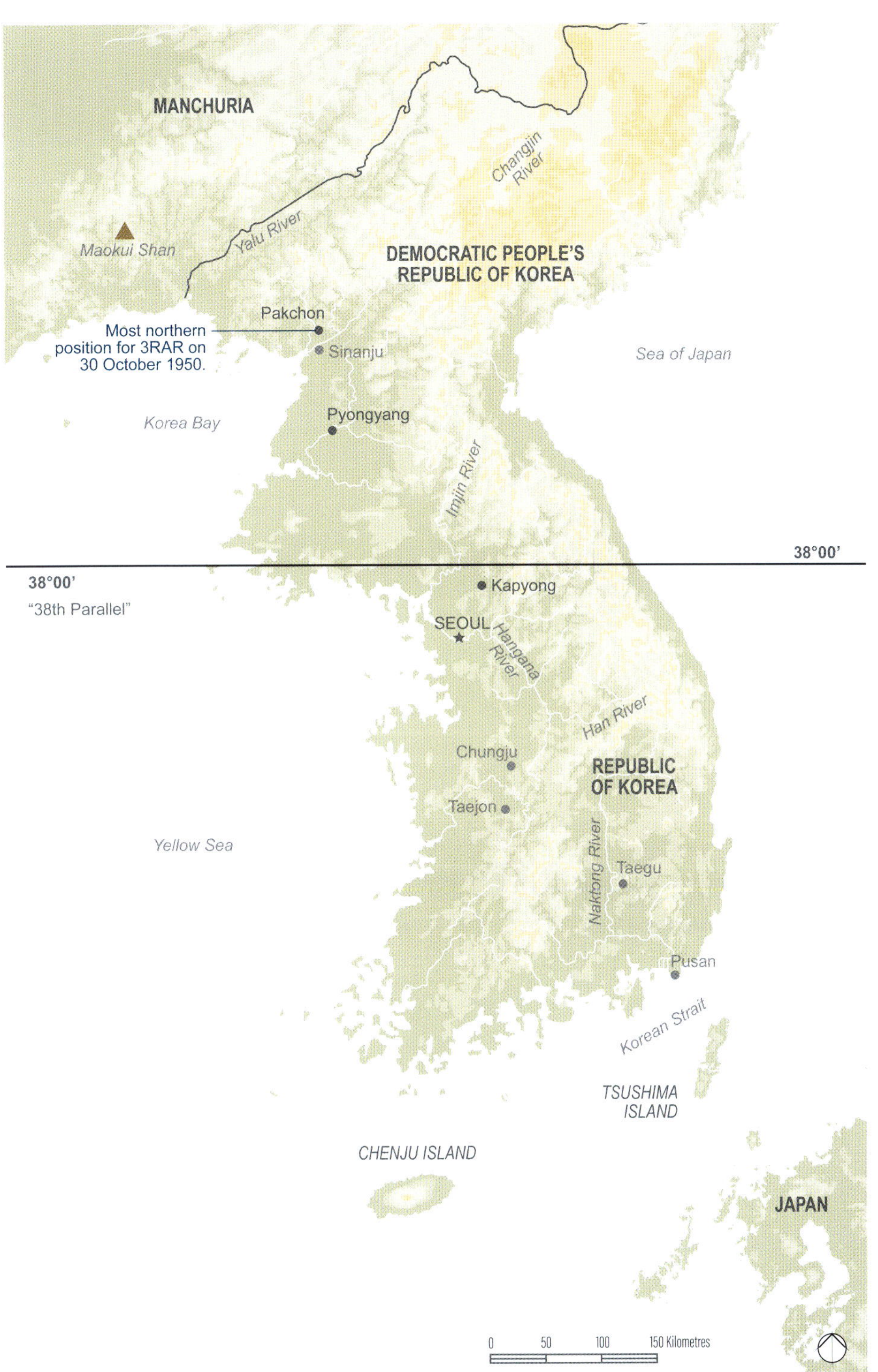

Map 1. The Korean Peninsula 1950–51

Members of the British Commonwealth Occupation Force (BCOF) in Japan sign on for operational service in Korea, 3 August 1950. (PHOTOGRAPHER: PHILLIP HOBSON, AWM HOBJ1038)

They had imbibed the AIF spirit and understood that survival depended on discipline in battle.[28] They enlisted for the hell of it but, having been there before, had no illusions about the consequences of battle. From experience, they understood that survival depended on that form of discipline peculiar to the AIF volunteer and so puzzling to British officers. They could be difficult at times in the rear areas but never lacking when the chips were down. In addition, based on a national characteristic of mateship, they easily developed the team spirit so essential under challenging situations.[29]

In August 1950, the situation in Korea was desperate for the hard-pressed UN forces then consolidating their positions at Pusan, on the peninsula's southern tip.[30] On the 22nd, Brigadier Roy King, BCOF's brigadier in charge of administration and commander of the Australian military component, ordered Walsh to have 3 RAR ready to move to Hiro in preparation for embarkation to Korea at first light on the 25th. Two days after King's order, on 24 August, Acting Prime Minister Fadden announced that 3 RAR would serve alongside two British battalions – the 1st Battalion, The Middlesex Regiment (hereafter referred to as the Middlesex); and the 1st Battalion, the Argyll and Sutherland Highlanders (hereafter referred to as the Argylls).[31] Both were under-strength, mainly comprising national servicemen accustomed more to ceremonial garrison duties than to combat operations. The Argylls and Middlesex had formed the British 27th Infantry Brigade. With the addition of 3 RAR, the formation was renamed the 27th British Commonwealth Brigade (27 BCB). It would later be joined by the 60th Indian Field Ambulance. 27 BCB became a light infantry brigade dependent on the US Army for firepower, communications and logistic support. The Americans would decide where and when it would deploy and set priorities for its support. Neither the British nor the Australian units had direct communications with deployed national headquarters or with their homelands.

As 3 RAR was in the process of moving, on 25 August, it learned that the Argylls and Middlesex had departed Hong Kong for Korea that day. Fadden had wanted the battalion to reach Korea before the British units, but senior army officers had prevailed. Neither Lieutenant General Sidney Rowell, the Chief of the General Staff in Australia, nor Horace Robertson in Japan wanted 3 RAR deployed before it was ready; equipped with essential weapons, stores and equipment; and refreshed in its training in infantry minor tactics and the use of mortars, medium machine guns, and small arms. On 26 August, the battalion was ordered to remain in Japan until it was at full strength. The brigade's British battalions were less fortunate. Although it deployed to Korea quickly and committed to patrolling immediately, they waited some time for their heavy equipment and stores to arrive.[32]

By 26 August, the required numbers for K Force recruits for service in Korea had been met. They joined members of 1 RAR and 2 RAR, who had also volunteered for service in Korea, for training at the battalion locations of 1 RAR and 2 RAR. K Force recruits from New South Wales and Queensland were attached to 1 RAR, based at Ingleburn near Sydney, for pre-deployment training. Recruits from the southern states of Victoria, South Australia and Western Australia reported to 2 RAR, based at Puckapunyal,[33] for similar

3 RAR recruits handle and learn about anti-tank 'bazooka' ammunition at a BCOF base camp in Japan, 1950.
(SLV: H2002.199/3960)

training and administrative preparation. 3 RAR received twenty-two officers and 450 men as reinforcements or replacements. These included four rifle company commanders, the acting officer commanding support company, a new regimental sergeant major and a new commanding officer.[34]

The influx of volunteers, many of whom were former warrant officers and non-commissioned officers, intensified existing rivalries between the groups of experienced and inexperienced soldiers in 3 RAR. One consequence of the arrival of K Force volunteers was that the newly formed A and D rifle companies consisted of experienced veterans who had offered themselves for service in Korea. In contrast, existing B and C companies primarily consisted of Interim Army garrison troops softened by service in Japan, as well as volunteers from 1 RAR and 2 RAR in Australia, eager for a change from peacetime soldiering. This mix would make a difference at Kapyong, where ex-AIF officers Ben O'Dowd and Norm Gravener commanded A and D Companies. If either had given ground under intense ground attack, 3 RAR's position would have cracked and been overrun.

Changing commanding officers

Shortly after the premature attempt to deploy 3 RAR to Korea, another decision unsettled the battalion. Senior officers at Army Headquarters in Melbourne assessed that Stan Walsh lacked the experience needed to command a battalion on operations in Korea. They resolved to find a more experienced officer with a proven record of commanding an Australian infantry battalion in combat. Rowell selected 30-year-old Lieutenant Colonel

The Regimental Sergeant Major of 3 RAR, Warrant Officer First Class William 'Bill' Harrison, addresses new reinforcements who have just joined the battalion from Australia, 1950. (PHOTOGRAPHER: ARTHUR GULLIVER, SLV H2002.199/3720)

Charles 'Charlie' Green, DSO, based on his stellar record of command during the last years of the Pacific War.[35] But Green was not his first choice. The stand-out Staff Corps infantry lieutenant colonels in the Army with combat experience at the time were Thomas 'Tom' Daly and Frank Hassett. In 1992, General Sir Thomas Daly wrote about how Green was selected ahead of him. In 1950, Daly was Director of Military Art and Commanding Officer of the Corps of Staff Cadets at the Royal Military College (RMC) in Duntroon. Duntroon's commandant would not release him without having an immediate replacement. Needing to act urgently, Rowell appointed Green instead. Daly wrote:

> *The Commandant, the then Major General Henry Wells, was requested by Army Headquarters to make me available to take command of 3 RAR, the reason being that as 3 RAR was the only unit representing Australia in an international theatre of operations, it was important that it was commanded by an officer who had already successfully commanded a battalion in action.*
>
> *General Wells – much to my chagrin – replied that with the end of the year and graduation approaching, it would not be in the best interests of the College for the Chief Instructor (DMA) to be released unless there was an immediate replacement. He nominated the then-LtCol Frank Hassett as acceptable. Hassett was then GSO 1 [Operations] for HQ Eastern Command under Lieutenant General Frank Berryman, who also expressed his unwillingness to release him.*
>
> *It should be remembered that the CGS [Chief of the General Staff], General Rowell, was having some difficulty with Generals Berryman and Robertson [Commander BCOF], two able and ambitious officers, so rather than continue a tiresome and time-consuming argument and since the appointment was a matter of urgency, the Military Secretary, Colonel Hurley, canvassed for another officer with the requisite qualifications. He came up with Charles Green, a student at the Staff College, whose removal to take command of 3 RAR would not ruffle any senior feathers. And so, the appointment was made. I cannot know whether I would have suffered the same fate as Green. I do know that I would not have led the battalion with the same – if any – distinction as he did.*[36]

Walsh discovered that he was being replaced when he was sitting in the 3 RAR Officers' Mess with his officers one evening, listening to Radio Australia. A news bulletin covered the Army Minister's announcement of a new CO for 3 RAR and reported Green's boarding a Japan-bound aircraft in Melbourne.[37] Walsh was rightly furious about his superiors' discourtesy and the embarrassment they caused him in front of his subordinates.[38] He was posted as a liaison officer to the US 8th Army Headquarters in Korea.[39]

Green was a good choice. In 1939, he was a farmer in Ulmarra, near Grafton, New South Wales. He had been in the militia since 1936, and after Menzies announced that Australia was at war, Green joined the 2/2nd Battalion. He was 20 years old. By 1945, he was a 25-year-old veteran of campaigns in the Middle East, Greece, Crete and Papua New Guinea. During the final battles of the South West Pacific campaign in late 1944 and 1945, he commanded the Western Australian 2/11th Battalion through several demanding operations.

On returning to Australia in 1946, Green decided, after spending three years farming, to make the army his career. He assumed command of 3 RAR on 10 September 1950, the day before Australia's last draft of reinforcements arrived in Japan. His leadership and example were desperately needed. Despite his rosy assessment of 3 RAR's morale in mid-1950, Alf Argent later said:

> *The basic material was there all right … but there was a distinct lack of cohesion, and the standard of sub-unit and unit training was poor. The parts did not fit well together … Yet in those difficult, tiring days, we wondered if we had absorbed the reinforcements and equipment [sic] or whether the reinforcements and equipment [sic] had swallowed us … the CO remained surprisingly calm and seemingly above all the turmoil.*[40]

On 27 September 1950, less than three weeks after Green assumed command, 3 RAR embarked for Korea. Private 'Snowy' Dicker remembered arriving at Pusan (now Busan) to a colourful, cheering crowd and bands. The Americans and South Koreans played their national anthems. The South Korean anthem, said Dicker, sounded like *The Road to Gundagai* and made everyone homesick. Green met the battalion, and it entrained for the 100km trip to Taegu (now Daegu) through what Dicker called 'some rather doubtful country'.

Members of 3 RAR take in the view of the Pusan harbour and lighthouse from the deck of the US troopship *Aiken Victory*, 28 September 1950. (PHOTOGRAPHER: PHILLIP HOBSON, AWM HOBJ1346)

Brigadier Basil Coad met the Australians at Taegu, and on 30 September 3 RAR became part of 27 BCB.[41] By this time, the British had nicknamed 27 BCB 'the Cinderella brigade' possibly because, like Cinderella, the brigade was impoverished and in a shabby condition compared to other 'sister' US brigades in its parent US Division. The Middlesex and Argylls comprised just 600 all ranks, lacked transport and heavy equipment, and had no organic artillery, relying instead on the Americans.[42]

By the time 27 BCB was hastily assembled and awaiting its first combat test, General Douglas MacArthur gambled with landings at Inchon behind the North Korean lines. This and the subsequent UN breakout north of Pusan broke the North Korean offensive. It was time to decide whether to respond to North Korea's invasion of South Korea with a 'counter-invasion' and pursue the North Korean army into its homeland, extinguishing the communist regime and re-unifying the Korean Peninsula, or stop at the 38th Parallel and return to the prewar status quo.

In October, strategic-level decisions in Washington and Beijing placed 3 RAR in danger. Historian Bruce Cumings wrote that restoring the prewar border went against America's strategic Cold War objectives. The United States wanted to force the communists north to the Chinese border along the Yalu River. Facing this threat to its ally, China's ruler, Mao Zedong, resolved to intervene.[43]

On 15 October 1950, US President Harry Truman flew to Wake Island to confer with General MacArthur, who assured Truman that there was 'very little chance of Chinese and Russian intervention in the war'. Meanwhile, a build-up of hundreds of thousands of Chinese troops across the Yalu River went unnoticed. On 17 October, MacArthur ordered a UN advance to the Yalu, unknowingly condemning his troops to face the might of the Chinese Army as it swept into North Korea.[44]

Four lessons for the contemporary Australian Army arise from the months following the North Korean invasion. The first is that sudden strategic events can lead to reflexive decisions by governments to deploy land forces with little or no notice. The Army must maintain forces at high levels of readiness for this contingency. The second lesson is that the Army needs to minimise high personnel turnover, particularly the churn of an annual posting cycle, and maximise the stability of tactical teams to sustain high-readiness forces. The third lesson is that high-readiness forces should not deploy until mission rehearsals have taken place and they are fully equipped for the coming operations. The fourth lesson is that if the Army allows its forces to be dependent on allied firepower and supply chains, the trade-off is vulnerability to allied priorities for firepower and resupply, including medical evacuation.

In 1950, 3 RAR benefited from the availability of seasoned veterans from Australia, as well as ex-AIF officers and other ranks serving in Japan. BCOF had sufficient stocks to 'top-up' the battalion, and the US military supply system backed them up in Korea. These exceptional personnel and materiel circumstances may not apply to future short-notice deployments.

CHAPTER 2

ADVANCE INTO NORTH KOREA AND THE BATTLE OF PAKCHON

THIS CHAPTER DISCUSSES 3 RAR OPERATIONS following the battalion's arrival north of Seoul. It gives a detailed account of the Battle of Pakchon, a debacle that influenced how the Australians fought at Kapyong six months later. At Pakchon, they experienced the chaos of a night-time withdrawal while in contact with the enemy. Company commanders exercised their initiative without effective command and control from Battalion Headquarters. The Battalion CO's removal from command demonstrated the consequences of ignoring a brigade commander's orders and making significant decisions, such as ordering a withdrawal, without prior consultation and approval.

For the push into North Korea, the Americans deployed a makeshift 27 BCB, consisting of battalions that hadn't trained or rehearsed together in a frontline position. Initially, the advance was straightforward, even exhilarating, as North Korean units fell back, many soldiers surrendering without resistance. But UN forces were heading into significant danger on the approaches to the Yalu River. Chinese messages warning the United States against crossing the 38th Parallel had been ignored, and as the UN's northward advance continued, China prepared to intervene.

On 17 October 1950, after being airlifted north of Seoul, 27 BCB became the vanguard of the UN advance.[1] The Americans might have used a more experienced formation, but there was no lack of enthusiasm for the chase in the 'Cinderella brigade'.

4 Section, 2 Platoon, A Company on the move through a paddy field near Pyongyang, 3 November 1950. (PHOTOGRAPHER: ARTHUR GULLIVER, SLV H2002.199/3612)

After advancing seventy kilometres on the first day along roads and through terrain crowded with withdrawing North Koreans, most of whom decided to surrender rather than fight, UN forces were eager to push north as quickly as possible. Resistance diminished further after 27 BCB moved through the North Korean capital, Pyongyang.[2] North Korean units encountered further north appeared to be more intent on getting out of the way or giving themselves up. The North Korean army, it seemed, was struggling to maintain morale and fighting spirit.[3]

Though the North Koreans were disadvantaged by a lack of air, artillery and logistic support, and were subject to relentless UN air, artillery, tank and mortar fire by day, especially before being attacked by infantry, they nevertheless remained a capable foe. During the next ten days, the Australians were engaged in several short, sharp battles, including three battalion attacks and two night-time defences against counterattacks.[4] Charles Green vindicated his 'last-minute' appointment to command 3 RAR by leading his men well and inspiring them with clear and concise orders, personal courage and coolness under fire.

On 22 October, as the Australians were again leading the Eighth Army's advance, North Korean forces opened fire on the lead company, C Company, commanded by AIF veteran Major Archer Denness. Charles Green, positioned forward behind C Company, directed

Denness to form his company into assault formation immediately and attack the North Koreans, firing at them 'off the line of march'. While he was giving these quick orders, a group of North Koreans opened fire on Green's headquarters team. Ben O'Dowd recalled being present as OC HQ Company and Battle 2IC. Green, he said, 'never missed a beat' by continuing to give his orders while the regimental policemen, drivers, signallers, batmen and whoever else was around fought off the North Koreans.[5]

Then Denness led his men into the fray, driving into the North Korean ambush without waiting for artillery or mortar support. Brigadier Coad, who witnessed the assault, described what followed as 'like driving snipe ... The Australians sprinted forward, shooting, bayoneting and butt-stroking hapless North Koreans'. Those who feigned death or hid were killed if they were discovered. The Australians, wrote Coad, 'thoroughly enjoyed it'.[6]

By lunchtime, the Australians had killed approximately 200 North Koreans and taken 239 prisoners, at the cost of seven diggers wounded.[7] For this action, Green received a US Silver Star. His citation read, in part, 'Superb leadership, daring tactics and cool courage displayed by Colonel Green in deploying his units resulted in victory for his command and was in keeping with the highest traditions of the military service'.[8] Denness received the Military Cross. He was proud of his three platoon commanders – Lieutenants Colin Townsend, Robin Morison and David Butler, all Duntroon classmates. Butler, whose performance was observed by a US Army officer accompanying 27 BCB, was also awarded the US Silver Star. Townsend and Butler had turned 23 and 22 years of age, respectively, on the same day, a month before their first taste of combat, in what was dubbed the Apple Orchard because the fight happened amidst apple trees. They commanded 6 RAR in Vietnam at different times, almost twenty years later.[9]

By 23 October, 27 BCB had advanced nearly ninety kilometres into North Korea and was back in the UN forces' vanguard with Sherman tank support. Coad put Green and the Australians 'up front' again on 25 October. In a swift attack off the line of march, preceded by air strikes, artillery and mortar fire, and following a challenging river crossing over a bombed bridge, the Australians cleared North Korean defenders from a ridgeline south of Pakchon. Major Wally Brown led B Company through the town and captured 225 North Koreans.[10]

During the night and into the early hours of 26 October, North Korean forces mortared and probed the Australian positions. Two T-34 tanks supported a probe on B Company, resulting in two soldiers being killed and three others wounded. Unfortunately, Sherman tanks supporting 3 RAR were unable to cross the river to the south, the only bridge in the vicinity being the ruin crossed earlier by the Australians who, denied armoured support, were forced to rely on their 3.5-inch M20 bazookas. Supporting fire from A Company, combined with return fire from B Company and the battalion's mortars, pushed the attackers back and forced their withdrawal from the area by first light.[11] The Australians estimated that over a hundred North Koreans were killed and thirty-eight taken prisoner in the battle, named for the area's most distinctive landmark as the Battle of the Broken Bridge.

A Russian T-34 tank knocked out by a napalm bomb that was dropped by supporting aircraft of the US 5th Air Force, 1950. (PHOTOGRAPHER: ARTHUR GULLIVER, SLV H2002.199/4222)

Australian losses were eight killed and twenty-two wounded. The dead were interred in a Christian churchyard at Pakchon.[12]

By nightfall on 26 October, 27 BCB had crossed the Taeryong River, south of Pakchon, with the assistance of US engineers, and had consolidated in defensive positions, co-located with Sherman tanks. Information gathered from a briefcase found with a dead North Korean colonel revealed that the enemy's supply system was struggling, and the 17th North Korean Tank Brigade opposing 27 BCB was having difficulties maintaining tanks and troops in the field.[13]

On 27 October, the Middlesex took over from 3 RAR in the van and conducted a battalion attack to clear the increasingly determined North Korean resistance ahead of them. The key to success was UN air and artillery superiority. Air strikes and artillery bombardments before ground assaults stunned defenders and caused substantial casualties and the destruction of several T-34 tanks, artillery pieces and mortar lines.[14] On 27 October, Captain Bill Chitts assumed command of A Company when Major Bob Gordon was injured in a vehicle accident. Less fortunate was the 27 BCB brigade major, Major Douglas Reith, who lost his life in a vehicle accident on the same day.[15]

Brigadier Basil Aubrey Coad (seated, front left), Commander, 27th British Commonwealth Brigade, pores over a map with Lieutenant Colonel Man, Commander, 1st Battalion, Middlesex Regiment (with moustache), and Lieutenant Colonel Charles Green (front, right), Commanding Officer, 3 RAR, following the Battle of Yongju, 22 October 1950. (PHOTOGRAPHER: IAN ROBERTSON, AWM P01813.658)

On 29 October, Green and the Australians faced their biggest test so far on the heights before the town of Chongju. Coad put them in the van once again. The brigade estimated that ahead of them on wooded slopes in rugged terrain were 500–600 North Koreans in camouflaged positions with strong, well-sited defences supported by several dug-in tanks and two self-propelled guns.[16] Green masterfully coordinated preparatory air, artillery and mortar fire onto his opponents before sending in his ground assaults. Air strikes by F-80 Shooting Star and F-51 Mustang fighters destroyed an estimated four to nine dug-in enemy tanks and the two self-propelled guns.[17]

D Company, led by Major Wally Brown, with two platoons of Sherman tanks in support, conducted an assault to capture the first objective, Hill 38. Lieutenant David Mannett, a graduate from Duntroon's class of 1948, led 10 Platoon in a critical flanking assault that split enemy fire and enabled the company's other platoons to seize forward trenches, shooting and bayoneting North Koreans as they went in. After two hours of savage close-quarter combat, he reported that the North Korean position had been 'cracked'.[18]

A 3-inch mortar crew of 3 RAR goes into action with a M4A3E8 Sherman tank waiting in support in the background, Pakchon, Korea, 5 November 1950. (PHOTOGRAPHER: CLAUDE HOLZHEIMER, AWM 146951)

Lieutenant Colonel Charles 'Charlie' Green, DSO (left) peruses a map in Korea and confers with the 3 RAR Intelligence Officer, Lieutenant Alf Argent (right). Green's radio operator, Corporal Lindsay Beeck, is in the background, October 1950. (PHOTOGRAPHER: LLOYD NORMAN BROWN, AWM 044768)

Captain Bill Chitts led A Company in a spirited second-phase assault, also supported by two platoons of Sherman tanks, to join Brown and his men on the ridgeline. Members of A Company destroyed three T-34s using 3.5-inch M20 bazookas. B Company, commanded by Captain Darcy Laughlin, followed up and consolidated on the ridgeline between A and D companies. Denness's C Company and the Battalion Headquarters staff moved to create depth, completing a comprehensive, mutually supporting battalion defensive position by nightfall.

That night at 8pm, the North Koreans counterattacked in strength. Mannett and his men bore the brunt of several assaults and were temporarily surrounded. They counterattacked with 'bullet and bayonet' and repulsed their assailants. The other two D Company platoons had to counterattack into Mannett's position several times to retake trenches occupied by groups of North Koreans. Several Australians lost their lives there in hand-to-hand fighting, but D Company was unyielding.

A company's most intense moment came later in the night, in what the 3 RAR War Diary described as a 'Banzai' assault on its position.[19] Artillery, 3-inch mortar and small-arms fire dispersed the attackers before they reached the company's trenches. Throughout the night, artillery shells fell sporadically on the Australian positions, but there were no more counterattacks. Artillery and airstrikes drove the North Koreans off after dawn. Mannett received the Military Cross for his leadership and personal bravery in the assault on the North Korean positions during the day and the defensive battle against counterattacks that night. The Australians lost nine killed and thirty wounded. They entered the town of Chongju on 30 October, killing twelve North Koreans in short engagements and taking ten prisoners – stragglers who had been too slow to keep up with their withdrawing comrades.[20]

After capturing Chongju, their final objective, 3 RAR hoped for a quiet night. The 21st Regimental Combat Team, part of the US 24th Division, had passed through 27 BCB positions to resume the UN forces' advance. The Americans' mission was, in the words of the 27 BCB War Diary, 'to spearhead the advance and make a dash for the Yalu River'.[21] After two weeks of arduous daily fighting and sporadic bombardment, 27 BCB was scheduled to become the 24th Division's reserve.[22] 27 BCB's War Diary notes that 'from 17 October, the Brigade had led the advance, save three days south of Pyongyang, and a rest and refit were in great need ... It appeared that one of the few enemy defences had been broken at Chongju and that the enemy was in a desperate plight'.[23]

During the previous two weeks, the Australians had borne the brunt of the fighting – three battalion attacks and two night defences against counterattacks, as well as daily skirmishes. Green had led 3 RAR with great skill. Companies, platoons and sections were forged in battle under experienced company commanders, competent young platoon commanders and seasoned section commanders. While they had inflicted hundreds of casualties on North Korean units, the Australians lost nineteen killed and sixty-two personnel wounded – the equivalent of two rifle platoons out of twelve platoons.

Private Jack Morrison on the Vickers Medium Machine Gun in the early weeks in Korea.
(PHOTOGRAPHER: ARTHUR GULLIVER, SLV H2002.199/3049)

3 RAR was now 'blooded' under a superb battalion commander. After a well-earned rest, the Australians would be ready to resume combat operations. Unfortunately, tragedy was about to strike. 3 RAR's War Diary records that at 6.10pm six high-velocity shells fell in the Battalion Headquarters area. One struck a tree in the rear of C Company's area, seriously wounding Charlie Green, who was evacuated to a surgical hospital at Anju. Major Ian 'Bruce' Ferguson MC, 3 RAR's Second-In-Command, took command.[24] Green died the following day. His loss cast a pall over the battalion, which was having its first day's rest since crossing into North Korea.

After receiving a signal in the morning that he was to command 3 RAR again, Stan Walsh arrived at Battalion Headquarters at 9pm on 31 October after a hurried trip from Eighth Army Headquarters.[25] He arrived at a difficult time, facing his first command of an infantry battalion on operations with no time to settle in.[26] As far as Walsh was concerned, his command was temporary. He assumed that Ferguson would be appointed in due course. Anticipating ill feelings, Walsh assured Ferguson on his arrival that he should expect to be given command soon.[27]

LIEUTENANT COLONEL CHARLES HERCULES GREEN DSO

The influence of Charles Hercules Green on 3 RAR's success at Kapyong was significant. He joined the battalion in Japan in September 1950 and built teamwork, competence and resilience in battle in October, honing 3 RAR into a fighting unit, before his death in early November. He was a role model for members of 3 RAR, who later included Vietnam War era battalion commanders and 1980s general officers who would refer to him as inspirational. The account of his performance in September–October 1950 in this chapter, along with this brief biography, should inspire all Australian Army officers.

Lieutenant Colonel Charles 'Charlie' Green DSO, pictured in Hara-mura, Japan, on 15 September 1950, soon after assuming command of 3 RAR. (PHOTOGRAPHER: CLAUDE HOLZHEIMER, AWM 146724)

Green was born on 26 December 1919 near Grafton, New South Wales, the son of a dairy farmer. Aged 11, he nearly lost his life when a horse kicked him in the face. After a year of facial and dental surgeries and a lonely convalescence, he returned to school with a full set of dentures, a thickened nose and a prominent facial scar. Conscious of his false teeth, Green seldom laughed, adopting an earnest countenance while maintaining the whiff of a closed-lip smile and a playful sense of humour in comfortable company.

Despite his accident, at the age of 13, he left school to work with horses and support his father's farm. At 16, he joined the Grafton company of the Citizen Military Forces' 41st Battalion, based at Coffs Harbour, later enlisting in the 2nd AIF on 25 October 1939, less than a week after recruiting opened, just two months short of his 20th birthday. He was commissioned as a lieutenant in the 2/2nd Battalion.[28]

Green's experiences during the Second World War strengthened his character and established his calm and deliberate leadership style. At the age of 21, he led a group of Australian soldiers to safety, evading capture and escaping Greece by boat after that failed campaign.[29] He returned to Australia in 1942 with the rank of major. He served as the 2/2nd Battalion's 2IC during its reconstitution and training on the Atherton Tablelands and on its deployment to New Guinea in 1944.

In 1945, aged 25, he took command of the West Australian 2/11th Battalion, where he was quickly nicknamed 'Chuckles', a mocking reference to his serious demeanour. Green restored the weary battalion's morale after a difficult settling-in period caused by the Army giving a New South Welshman, who had not established his credentials, command of a Western Australian battalion. He led the battalion skilfully and courageously until the end of the war, earning respect, if not affection, and receiving the Distinguished Service Order.

Green returned to Grafton for three years after the war ended. When the CMF was reformed in 1948, he commanded his original unit, the 41st Battalion. In early 1949, he joined the Interim Army as a lieutenant colonel. He was posted to instruct at the School of Tactics and Administration in Victoria, before being selected for the Army's Staff College, located at Queenscliff. There, he was ordered to assume command of 3 RAR, which was then preparing for deployment to Korea. He did so on 12 September.[30]

In Korea, Green won the early respect of brigade commander Basil Coad. Coad kept a photograph of Green and himself in his home for the rest of his life.[31] By mid-October, 3 RAR was the forward unit of the Eighth Army's advance into North Korea. Green had settled the battalion down in three weeks, enforced its battle drills and boosted morale with success in battle.

Alf Argent described Green as tall, dark and sinewy, unfazed by pressure and a natural leader. In Korea, his leadership was firm and sure, and his orders clear, concise and effective. In operations, he was always immediately behind the lead company group.[32]

On 1 November 1950, just before his 31st birthday, Green died of wounds caused by shell fragments the previous evening. In David Butler's opinion, Green's most significant legacy was the way 3 RAR performed after his death through the difficult 1950 winter, the see-sawing war of movement in early 1951, and the courageous defence and withdrawal under fire at Kapyong.[33]

Prelude to Pakchon

Further north, the clouds of disaster had darkened over MacArthur's planned advance to the Yalu River. There had been warning signs. On 26 October 1950, a 6th ROK Division reconnaissance platoon reached the Yalu River and was 'wiped out by unknown forces'.[34] That night, while 27 BCB crossed the Taeryong River south of Pakchon and settled into defensive positions in reserve, hoping for a few days of rest, Chinese forces smashed into the 7th ROK Regiment as it approached the Yalu. It and the two regiments sent to assist were annihilated, while the 1st ROK Division was also in trouble at nearby Usan. A United States cavalry division sent to help had its lead regiment surrounded and a battalion destroyed. Soon afterwards, enemy jets appeared in the skies over North Korea.[35] During the final days of October, the North Koreans, reinforced with Chinese regulars, ambushed and slaughtered two of the 6th ROK Division's regiments.[36]

November withdrawal

The setbacks in the last week of October were the prelude before the Chinese struck in full force during the first days of November 1950. The hapless 1st ROK Division was overwhelmed in a 'series of crushing attacks' and Chinese MiG-15 jets appeared in increasing numbers over the following days.[37] In retaliation for China's entry into the conflict, MacArthur received permission to bomb bridges on the Yalu River, cutting off Chinese supply lines into North Korea, but nature intervened to overcome this setback. In winter, the Yalu froze, and bridges were not needed.[38] More surprises were to unsettle UN forces in the coming days.

Having advanced almost to the Chinese border, UN troops were now in full retreat, suffering heavy casualties under the weight of the communist offensive. 27 BCB was 'puzzled and frustrated' as it began to retrace its steps of the previous week.[39] The brigade was ordered south to the Pakchon–Chongju–Taechon–Kusong area as part of the Eighth Army's consolidation of its front line. That night, 1 November 1950, Charles Green died of his wounds. His body was interred in the same churchyard as Australia's dead from the fighting in the Battle of the Broken Bridge and at Pakchon.[40]

On 3 November, 3 RAR moved into its defensive positions on high ground one-and-a-half kilometres west of Pakchon. For twenty-four hours, the battalion was alone far in advance of the UN lines, with no other UN troops between itself and the Manchurian border.'[41] There were insufficient trucks to move it south to rejoin the brigade.[42] Its luck held, and the battalion consolidated with 27 BCB in the Pakchon area on 4 November. US, British and South Korean units had withdrawn through them to positions in the south, where they prepared to counterattack to the Yalu River.

US intelligence estimated that by the beginning of November, 90,000 Chinese troops were in North Korea. In reality, six armies comprising eighteen Chinese divisions had crossed the Yalu. Moving fast on foot at night and lying up under camouflage by day, almost 300,000 Chinese troops, along with the remnants of the North Korean army and guerrillas numbering as many as 80,000, waited to clash with some 150,000 UN soldiers.[43] General Walker was about to push his UN troops to Armageddon, south of the Yalu. As they detected the Eighth Army shuffling forces into a consolidated position to resume their advance, the Chinese showed their hand. They decided to throw several punches and start a contest in the air over North Korea to test the US resolve and cause second thoughts about closing in on China's border.

27 BCB had consolidated in the Sinanju–Anju bridgehead, a major road junction south of Pakchon and the only crossing over the Chongchon River. Brigadier Coad was concerned about the eight to ten kilometre gap between 27 BCB and the US 19 Regimental Combat Team to the east. His fears were realised when, on the night of 4–5 November, a Chinese attack threatened the bridge at Anju. As refugees streamed south, senior officers assessed that they might conceal Chinese troops infiltrating 27 BCB's rear.[44] The 27 BCB War Diary for 4 November records presciently: 'It is believed that there are six Chinese divisions in Korea who are well-trained in mountain warfare and night fighting. They have been heard to use whistles and bugle calls to control their movements'.[45]

Though no one could have known it, the scene was set for a rehearsal of Kapyong: large numbers of Chinese troops moving at night, intent on attacking under the cover of darkness, and thousands of refugees clogging roads and concealing enemy infiltration around hastily occupied defensive positions. The Chinese tactics were to approach through the hills, then encircle and cut off UN forces while launching a frontal assault.

In the early morning of 5 November, the Australians heard small-arms fire to the south near the 61st US Field Artillery Battalion's artillery positions. The Chinese, remembered Jack Gallaway, were 'swooping down on the US gun lines in the manner of an Indian attack on a wagon train'.[46] The assault was part of a joint Chinese and North Korean assault on the US 24th Division. Realising that the Australians were isolated forward of the UN line, Coad permitted Walsh to withdraw 3 RAR and regroup.[47]

The Chinese appeared to be trying to cut the road further south and trap 27 BCB.[48] Australia's Official Historian described 27 BCB's position as 'perilous'. The Chinese had opened a route to Anju, where possession of the bridge over the Chongchon would isolate US troops to the east. 27 BCB was also in danger, so Coad ordered his battalions to turn south, determined to fight back down the road towards new defensive positions south of Pakchon.[49] '27th Brigade was in a race for survival: a 6-mile fight past or over any enemy in its path', wrote historian Andrew Salmon. 'If the Chinese halted them or beat them to the Chonghon crossing, they would be cut off from their rear, surrounded and destroyed.'[50] Coad redeployed the Argylls back across the Taeryong River. It was time to push the Chinese off the 150 foot–high ridgeline covering the brigade's withdrawal route along the north–south road to the Chongchon River and the Anju junction. A company of Argylls formed up for the attack in paddy fields overlooking the north–south road.[51]

Attacks at Pakchon

Major David Wilson, the Argyll company commander, always recognisable by a hunting horn slung over one shoulder, was assigned four Sherman tanks and C Battery of the US 61st Field Artillery Battalion to support his assault.[52] Ben O'Dowd wrote that the US guns were formed into a semi-circle and 'engaged the enemy over open sights at almost point-blank range [approximately 500 metres] ... the shells bounced off the frozen paddy and exploded in the enemy's faces'.[53] Presumably, tank and mortar fire were also brought to bear. The Chinese responded with small arms, machine guns and mortar fire on the gun line. Wilson reported 'gunners being shot up behind their gun shields while others took their place. It was like seeing something from a war in the Napoleonic era'.[54]

Wilson blew his hunting horn to signal the start of the assault. Chinese in forward positions fell back deceptively, inviting the Argylls to follow them up the slope to the ridgeline, where the defenders were dug in. The next blast of Wilson's hunting horn sounded a resumption of the advance, but this time the Chinese counterattacked, killing six Argylls and wounding five in the forward platoon and forcing them back 'to be pinned down on a reverse slope, guarding their dead and wounded'.[55] Coad decided to send in the Australians.

This 5 November attack was Walsh's first test of combat command. Major Cyril Hall, OC Support Company, thought he did not appear confident enough to give complete orders. Walsh instructed the battalion to launch their assault from a start line along the road and cross 4,500 metres of open paddy fields to the ridgeline. He nominated A Company (Bill Chitts) and B Company (Darcy Laughlin) in the lead, with D Company (Wally Brown) behind them and C Company (Arch Denness) in reserve. A Company was to seize the first of two Chinese-occupied crests, and B Company the second. Walsh invited the company COs to 'get together and work out the details', adding that H-Hour would be at midday.[56] Lieutenant Noel 'Chic' Charlesworth overheard Walsh's orders to Hall: 'Cyril, you organise the companies for the attack and give what support you can'.[57] In the little time left to organise their companies, the OCs discussed the attack 'in committee, as it were', and 'agreed on a plan', said Hall.[58]

The assault was preceded by British artillery support and close air support from a flight of No. 77 Squadron RAAF Mustangs. It was the first of very few occasions on which Australian aircraft supported Australian ground troops in Korea.[59] 3 RAR's 3-inch mortars and medium machine guns also supported the attack, but their crews had to endure the Chinese response in kind.

The assault began at 2pm under heavy mortar and machine-gun fire, with A and B companies, bayonets fixed, in the lead.[60] The Argylls, trapped under fire on the ridge slopes, looked back to the road to see two Australian companies advancing in extended-line assault formation and another two following. A British soldier recalled, 'One was amazed that they were doing this with the fire coming off the hill; it was awesome – a lot of people, the full monty! – I was in a position that you would never see it from unless you were enemy'.[61]

Charlesworth's Platoon Sergeant, George Harris, said, 'Two platoon took the first casualty. I saw Mick Servos go down, and the way he fell, I thought he was dead. When he told us he was only shot in the leg, we left him for the stretcher-bearers'.[62] Servos joked later, 'I almost got a DSO – dick shot off! I was lucky; (the bullet) shot all the muscle out of my leg but did not hit bone'.[63] The company clerk fell next to Private Stan Connelly in B Company: 'His head exploded like a watermelon; he dropped dead beside me. This upset me, but the attack had to go on'.[64]

George Harris remembered the Chinese on top of the hill making a fatal mistake. Standing up to fire down on the Australians, they made themselves easy targets.[65] It took the two assault companies two hours of close fighting to gain their objectives and clear the Chinese from the ridgeline.[66] Walsh had demonstrated some skill by ordering D Company to attack the enemy's right flank in support of A and B companies at a crucial time.[67] He was well supported by Captain Ben O'Dowd, his 'Battle 2IC', appointed by Charles Green, who had trusted O'Dowd to execute operations, leaving himself able to respond to changing circumstances, adapt plans and work out the next tactical move.

Brigadier Coad was pleased, and visited Walsh, telling him so.[68] Walsh decided to 'keep the Chinese busy' by directing the US artillery to fire new shell types that exploded above the ground at the same height, whatever the terrain. Walsh could easily hear the Chinese yells.[69] The Australians quickly settled into new defensive positions to cover the remainder of the brigade's move down the road from their new posts on the high ground. Coad 'left 3 RAR behind as a rear guard' to face inevitable Chinese counterattacks.[70] According to Walsh, Coad ordered him to detach a company to monitor road traffic at a junction further south, to ensure that Chinese troops were not infiltrating past the Australian positions among refugees to trouble the remainder of 27 BCB, consolidating defensive positions overnight. Walsh recalled in a testimony to Jack Gallaway decades later that he assessed that this would weaken his main defensive layout and decided not to detach a company for this task.[71]

On Guy Fawkes Night, 5 November 1950, 27 BCB's battalions ended up in separated positions with the Australians isolated 'up front', as would be the case at Kapyong, covering 'some six kilometres of the Pakchon–Maenjung–Anju road'.[72]

Defence and withdrawal at Pakchon

Walsh deployed 3 RAR into an elongated defensive layout on the captured ground overlooking the road. A Company held a prominent conical pimple at the northern end of the high ground, and D Company held the dominant hill at the southern end. He left B Company on its crest in the saddle between A and D companies. C Company, on the flat, covered the gap between A Company and the road facing north, from where the Chinese were expected to come. Ben O'Dowd located battalion headquarters with Cyril Hall's

Support Company Platoons: mortars, anti-tank, assault pioneers, machine gun and signals, less sections and personnel allocated forward to companies west of the road in the area between it and the river.

As A company was reorganising on the ridgeline, it was hit by three mortar bombs. One man, a section 2IC, was killed, and company commander Bill Chitts was wounded and had to be replaced.[73] The company's senior lieutenant, 22-year-old Lawrence 'Algy' Clark, took over from Chitts.[74]

Clark was probably not at his best for commanding A Company – he had been wounded but chose to remain on duty. His platoon had taken the brunt of the casualties during the assault. Platoon Sergeant George Harris had been wounded and replaced by Corporal Jack Shepherd. Clark had lost his good mate Eric Larson, who fell in the B Company assault, and he witnessed the death and wounding of several of his men. He organised the evacuation of his seriously injured company commander and several wounded men. The dead were laid out side-by-side at company headquarters, a sombre reminder to everyone of their possible fate in the coming hours. Clark, said Jack Gallaway, had 'undergone a good deal of trauma during the attack and subsequent consolidation on the feature ... In taking command, Lt Clark had to improvise a [company headquarters] staff from very few resources.

Lieutenant Colonel Bruce Ferguson (centre) briefs Lieutenant General Sir Horace 'Red Robbie' Robertson (left) and Brigadier Basil Aubrey Coad (right), 1951. (AWM 044498)

Algy had his own batman with him, the CSM Warrant Officer 'Sticks' McGavin, and a 3.5-inch bazooka team of two men'.[75]

Meanwhile, in the gloom before nightfall, Lieutenant Bill Keys came forward with some K Force reinforcements from Australia for A Company. After a brief discussion with Lieutenant Noel Charlesworth, 2 Platoon's commander, Keys took command of 1 Platoon, which had been in reserve during the afternoon assault and was relatively unscathed.[76] The other companies occupied defensive positions without incident, following well-practised drills. The proximity of 3 RAR's mortar line, where soldiers were 'energetically pumping out bombs in response to defensive fire task requests ... attracted generous Chinese retaliation, some enemy mortar bombs landed disturbingly close to the headquarters area, although none came in [causing casualties]'.[77]

As soon as it was dark, A Company was attacked, and mortar bombs thickened with heavy machine-gun fire pouring in on fixed lines began to fall on C Company, close to the Battalion Headquarters and Support Company positions. Amidst this ear-splitting noise, battalion communications became difficult.[78] The other companies were soon under fire as the Chinese probed the Australian positions, looking for weaknesses. Mortars and heavy machine-gun fire were softening up 3 RAR. Ominously, said the Official Historian, 'Accompanied by bugle calls and whistles, Chinese and North Korean infantry pressed in against C Company on the road and A and B Companies on the ridgeline'.[79]

Walsh differed with O'Dowd regarding the threat Chinese mortar fire posed to Battalion Headquarters (BHQ). He said many years later that it was 'heavy and quite accurate and deadly ... and my first action was to move battalion headquarters off and back down the road to avoid useless casualties, and this we did'.[80] The closeness of the mortar fire unsettled Walsh, and it must have become apparent through radio and line communications, as well as by his own hearing, that the companies were now fully engaged. Walsh ordered O'Dowd to move the battalion headquarters a thousand yards to the rear, despite O'Dowd pointing out the difficulties of pulling down a functioning headquarters in the dark, and the communications and casualty evacuation problems it would cause.[81]

Stepping back a battalion headquarters with its protection elements at night when forward companies are engaged and the enemy is dropping mortar bombs and firing machine guns into the area is tricky. This would be the case at Kapyong, the following April. In such circumstances, commanding officers should command within a tactical headquarters group comprising artillery and mortar fire controllers, signallers, runners, drivers, a batman for close personal protection, and an intelligence operator to update maps. They should dispatch a group from the headquarters, typically consisting of an officer with a driver, a signaller and a guide group, to conduct a reconnaissance of the new location, plan the layout of the headquarters in that location, and then act as guides to show where headquarters elements should position themselves upon arrival. Commanding officers and their tactical headquarters staff should maintain continuous communication and direct operations while the main headquarters is in motion. Amidst all this, regimental medical officers (RMO) must ensure that medical support and evacuation arrangements for casualties are uninterrupted.

Although Walsh had O'Dowd as his 'Battle 2IC', he was still responsible for command and issuing orders as forward companies came under Chinese pressure, but he seemed more intent on moving further south. O'Dowd recalled:

> *Prior to leaving to select the new HQ site, the CO contacted the brigadier on the rear link, advising him of the enemy counter-attacks in progress, the mortaring and the intention to move his headquarters to safer ground. The brigadier's reply was broadcast [on radio speakers] loud and clear: 'If your headquarters is being mortared, then it may be wise to move it, but the rifle companies must remain in present localities'.*[82]

Cyril Hall visited the battalion headquarters and spoke with Walsh, who, after telling him that A Company was 'lost', said that BHQ was going to withdraw. Hall was concerned at the vagueness of Walsh's planning; there were no discussions on exactly where HQ was going to be established, but he did what he had to do to begin the withdrawal.[83]

Walsh drove off down the road, accompanied by his signaller, the Adjutant, Captain John Callander, the Intelligence Officer, Captain Alf Argent, and two British signallers operating the Brigade Rear Link radio, giving him the means to maintain communication with his companies and with his brigade commander. O'Dowd took over responsibilities for packing up and dispatching the headquarters to follow Walsh south. It was, he remembered, an:

> *... extremely unpopular and confusing task of striking and loading tents and dispatching headquarters vehicles in the dark. The RMO protested the loudest, being heavily involved with attending to casualties in various stages of preparation for evacuation.*[84]

After arriving at the new headquarters near a railway junction, Walsh ordered the forward companies to withdraw to his location without consulting his brigade commander.[85] According to O'Dowd, Walsh radioed this order at around 8pm 'without selection of alternative defensive positions, provision of rear reconnaissance, timings, order of company movement or any other planning data'.[86]

Reactions among the rifle company commanders differed. Darcy Laughlin (B Company) and Wally Brown (D Company) were Second AIF veterans who knew Walsh when he commanded 3 RAR in Japan.[87] They were occupying high ground in advantageous defensive positions. The Chinese were attacking A Company in their northern crest position and C Company on the flat, down from A Company and closer to the road. A Company's Algy Clark heard that Laughlin and Brown told their radio operators to turn their radios off and pretend they didn't hear the withdrawal order. Both companies remained where they were without suffering any casualties.[88] Brown told Walsh he would see him about his order in the morning.[89]

Clark later said that on 5 November 1950 his 'very young and inexperienced' self was 'stupid' for, unlike his fellow company commanders, having done 'exactly as I was told', although he, Keys and Charlesworth agreed that withdrawal was not wise.[90]

> *The order to withdraw was simply just that – 'Withdraw' – with no indication of where to, when or what route to follow. Algy, Bill, myself and McGavin [now commanding 3 Platoon] discussed it and worked on the assumption that any counter-attack would come from the direction the Chinese had gone after the assault. We would hold forward with 3 pl and 2 pl (Charlesworth) and 1 pl (Keys) would withdraw through 3 pl and 2 pl [and CHQ] down behind B Coy. When 1 platoon cleared my position, I would go through [with] 2 Platoon and follow 1 Platoon. (THAT [Charlesworth's emphasis] was the idea).*[91]

Bill Keys began his withdrawal through the gap between 2 Platoon and 3 Platoon. 'By removing his forward platoon', said Jack Gallaway, 'Algy Clark left the front door open for an attack upon his company headquarters'.[92] Charlesworth counted 1 Platoon off to know when it was time to begin his platoon's withdrawal. He knew that Keys had brought reinforcements, but when his count reached forty, and more soldiers were following, Charlesworth suddenly realised something was wrong. Many more men were coming, but they neither spoke nor moved like Australians. He opened fire, describing the moment as, 'the start of a most confusing night'.[93]

Charlesworth's men saw and heard what was happening and joined the firing. Soon, the left section of 2 Platoon and Company Headquarters were under attack – seemingly from all directions.[94] The Chinese had breached A Company's position and were between 2 Platoon and 3 Platoon. Keys and 1 Platoon were clear, but the remainder of A Company was now threatened with being overrun. Charlesworth had been poised to withdraw. He directed his soldiers to return to their fighting pits to face the Chinese following 1 Platoon. The fighting continued for some time, during which the platoon was split into two. Both groups eventually withdrew independently amidst much confusion and intermittent contacts with Chinese troops in the dark.[95]

Meanwhile, Walsh appeared overwhelmed by events, confused and fixated on what had happened to A Company before and after his order to withdraw. When Cyril Hall spoke with him later that night, after putting his Support Company platoons on the ground in the new position, about 1,000 metres south, Walsh repeated that the A Company position was lost. Still, he said, the other companies were 'standing fast'.[96] He did not appear to know that D Company was still in position, but Laughlin and Denness had decided to withdraw after the Chinese had ceased their probing around midnight to achieve an easy, clean break. Corporal Jeff Jones, who now commanded 5 Platoon, B Company, after Eric Larson's death, said that Darcy Laughlin waited until 11pm before gathering platoon commanders to issue orders for a withdrawal. B Company had been repelling Chinese probes comfortably and had not sustained any casualties.[97] B and C companies were both able to withdraw during lulls in the fighting.[98]

In effect, 3 RAR, against Coad's orders, was relinquishing hard-won ground without a fierce fight – in A Company's case, at a high cost, after Chinese troops broke into the middle of the withdrawing Australians' position, causing heavy casualties. Only Keys' platoon escaped unscathed.[99]

Walsh's next challenge was to establish his battalion in its new location. The movement and relocation of the Battalion Headquarters had not gone well. O'Dowd said:

> *Absolutely nothing had been done to re-establish the headquarters; four unmanned 17-pounder guns of the Anti-Tank Platoon were strung out along the road, headquarters vehicles remained loaded where they had halted on arrival, and the RMO was treating casualties on the roadside and pushing them up culverts to provide scant protection from the night air. A sort of ad hoc tactical headquarters had evolved around the brigade rear link vehicle.*[100]

Leaderless, Argent, Callander and the Signals Officer, Captain Watts, were standing together with the signallers and their command net radios: 'Absolutely nothing had been done about security, and there were groups of soldiers, including the recently arrived reinforcements, standing around waiting for instructions'.[101]

The withdrawal had not gone unnoticed at brigade headquarters. Australia's Official Historian wrote:

> *When Coad heard on the radio that Walsh had ordered the forward companies to withdraw from the ridge that prevented the enemy from dominating the road, he was most disturbed. Coad believed that it was essential for the defence of the bridgehead north of the Chongchon River that this part of the road … [that] protected the entire left flank of the brigade … be held.*[102]

He ordered Walsh to stop the withdrawal of the forward companies, but it was too late.[103] A Company was in disarray, unable to turn and retake its old position, and B and C Companies were on the move in the dark. O'Dowd wrote:

> *Even with fresh full-strength companies, the task of mounting an unsupported night attack against a numerically superior enemy, without daylight preparation, would have had a dubious chance of success. With the current strengths, location and condition of A and B Companies, night attacking was not a proposition … D Company [held its position and] refused to answer any further radio traffic for the remainder of the night.*[104]

Now knowing about Coad's displeasure, Walsh had the challenge of consolidating 3 RAR on the ground in its new location. When Cyril Hall informed Walsh that he had observed B Company coming out of their position in the saddle, Walsh told him to meet it and get Laughlin to deploy 'over there, waving his arm with an expansive sweep into the blackness of the night in the direction of our right front'.[105] Hall met Laughlin coming off the rear slope of D Company's hill and passed on the CO's order with a similar sweeping gesture. Laughlin, said Hall, 'was not amused (and) trudged off to the right front of the new position'.[106] In the darkness and confusion, the risk of Australians firing on each other increased. Lieutenant Paddy Outridge almost ordered his Anti-Tank Platoon to fire on B Company coming into position. Hall mused that 'B [Company's] enjoyment of the night's activities would not have been enhanced had they been, in fact, "shot up the arse like hedge sparrows" by Paddy's braves'.[107]

Meanwhile, Charlesworth and his group were making their way to safety. He wrote later:

> *The next problem was to get into our own lines without being shot up. Anytime we called out, we met small arms fire. Finally, after what seemed like hours, we made contact with C Company ... and reported to Archie Denness [OC C Company]. They were about to withdraw – I think it was sometime after midnight. In the event, they loaded Kirby and me onto a jeep. It was the last time I walked for some considerable time ... The platoon casualties were disastrous – 8 KIA, as I remember, and about 17 WIA ... to my knowledge, Vic Carr was the only member of the original platoon who completed a full tour without being wounded.*[108]

It was a busy night for Cyril Hall. After putting his company and B Company on the ground, he reported back to Walsh, who told him to gather A Company's survivors as they straggled in and put them into position on the left front of BHQ. Hall met Bill Keys and his platoon, which had withdrawn in good order. While Keys put his soldiers into position, Hall met others from A Company and, after 'offering a few words of comfort and encouragement, placed them at two-yard intervals along the railway embankment that ran obliquely across the left front of the new position of the road'. Hall then reported to the CO, 'and went off to dig my own "splitty" [fighting pit], clean my rifle and prepare to meet my Maker, an event that I assuredly thought would follow come first light'.[109]

First light ushered in an anti-climax rather than a slaughter. On the morning of 6 November, the immovable D Company sent a clearing patrol forward to the old A and B company positions. Sergeant Buck Buchanan and his platoon found scores of dead Chinese amid heaped quantities of abandoned equipment and blood trails – the detritus of their defeat and A Company's confused withdrawal of the night before. According to Buchanan, 'A and B Companies had certainly stuck it up the Chinks [Chinese]. We walked all over their objective the next morning without having to fire a shot'.[110] Knowing that the Chinese recovered as many dead and wounded as they could, the Australians estimated that they had suffered 200 dead and a further 200 wounded.[111]

Walsh's dismissal

As the sun rose on the morning of 6 November 1950, Walsh faced a reckoning. Twelve Australians had been killed and sixty-four wounded in a single night, almost as many as the seventeen who had lost their lives during the previous two months.[112] True, his subordinates had either disobeyed or been slow to obey his orders. Wally Brown had ignored the order to withdraw and then severed communications. Both Laughlin and Denness waited several hours before effecting their own withdrawal.

Walsh may have hoped that Brown's disobedience and Laughlin and Denness's slowness in carrying out his orders would save him from Coad's wrath. But his own decision to disobey Coad's order and direct the forward companies to withdraw, refusing to detach one of his companies to monitor refugees and stop Chinese infiltrators from using them as cover, should have concerned Walsh more when he was summoned to Coad's headquarters.

'There were just the two of us present', remembered Walsh:

He informed me that he was not happy with the events of the night before, particularly my refusing to detach a company and that he had arranged for my relief by Bruce Ferguson. My reaction was, of course, extreme disappointment ... He showed me a signal from Lieutenant General Robertson's Headquarters saying that I was to return to Eighth Army Headquarters and then resume duties as an observer. I went forward again and found to my surprise and anger, that Bruce [Ferguson] had already been informed, which, of course, was a completely unethical manner of dealing with the situation.[113]

Walsh rationalised in 1992 that his removal was more about his disobeying Coad's order to detach a company to monitor road traffic than his unauthorised order to withdraw the rifle companies.[114] He also lamented that Ferguson, whom he felt should have been given command after Green's death, did not establish himself in battalion headquarters to assist during his first days in command. Gallaway observed that Ferguson spent a great deal of time at battalion headquarters when Green was in command, leaving the impression that Ferguson may have sulked back in A and B Echelon rear areas after Walsh arrived. O'Dowd, he said, agreed with this assessment.[115] Decades after the war, Ferguson confirmed his close relationship and proximity to Green during the advance into North Korea, reporting, 'I was able to stay close to the action ... and to study his technique of command, little knowing how this knowledge was to help me in the times ahead'.[116]

Army Headquarters confirmed Ferguson's command of 3 RAR shortly after the Pakchon withdrawal and temporarily promoted him to the rank of lieutenant colonel. Reflecting later about his feelings on being given command, Ferguson wrote:

It is one thing to take over a command in peacetime and enjoy the luxury of a new appointment, but quite another to assume command of a unit in combat.

That day left me with agonising doubts as to my ability. It was clear to me that the Battalion had not recovered from their recent setback [death of Green and then Pakchon], and I was still under assessment by every digger. That night I got to thinking about how Charlie Green would have tackled the problem, and it was then that I realised he had left behind a legacy I should try to carry on.

It was not long before it became apparent to me that I had inherited the loneliest command any man could have. Being the senior Australian, I was solely responsible for anything that might befall the Australian battalion in Korea ... With no one to turn to for advice in whatever situation I might find myself, it was, as I have said ... the loneliest command ever allotted to an Australian battalion commander on foreign soil.

Pakchon impact on Kapyong

Walsh's fate demonstrated the consequences of disobeying a brigade commander's orders. Before and during the battle of Kapyong, Ferguson accepted his brigade commander's direction to site 3 RAR on the allotted terrain, despite the wide frontage and compromises he and his company commanders had to make on all-round defence. He accepted that he and his headquarters would not be located forward with the rifle companies but would be two kilometres to the rear on the valley floor, monitoring road traffic and attempting to give confidence to a South Korean divisional commander to rally his troops to consolidate with the Australians for a fight. During the night battle at Kapyong, Ferguson would emulate Walsh in ordering the withdrawal of his headquarters, but, unlike Walsh, he moved back to consult with his brigade commander in person about withdrawing the forward companies.

As stated at the beginning of the chapter, Pakchon demonstrated how not to withdraw under fire. Though there are no explicit references by Kapyong veterans to the lessons of Pakchon, it is reasonable to conclude that those who experienced the debacle at Pakchon would not repeat the mistakes of not delivering clear orders, moving BHQ haphazardly and, in A Company's case, not ensuring a clean break before leaving forward positions.

Among its impacts on 3 RAR's approach at Kapyong, Pakchon set the scene in another way. It gave the new A Company a creation story. Though a self-described student of Green's command techniques, Ferguson did not want a Battle 2IC and was not close to O'Dowd, whom he assigned to command the decimated and demoralised A Company. After substantial reinforcement with officers, NCOs, and K Force reinforcements from Australia, as well as some soldiers from other 3 RAR sub-units, O'Dowd declared:

We had a full-strength rifle company, but we had little idea how it would perform in the confusion of battle. Four of the five officers, including me, were newly posted. A large portion of the reinforcements' 'other ranks' were scattered among the survivors of the Pakchon battle ... I prayed for a few cardboard pushovers [easy missions] to come our way before we got a big one. Something my officers and their platoons could cut their teeth on. A period of 'running in'.[117]

The fate of Algy Clark, A Company's young lieutenant in his first combat command, deserves mention and reflection. Clark wept uncontrollably in Walsh's arms the morning after Pakchon. He was the only officer left in A Company, and if anyone was concerned at his emotional display, it did not colour O'Dowd's opinion. O'Dowd mentored Clark, appointing him as A Company's 2IC, effectively a promotion in the field. O'Dowd saw Clark's potential and was a powerful role model.

Lieutenant Colonel Charles Green DSO and Major Bruce Ferguson in Pusan Port, Korea, 28 September 1950. (PHOTOGRAPHER: CLAUDE HOLZHEIMER, AWM 146786)

Clark's subsequent career validated O'Dowd's judgement. He joined his 3 RAR Duntroon classmates when they were withdrawn from Korea in late November to serve with new National Service battalions in Australia.[118] In 1951, he returned to 3 RAR in Korea and was awarded the Military Cross as a platoon commander at the Battle of Maryang San that October.[119] After graduating from Ranger and Airborne courses in Fort Benning, USA, Clark assumed command of the Australian Army's new Special Air Service (SAS) Company, inaugurating the SAS selection course in 1961. These US special forces induction courses would have informed the design of the Australian SAS's unique, physically and mentally demanding course. He may have reflected on his emotions after Pakchon and designed this course to ensure that young officers, NCOs and soldiers in Australia's special forces would be less likely to break down emotionally under pressure.

The aftermath of Pakchon set the scene for the next six months of combat operations, leading to the battle of Kapyong, and would testify to Green's legacy. He had given Bruce Ferguson and 3 RAR's company commanders a masterclass in tactical command of offensive operations and defence against Chinese counterattacks. He demonstrated how to coordinate close air support, artillery and mortar fire to advantage. Unfortunately, he was killed before demonstrating how to command a battalion fighting withdrawal. Green epitomised coolness under fire and sound judgement amidst the dangers of battle. His subordinates now had the challenges of emulating those characteristics over the coming combat operations during the Korean winter.

A group of 3 RAR soldiers celebrate at Christmas time in Korea, 1950. (SLV: H2002.199/3532)

CHAPTER 3

THE 'RUNNING IN' PERIOD

MAULED BUT UNBOWED AFTER Pakchon, 3 RAR, under its new commanding officer, faced a cold winter of limited patrolling operations until the weather changed. If there were no ceasefire, combat operations would start again. This chapter covers the period from Pakchon in early November 1950 through a bitter winter to the Battle of Kapyong in late April 1951. After combat operations resumed towards the end of winter, 3 RAR developed as a formidable fighting unit, leading up to Kapyong, deeply bonded in an ethos of mateship forged in combat.

Initially, Ferguson struggled with the loneliness of his new command and agonised over his fitness for the role. He found a confidant in late December when Don Beard arrived from Japan to be 3 RAR's new RMO. Beard recalled:

> *I left the RAAF base Iwakuni in a Dakota [aircraft], cold, tired, fearful and with a king-size hangover ... I reached the battalion, which had been in the 'the big bug out' ... Colonel Ferguson was ... CO. I reported to him, and he received me warmly and said there were ... casualties and sick needing my care. The RAP [Regimental Aid Post] was in a ditch ... By now, it was mid-winter, and both armies ground to a halt with only patrolling activity possible.*
>
> *Colonel Ferguson 'took me under his wing'. Every evening at about 1700hrs, I reported to his 'caravan' or his tent. It really was a personal O Group [orders] ... I appreciated being taken into his confidence.*[1]

Ferguson warmed to Beard's intelligence, civility and character. He used Beard as his 'eyes and ears' for how the battalion was coping with operations, and for officers' and soldiers' physical and mental health. 'He was very concerned as to whether all officers were looking after the soldiers', remembered Beard. 'A liaison developed between the CO and the RMO for mutual benefit for each other and overall benefit of the Battalion.'[2]

Lieutenant Colonel Bruce Ferguson, newly appointed commanding officer of 3 RAR, Pakchon, Korea, 7 November 1950. (PHOTOGRAPHER: CLAUDE HOLZHEIMER, AWM 146990)

LIEUTENANT COLONEL IAN 'BRUCE' FERGUSON DSO

It is important to include a deeper exposition of the career and character of 3 RAR's new commanding officer, to better understand the conduct of 3 RAR's combat operations leading up to and during the Battle of Kapyong. He was well known in the battalion and had served as the battalion 2IC under Stan Walsh in Japan; under Charles Green from September 1950 until his death in early November; then briefly under Stan Walsh again, until Walsh's dismissal and his appointment to commanding officer after the debacle at Pakchon. His subordinates deemed him competent but aloof. His personal writings and the reflections of his RMO, Don Beard, suggest some insecurities, and there is controversy about his command during the Battle of Kapyong and the truthfulness of his accounts of the battle before his passing in 1988.

Bruce Ferguson was born in Wellington, New Zealand, on 13 April 1917. Educated in Wellington, Melbourne, London, Paris and Dunedin, he began his working life as a cadet journalist in Wellington and was with *The Sun* newspaper in Sydney when the Second World War began. On 3 November 1939, he enlisted in the 2nd AIF. Allotted to the 2/1st Battalion, he was soon transferred to the intelligence section of headquarters, 16th Brigade, 6th Division.

In February 1940, he arrived in the Middle East and was promoted to sergeant. He was commissioned probationary lieutenant on 27 June. As a brigade intelligence officer, he was active in the capture of Bardia and Tobruk, in Libya, in January 1941. He joined the 2/2nd Battalion in May and served with it in Egypt and Syria before its deployment to New Guinea in 1942. Ferguson led his company across the Owen Stanley Range to Sananandа in October–December that year, spending the next nine months in and out of hospitals with malaria and dengue fever. He was awarded the Military Cross for his leadership at Templeton's Crossing.

Ferguson joined HQ 7th Division in October 1944. He served on Morotai and was at Balikpapan, Borneo, when the war ended. Volunteering for the British Commonwealth Occupation Force (BCOF) in Japan, he commanded a company at Kaitaichi, near Hiroshima, and then on Etajima Island. In 1947, Ferguson became second-in-command of his battalion and was attached to Headquarters, BCOF, in 1948. On 26 June that year, he married Alice Elizabeth (Betty) Browne.

He took command of 3 RAR on 8 November 1950 as a temporary lieutenant colonel, after Charlie Green was mortally wounded. Ferguson led the battalion through the winter of 1950–51, through the advance and withdrawal and at Kapyong, for which he was awarded the Distinguished Service Order. His command of 3 RAR officially ceased on 5 July 1951.

Lieutenant Colonel Bruce Ferguson, commanding officer during 3 RAR's participation in the Battle of Kapyong, 23–26 April 1951, pictured after the Battle of Pakchon in November 1950. (PHOTOGRAPHER: PHILLIP HOBSON, AWM HOBJ1745)

After Korea, Ferguson commanded 1 RAR and the 13th National Service Training Battalion. He served in Japan from 1952 to 1953, instructed at the Royal Military College, Duntroon, in Canberra from 1959 to 1962, and performed staff duties with the Southeast Asia Treaty Organization in Bangkok from 1963 to 1966. On 14 April 1967, he retired with the rank of colonel. He was the secretary of the Union Club in Sydney from 1969 to 1974. Survived by his wife, Betty, and their three sons, he died on 21 December 1988 in Canberra.[3]

Resumption of combat operations

After a respite in reserve conducting local patrolling operations in the snow, 27 BCB returned to the front line in early February 1951 as the weather warmed. Several changes had occurred to 27 BCB. The 16th Field Regiment, Royal New Zealand Artillery (RNZA), was now 27 BCB's direct support regiment, and the 2nd Battalion, Princess Patricia's Canadian Light Infantry (2 PPCLI), had arrived to become a fourth battalion. The 27 BCB had taken on a richer British Commonwealth flavour and had more tactical punch.

For the remainder of February 1951, the British, Australian and Canadian infantry, supported by their New Zealand gun regiment, were shunted to and fro across the battlefield, counterattacking Chinese units that had broken through the UN line. These were exhausting, dangerous operations characterised by changes of plan, rapid movement and resupply difficulties. General Ridgeway was trying desperately to halt the Chinese, buy time to reinforce and restock his formations, and regain the tactical initiative.[4]

Return of the initiative

By 28 February 1951, the last Chinese resistance south of the Han River collapsed. US General Matthew Ridgeway had achieved a masterful turnaround in the Eighth Army's fortunes. He now ordered the start of Operation Ripper, to recapture Seoul and drive communist forces back across the 38th Parallel, with an advance by two corps across the Han River. Ripper was launched on 7 March, while a general United Nations offensive to the north was underway.

Coad put the Canadians and Australians up front to capture the first line of hills on the brigade's axis of advance. Heavy machine-gun and mortar fire slowed the assaults and neither battalion had captured its objectives by the late afternoon. The Australians lost twelve killed and twenty-four wounded, and the Canadians six dead and twenty-eight wounded. It was probably the hardest day's fighting for the Australians since the defence of the Chongchon bridgehead the previous October. The following day, the battalions advanced again and discovered that the Chinese had withdrawn through the night, leaving eighty-two bodies, and had dragged many more away. Over the next four days, 27 BCB, with the Argylls and Middlesex in the lead, advanced with little contact to their first objective, north of the Han River. The Chinese had made a clean break and were regrouping further north.[5]

On 11 March, the Australians were again in the van, fighting for two more days before being relieved and sent into reserve. By the middle of the month, UN forces had retaken Seoul and were poised just south of the 38th Parallel. On the UN side, senior political and military leaders questioned whether that line should be crossed again.[6] After some fractious political manoeuvring in the United States that left MacArthur's authority to advance into North Korea unaltered, he authorised Ridgeway to mount another offensive. For the second time, UN forces were about to enter North Korea.[7]

On 24 March 1951, 27 BCB was ordered to join the US 24th Division in the advance. Brigadier Brian Burke, of the 29th British Commonwealth Brigade (29 BCB), had taken command only the day before. Coad had left unexpectedly for Hong Kong on compassionate leave. Burke had little time to settle in before his brigade was on the move.[8]

For 3 RAR, advancing up the Chojong Valley through mud, slush and snow in vehicles that frequently broke down was tedious and uncomfortable. Major Walter 'Wally' Brown commanded the battalion while Bruce Ferguson was on leave in Japan. The enemy had withdrawn from the valley, and there was only fleeting opposition from stragglers. After eight days of this slogging, stop-start advance, the brigade occupied temporary positions.[9] Three days later, on 3 April, Operation Rugged began. Its objective was a line between three to ten kilometres inside North Korea, running from the Imjin River east to the Whatch'on (Chosin) Reservoir. The 27 BCB axis of advance ultimately took it into the Kapyong Valley, north of the 38th Parallel.

Members of 3 RAR ride on a US Sherman tank as it moves along the metal tracks of a Ponton Treadway bridge.
(PHOTOGRAPHER: IAN ROBERTSON, AWM P01813.637)

The advance up the valley was harsh and arduous. 3 RAR had to climb the heights on either side and force the Chinese back along the flanking ridges and hilltops while the brigade's heavier elements moved along the poorly constructed track on the river's east bank.[10] The Australians on the ridges sometimes had to move 'one man up', in freezing wind, waiting for the inevitable 'crack' of rifles and automatic weapons from small rearguard groups of the enemy.

Forward scouts were under intense pressure to detect the Chinese before they could open fire. Tensions rose further when the scouts discovered old antipersonnel mines laid in late 1950 by South Koreans fleeing the North Korean invasion. Fortunately, the Chinese usually opened fire inaccurately at long range. They withdrew quickly when New Zealand forward observer teams, Australian mortar fire controllers and US forward air controllers called in artillery, mortar fire and close air support on their hastily constructed positions. The brigade reached its objective on the Kansas Line on 8 April.[11]

Don Beard remembered the pressures on the Australians during these operations. The cold climate caused most medical issues. He observed that late winter operations demanded 'tremendous physical and mental fitness, which tested many of the members to the limit'. Service in Korea meant forced marches, brief battles, more marches and living outdoors for days on end without relief. 'I very quickly became proud to be an Australian because of their efforts', said Beard.[12]

The Korean weather claimed more Australian casualties on 11 April. During a severe electrical storm, lightning struck three diggers. They were evacuated, suffering from shock. On the same day, the US Armed Forces Radio announced that two Australian officers – 36-year-old Major 'Arch' Denness, OC Support Company, and 22-year-old Duntroon graduate Lieutenant David Mannett – had been awarded the Military Cross for bravery, and Lance Corporal John McMurray had received the Military Medal.[13] News of the Military Cross award to Denness and Mannett enhanced their reputation and recognised Australian fighting qualities. The broadcast also announced that President Harry Truman had sacked the US Commander of UN Forces in Korea, General Douglas MacArthur. MacArthur had publicly disagreed with Truman about how to fight the war in Korea and was replaced with Matthew Ridgeway. General James Van Fleet assumed command of the Eighth Army.[14] 27 BCB resumed the UN advance to objectives five kilometres to the north. Chinese defenders, who were buying time for their compatriots' withdrawal further north, awaited them.

The two weeks from 9 April until the Battle of Kapyong began on 23 April were exhausting, though Ferguson was refreshed from leave and in his stride. The Australians were preparing for, or conducting, attacks against Chinese positions daily. 27 BCB reached its objectives further north on 8 April, ending this advance to contact phase. Orders were received to advance a short distance to take further objectives in two or three days' time. The brigade was scheduled to consolidate as a divisional reserve for a rest. The 6th ROK

Division was scheduled to move into a position astride the Kapyong Valley north of 27 BCB, to consolidate before resuming the UN advance into North Korea.[15]

On 11 April, Burke ordered the Middlesex forward to capture four small hills nicknamed 'Sole', 'Kipper', 'Dab' and 'Cod'.[16] The 2 PPCLI moved to the right to secure the brigade's flank on a 'Pike' feature while the Middlesex conducted their assaults. Tired from day and night combat, 3 RAR remained in reserve further south 'on call'. After meeting stiffening resistance over the next forty-eight hours, the Middlesex captured the last objective, 'Cod', on 13 April.[17]

Burke, continuing to name objectives after fish, assessed that the Chinese held four features ahead – 'Turbot', 'Sardine', 'Salmon' and 'Trout' – preventing 27 BCB from reaching and occupying final objectives and being relieved by the 6th ROK Division. Burke planned to capture all four on 15 April after subjecting the Chinese to heavy artillery, mortar and aerial bombardment.[18] Brigadier George Taylor, Commander 28 BCB, arrived at 27 BCB Headquarters on the eve of these attacks. This reconnaissance was a tangible reminder that his relief and that of his two British battalions were not far away.[19] The new British brigade headquarters was inbound with two fresh infantry units – 1st Battalion, The King's Own Scottish Borderers, and 1st Battalion, The King's Shropshire Light Infantry.

Burke's decision to continue attacking with British units to achieve the final objectives was understandable from a tactical point of view, but possibly psychologically inopportune. Earlier that day, he issued orders that Headquarters 27 BCB, the Middlesex and the Argylls, would return to Hong Kong in two weeks. In the Australians' opinion, the Middlesex were circumspect about attacking 'Sardine' after they had captured 'Pike', 'Dab' and 'Cod'. 3 RAR's War Diary reads, 'A lesson was learnt in the premature announcement of the relief of 27 BCB which coming during active operations tended to restrain any aggressive action by the units concerned'.[20] The Middlesex were ordered to assault 'Sardine', and the Canadians to take 'Turbot', on 15 April.[21] In O'Dowd's opinion, 'The Middlesex had an obvious morale problem. With their battalion close to relief and a return to the good life in Hong Kong, they regarded [the attack] as a rather inappropriate time for heroics'.[22]

Ben O'Dowd re-joined 3 RAR from the BCOF Hospital in Japan on 9 April, where he had been recovering from wounds sustained on 11 March. He reassumed command of A Company from Captain Jack Gerke, who temporarily took over command of B Company while Captain Darcy Laughlin was on leave in Japan. O'Dowd's return proved challenging: 'In my keenness to get back, I had cut convalescence short and, as a consequence, was in poor condition'. Six days later, having reached A Company HQ, he was ordered to lead an attack on 'Salmon'.[23]

After several assaults, supported by artillery, air strikes and tank fire, the Middlesex had failed to capture 'Sardine' on 15 April. Adding to the battalion's distress, supporting US medium artillery fire fell into their positions, causing further casualties.[24] Burke decided to use O'Dowd's company, then in reserve in the gully behind and adjacent to the Middlesex, to take 'Sardine'. O'Dowd thought it was obvious that A Company would get the task:

Ferg's briefing gave me great encouragement to succeed. He said, 'The Brits have been unsuccessful twice, and now all eyes are on the Australians. Don't you come back without it'. I knew he was not kidding!

'Sardine' was on a ridgeline, with a deep heavily timbered gully between it and A Company. Unwilling to make the kind of frontal attack tried unsuccessfully by the Middlesex – descending into the gully and charging up a steep slope towards an entrenched and prepared enemy, 'going up the guts' in the diggers' idiom – O'Dowd had 3 Platoon under Lieutenant Harold Mulry lead the assault, knowing that he and his men 'required no encouragement when it came to close-quarters work'.[25]

Mulry was one of O'Dowd's favourites – loyal and aggressive, he always bravely did as he was told. He was an older, experienced ex-AIF officer who avowed to fellow officers that he had left a wife and family in Australia to fight communism in Korea, unlike many others who said that they had left wives and families to fight in Korea, ignoring ideology entirely.[26]

O'Dowd planned a two-prong attack with 3 Platoon leading. 2 Platoon, commanded by Sergeant George Harris, was in the backup role, hitting the Chinese left flank while Mulry's frontal assault went in. Harris was another aggressive combat leader, known for his harsh treatment of young officers who did not meet his standards. O'Dowd's aim in sending Mulry to hit and hold, and Harris to hook, was to split enemy fire and create an opportunity for either platoon to follow through and seize the objective when they sensed that the Chinese were confused by the two assault forces.

The plan worked. Mulry carried his assault forward when he saw the enemy panicking and turning their fire onto Harris's flanking assault. He and his diggers charged up the hill and drove the Chinese from their positions with bullets and bayonets, killing over thirty. Grenade fragments slightly wounded eight Australians during this spirited assault. O'Dowd and his soldiers reorganised on 'Sardine', evacuated the wounded, took a resupply of ammunition and water, and settled in to repulse any counterattacks.[27]

That night, Burke ordered Ferguson to capture Objective 'Salmon' the following day. C Company, now led by Captain Reg Saunders, launched the assault, but the Chinese had abandoned the position after witnessing the fate of their comrades on 'Sardine'. C Company occupied the area without firing a shot. The Australians suffered a total of ten wounded during the attacks on 'Sardine' and 'Salmon' and in the subsequent occupation of these hills while being shelled by Chinese mountain guns.

The Canadians captured 'Trout' the next day. This completed 27 BCB's seizure of its objectives before their scheduled rest period in reserve. Snow fell each night as the British, Australian and Canadian infantry dug their defences and patrolled forward to keep the

Private Edward 'Bomber' Brown, A Company, wounded during the attack on Hill Sardine, Korea, 15 April 1951. (PHOTOGRAPHER: CLAUDE HOLZHEIMER, AWM 147334)

Chinese at bay. For the Middlesex and the Argylls, relief and return to garrison duties in Hong Kong was a little over a week away.

3 RAR stayed in the field because the Australian Army rotated individuals instead of whole units, unlike the British Army. This policy of replacement was disruptive and strained the cohesion of platoons and sections. Junior leaders and small teams were constantly 'churning' through personnel. They saw mates killed, or leave after 'doing their time', or due to wounds or illness. A steady flow of reinforcements, made up of experienced Second World War veterans and eager young blokes looking for action, came in to replace them. It was common for soldiers to leave their sub-units on the day their 12-month tour finished so they wouldn't test their luck. Officers didn't hold anyone back, probably worried that doing so might lead to a soldier getting killed or wounded after their legal obligation had ended.

On 16 April, 27 BCB was ordered to hand over its defensive positions to 6th ROK Division units. The next day, the South Korean division's 19th Regiment relieved 3 RAR. After six months of continuous combat operations, 27 BCB was given a rest before the headquarters, and the Argylls and Middlesex, left for Hong Kong. The brigade moved south to a rest area in reserve near the village of Chuktun-ni in the Kapyong Valley. The new 28 Brigade Headquarters was inbound with two fresh British battalions to join the Australians and Canadians. It was a welcome respite. By mid-April, South Korea was cleared of enemy, and the front advanced by some 100 kilometres to the north, into North Korea. 3 RAR had proven itself a tough fighting force, proficient and reliable in demanding weather and tough terrain.[28]

The Australians moved thirty-six kilometres by truck back down the Kapyong Valley. Ben O'Dowd thought the tension built up in each man over the past six months of combat operations began to ease as each kilometre went by. Late that evening, 3 RAR settled into a peaceful chestnut orchard far from the lethal mortars and artillery and the constant danger of being killed or wounded. The diggers dubbed the area 'Sherwood Forest'.[29] 27 BCB was almost fifty kilometres behind the front lines. Between the brigade and the enemy was a division of South Koreans, flanked by battle-tried US divisions.[30]

Events following the deployment order to Korea testified to the resilience of 3 RAR's commanders and their soldiers under pressure. They had endured hasty and exhausting pre-deployment preparations in Japan, which included high personnel churn, rapid reinforcement, and newly raised platoons learning to operate mortars, heavy machine guns and anti-tank weapons. After his sudden appointment, Charlie Green's pre-deployment training in Japan and command masterclass during the exhilarating advance into North Korea established 3 RAR's credentials as a fighting battalion for offensive operations and stubborn defence against counterattack.

3 RAR's resilience was tested again after the shock of Green's sudden death, and the withdrawal nightmare at Pakchon under his successor's command. By mid-November 1951, after weeks of continuous combat operations, the battalion had lost the equivalent of four rifle platoons of twelve – a third of its fighting strength – killed, wounded or sick. Another new commanding officer, Bruce Ferguson, had to find his feet. At the same time, A Company had to be rebuilt under a new command team, and other companies reorganised and retrained because of the churn of personnel leaving and arriving.

The winter months spent just south of the 38th Parallel allowed Bruce Ferguson and his commanders to consolidate before the resumption of the UN northern advance in late February 1951. Winter conditions limited Chinese and UN operations to routine security patrols of their areas. Patrolling during mid-winter was uncomfortable but not excessively dangerous. This period was a valuable time for reinforcements to settle in, for commanders and their teams to bond and develop, and for Bruce Ferguson and his company commanders to become familiar with each other and work cohesively.

Kapyong landscape, by Ivor Hele, 1953. (OIL ON HARDBOARD, 75.8 × 91.2CM, AWM ART40313)

The March attacks under their new brigade commander, Brian Burke, confirmed that the Australians had recovered well after Pakchon. Ferguson and his sub-unit commanders demonstrated the ability to execute well-coordinated attacks when 27 BCB resumed the advance into North Korea. Although the weather remained bitterly cold, 3 RAR performed strongly, achieving all its objectives and assisting in capturing others when needed. 3 RAR had reunited in combat and benefited from the influx of experienced K Force volunteers and others who operated under the guidance of experienced section corporals and both junior and senior officers.

Although 3 RAR was exhausted when it reached Sherwood Forest late on 17 April and felt entitled to a break, the men were used to orders changing and the battalion being redirected to handle the next crisis. Seeing the British and Scottish battalions they had fought alongside for the past six months preparing to depart might have caused some to think of their own homes. But K Force volunteers had signed up for twelve months' service in Korea, and they, along with former BCOF personnel and soldiers from 1 and 2 RAR, still had a few months left before they could go back to Australia or Japan.

CHAPTER 4

PRELUDE TO THE BATTLE OF KAPYONG

THIS CHAPTER COVERS THE days leading up to the first contact with Chinese forces on the hills overlooking the Kapyong Valley in the late afternoon of 23 April. Along with describing the calamity that befell the reconstituted 6th ROK Division north of Kapyong, it considers the risks of deploying units in isolated positions to defend a large area of ground against an enemy advancing on a wide front. Such risks are compounded when command and control arrangements among infantry, armour and artillery units lack proper rehearsal, efficiency and reliability.

The saying 'united we stand, divided we fall' applies well to combined arms warfare. In April 1951, while 27 BCB stemmed a Chinese advance at Kapyong, its truth was made manifest on the Imjin River forty kilometres to the west, where other enemy formations inflicted a significant defeat on a British brigade. Its closeness and timing make the Battle of the Imjin River important to this study, offering more lessons that the Australian Army can learn from defensive actions fought alongside allies.

For the soldiers of 3 RAR, the Chuktun-ni area felt like paradise compared to the cold, barren, freezing rocky hills they'd encountered further up the Kapyong Valley. They relaxed in a base camp setup and enjoyed daily baths, a luxury after months of washing only parts of their bodies, never fully stripping off their filthy, grimy uniforms. Soaking in hot, soapy water was a welcome relief. They slept under canvas tents on canvas doonas stuffed with straw, played football and watched films every night. Bruce Ferguson remembered they:

> *... really enjoyed the spell of relief from the line in a little orchard below the area of Kapyong. We were scheduled to be there for a fortnight, and all the soldiers sat down once a day for a long bath and came home every night for a beer. Life was very relaxing and pleasant.*[1]

The mood in 27 BCB was cheerful because the headquarters and two British battalions were heading back to Hong Kong. On 20 April, the brigade's advance party, made up of representatives from the headquarters, Middlesex and Argylls, left. Waiting for them was a warm, colonial-style setting, offering a more comfortable lifestyle with their wives and families, as well as a lively local social scene. That night, the Argylls hosted a gathering for the rest of 27 BCB. Many jokes were aimed at the Australians, Canadians and New Zealanders who would be staying on in Korea. Sometimes, the mix of alcohol among tired, tense and spirited men, proud of their countries and battalions, led to a flurry of fists. Others stepped in to stop these brief melees, with more – often teasing but good-natured – jibes.[2]

Though 27 BCB was resting, sending battalions home and individual personnel on leave or for recuperation, it was still IX Corps Reserve on three hours' notice to move in support of the corps' frontline formations, two US and a South Korean Division.[3] Chinese forces had broken contact at the time, and the battlefield was quiet. Lieutenant General James Van Fleet, the new Eighth Army commander, planned to push his forward divisions out in advance to contact on 21 April, to disrupt an expected Chinese Spring Offensive. US intelligence estimated that approximately 700,000 Chinese troops would participate in the offensive, 337,000 of them committed to a thrust against Seoul.[4]

During the respite in 'Sherwood Forest', there had been a steady flow of 3 RAR personnel to and from Japan. Major Arch Denness, MC, and Lieutenant Colin Townsend left for Tokyo on leave; Captain Darcy Laughlin returned to resume command of B Company, and Captain Jack Gerke moved to command Support Company while Denness was away. Others departed to receive overdue medical treatment for injuries and wounds sustained over the past weeks.

Darcy Laughlin and Jack Gerke were ex-AIF officers commissioned from the ranks during the Second World War. Laughlin had fought with the 2/3rd Battalion during campaigns in the Middle East and the South West Pacific. He was gregarious and enjoyed social occasions and good company, playing piano to entertain his fellow officers. Many songs were sung and many beers drunk in Kure, Japan, while Darcy Laughlin sang and played with gusto.[5]

Gerke had fought as a young soldier with the 2/16th Battalion on the Kokoda Track in 1942. He was a vigorous and decisive man who did not tolerate much questioning from subordinates. He was a first-class infantry officer who maintained a tight grip on the soldiers he commanded. O'Dowd described him as 'a fine soldier but one who could be blunt to the point of rudeness'.[6] Gerke knew all 3 RAR sub-units intimately as the 'permanent' temporary company commander. Ferguson seemed to have assessed that it was better to have a veteran like Gerke in temporary sub-unit command on operations than to allow inexperienced company 2ICs to command while company commanders were away on leave or convalescing from wounds or illness.

Among the other arrivals during this period was Lieutenant 'Lou' Brumfield, an experienced junior officer, re-joining the battalion for his second tour, having served with 3 RAR in Japan in 1948 and 1949. Brumfield fitted the mould of many of his Duntroon contemporaries: outgoing, self-confident and occasionally brash. He commanded 1 RAR in Vietnam during 1965.

On Saturday 21 April, Ferguson ordered a muster parade of all companies. Many diggers might have been unimpressed as they dressed in clean uniforms, polished boots and brass while suffering from the after-effects of the party with the Argylls. Ferguson had called the parade to read letters of congratulation from the Australian Chief of the General Staff, Lieutenant General Sir Sydney Rowell, and their erstwhile Brigade Commander, Brigadier Basil Coad, commending 3 RAR's performance over the previous months. The 6th ROK Division Band entertained the assembled Australians for an hour in the afternoon.[7]

22 April – church, another farewell party and looming danger

On Sunday morning, 22 April, the brigade held a united church service in the paddy fields of the Kapyong Valley as the rice stalks were beginning to turn green. Spring sunshine bathed the assembled British, Australian, Canadian and New Zealand troops, a welcome change from the bitter wind and snow of recent months. The service moved many to quiet reflection. Prayers were said for the dead and the seriously wounded. Eyes closed and heads bowed, men likely thought of fallen friends. Perhaps they offered up prayers for their own safety, for their mates to be spared, and for loved ones at home to be kept from harm and worry. Members of the Middlesex and the Argylls may have given thanks for their deliverance. The main body of the Argylls was about to leave for Hong Kong the next day, and the Middlesex would leave as soon as the first of the 28 BCB battalions arrived. That night, the New Zealand 162nd Field Battery gave the Argylls a final farewell dinner party, with sides of meat and vegetables cooked in rock ovens under the ground, in the style of a Māori hāngī.

Prelude to the Battle at the Imjin River

In a similar mood of reflection on the same day, padres conducted Sunday services for the 29th British Commonwealth Brigade (29 BCB) on the Imjin River. 'As ever, the expectations of battle swelled the congregations', wrote British Official Historian Anthony Farrar-Hockley. 'There had been sightings of a Chinese build-up all day – groups of men from tens to hundreds, batteries of guns, some horse-drawn, some towed by trucks.'[8]

The Chinese Third Army Group had arrived, its commander confident that after an approach march of thirty-two kilometres, his troops would attack, stopping for nothing.[9]

General Van Fleet was aware of his opponent's objectives. Chinese prisoners revealed that their commissars told them they would celebrate May Day in Seoul in a week. There had also been aerial reconnaissance reports of roads being prepared to the north and telltale smoke clouds masking the movement of troops and supplies.[10]

Where at Kapyong 27 BCB had the 6th ROK Division in defensive positions to the north up the valley, 29 BCB was in the front line on the Imjin. After its defeats several months earlier in North Korea, the 6th ROK Division had been retrained, re-equipped, and, with embedded US advisers, was expected to fight. They and 29 BCB would be the first formations to experience the Chinese offensive.

29 BCB's Commander, Brigadier Tom Brodie, had located his four battalions loosely along a twelve-kilometre front in separate positions on critical hills. He placed the 1st Battalion, The Belgian–Luxembourg Corps (the Belgians), on the far right, north of the river. Further south on the south bank, he positioned his two British battalions – 1st Battalion, the Northumberland Fusiliers (the Fusiliers) on the right flank; and 1st Battalion, the Glosters, on the left. He held 1st Battalion, the Royal Ulster Rifles (hereafter the Ulsters) in reserve.[11]

Separating battalions along a broad front resulted in widely dispersed companies unable to support each other with direct fire. Fusilier companies were up to three kilometres apart. The British, believing they would soon resume the advance, dug shallow positions, laying neither barbed wire nor mines for protection.[12]

The absence of activity to the brigade's front before 22 April suggested that the Chinese would strike elsewhere. However, there was an expectation that they might close up on the Imjin River on the night of the 22nd and launch some probing attacks as a preliminary move.[13] The atmosphere at 29 BCB resembled 27 BCB's relaxed mood as it prepared to occupy dispersed positions astride the Kapyong Valley. Aerial reconnaissance reported no sign of significant enemy forces and neither formation expected trouble.[14] Meanwhile, the Chinese were once again moving large formations unnoticed to the battle area.[15]

Brodie and his commanders were astonished at the appearance of large numbers of enemy on their front after dark on 22 April. They had no idea that the brigade area was a primary Chinese target for the offensive's opening phase.[16] Enemy infantry immediately began probing the Belgians north of the river, and by midnight men of the 187th and 188th Chinese Divisions were crossing into 29 BCB's sector in their thousands, driving towards the forward British battalions in waves, throwing themselves against the Fusilier and Gloster forward companies in an attempt to remove them from the route to Seoul.[17] Covered by Centurion tanks of the 8th Hussars, the forward companies withdrew to their main battalion headquarters, leaving the high ground to the Chinese, who began firing on the infantry and artillery positions below. Losing this vital ground so early in the battle set the scene for future challenges.[18] Each British battalion had faced the Chinese alone as the unsuitability of the brigade's dispositions and defences was made clear.

At the same time, other Chinese troops poured into the several-kilometre wide gap between the Glosters and the Fusiliers, cutting off the former.[19] In the hours before dawn on 23 April, after repelling attacks all night, the Glosters were spent and surrounded. Their rear area B Echelon resupply group had been slaughtered, and the battalion was cut off near what was to become known in British Army folklore as Gloster Hill.[20]

The fate of both the Belgians and the Glosters hung in the balance. Brigadier Brodie had the twin challenges of withdrawing the Belgians to consolidate his position while saving the Glosters, who were trapped and accessible only by a single track to their rear.[21] The US deployed the 1st Battalion, 7th Infantry Regiment, and two platoons of tanks to occupy the centre of the 29 BCB position. Helicopters flew in to evacuate seriously wounded soldiers. A US medium gun battery joined the British field regiment's guns to inhibit Chinese manoeuvres.

The Belgians were withdrawn with the support of US infantry, artillery and tanks. The Fusiliers and the Ulsters consolidated and were secure in new positions by nightfall further south. The 45th British Field Regiment had set up a new gun line, and the Philippine 10th Battalion Combat Team (10 BCT) arrived to become the 29 BCB reserve at 8pm.[22] The Glosters held their ground through four major attacks overnight on 22–23 April, and more after sunrise, aided by UN aircraft bombing and strafing the Chinese. Shells from forty-eight field and twelve medium guns falling simultaneously around A and D Companies forced the enemy back.[23]

Even with this array of fire support, the Glosters still suffered substantial losses on 23 April, making it difficult for them to disengage cleanly while carrying their wounded. In the words of historian Max Hastings, 'Like so many sacrificial actions which pass into military legend, that which was now unfolding on the Imjin should never have been allowed to take place'.[24]

While the assault against 29 BCB in the Imjin River Valley went in on the night of 22–23 April, the Chinese 60th Division, 3rd Field Army, attacked the 6th ROK Division's two forward regiments forty-eight kilometres north of where 27 BCB was having its farewell party.[25] Headquarters 16 RNZA Regiment and two batteries, accompanied by a US 105mm field battery, supported the South Koreans when the attacks began. By 11pm, their communications with the ROK regiments were lost, and by 3am on 23 April, the New Zealanders were hearing small-arms fire forward of one of their battery positions. At 4am, with gunfire now immediately in front of one battery and a steady stream of South Korean soldiers retreating south in disorder, the New Zealanders withdrew to a position six kilometres north of the 27 BCB position. The South Koreans steadied forward of them, about fifteen kilometres north of 27 BCB. By 8am, the New Zealand and the US gunners settled in to await further orders, hopeful that the South Koreans would hold their line.[26]

Just after dawn on 23 April, UN reconnaissance aircraft reported on the size of the Chinese offensive. The South Koreans defending the Kapyong Valley faced another night of close combat on 23 April. At 8.30am, General Van Fleet ordered 27 BCB, as the

US IX Corps reserve, to deploy further north into blocking positions south of where the 6th ROK Division was consolidating, encouraged by US military advisors to resist the inevitable Chinese assaults expected at last light. There was a slow passage of information about what was going on.[27] Ferguson was uncertain about his role until the brigade commander ordered him to establish a blocking position north of Kapyong to prevent any Chinese advance on Seoul.[28]

3 RAR's company commanders were to place their men on one hour's notice to move, and to rendezvous with Ferguson just north of the hamlet of Chuktun-ni, west of Hill 504, for an O Group. Lieutenant 'Alf' Argent, the Battalion Intelligence Officer (IO), who accompanied Ferguson that day, said many years later, 'that morning the CO and I recced the area and later held the O Group. It was a beautiful, warm day with clear, blue skies. War seemed a long way off'.[29]

At the O Group, Ferguson stated that the 6th ROK Division was fifteen kilometres north and about to come under heavy Chinese attack after being forced from their defensive positions overnight. 27 BCB were ordered to occupy a blocking position to buy time for UN formations to consolidate further south if the 6th ROK Division was unable to hold ground over the coming days. After receiving Burke's order to deploy immediately, Ferguson directed the company commanders to reconnoitre the positions he had pointed out on the map. He returned to the rear and sent companies to join their OCs.[30] Don Beard wrote later, 'There was disappointment and fury and a feeling that 3 Battalion was being used again'.[31]

At daylight on 23 April, the Chinese attacks in the Kapyong and Imjin River Valleys eased as they sought cover from UN aircraft, artillery and mortars, and rested and resupplied. But in the Glosters' sector, with the high ground in their possession, the Chinese appeared to see an opportunity, with superior numbers on hand, to crack the 29 BCB position despite the inevitability of conducting assaults under UN air, artillery and mortar bombardment. Farrar-Hockley summed it up:

> *When daylight dispelled the leaping uncertainties of darkness, the situation disclosed was grim. The Chinese held the abandoned centre of the brigade position ... many of the heights were occupied by the Chinese ... In the Glosters' sector, fresh attacks were being mounted on A and D Companies by about 1,000 enemy – an estimate confirmed soon after 0715 by an air observer.*[32]

By mid-morning, A Company, the Glosters' forward company, had only one officer left unwounded and fit for duty. Most of its men lay dead or wounded. A counterattack by the Fusiliers to reclaim their forward company position failed. Fifty per cent of the soldiers conducting the attack did not return.[33] It was during this assault that the Belgians were able to be withdrawn from their precarious position north of the river. The Glosters remained surrounded, with ammunition running out and food and water scarce.[34]

British commanders must have dreaded what the coming night would bring. On the Kapyong Valley front, the Chinese had mauled the 6th ROK Division overnight on 22–23 April and were poised to force it from its hasty defensive positions as night fell on the 23rd. Further south, 27 BCB was deploying to defensive positions to await its fate.

27 BCB defensive layout

Late morning orders to form a new defensive line by last light on 23 April truncated 27 BCB's planning and reconnaissance, resulting in weaknesses, compromises and risks in the brigade's defensive layout. The Argylls had departed earlier that morning, leaving Burke with the Middlesex, 3 RAR and 2 PPCLI to defend a front where the Kapyong Valley narrowed into a natural blocking position. Two lines of hills and ridges rose steeply on either side and three high features dominated: Hill 677 formed the summit of a string of hills that rose 600 metres from the valley floor to the west; a line of hills climbed 400 metres to the east and was crowned by Hill 504; and Sudok San was a massif rising almost 800 metres to the north-west at its highest point.

The difficulty for Burke was that he did not have sufficient troops to occupy this natural triangular fortress of hills and ridges. It would have been handy for him to have had the Argylls, but there was no chance of bringing them back for a fight now. The northern base of the triangle between Sudok San and Hill 504, which faced the Chinese, was just under seven kilometres wide. Hill 677, which formed the southern apex of the triangle, was four kilometres south of Sudok San and five kilometres west of Hill 504.

Burke could not establish a continuous defensive line of mutually supporting battalions; he had to make compromises by positioning them at the key features dominating the valley floor. He assigned the hills rising to Sudok San to the Middlesex, Hill 677 to 2 PPCLI, and Hill 504 to 3 RAR. If the Chinese attacked in sufficient numbers, nothing could stop them exploiting the gaps and getting behind the Australian positions.[35] In effect, 27 BCB's defensive layout was like that of 29 BCB; units forced to defend along a broad front that reduced depth broke the rule of mutual support within units and left flanks open.

At 10am on 23 April, US IX Corps headquarters compounded Burke's challenges by ordering the RNZA 16th Field Regiment's deployment further north to support the 6th ROK Division for the coming night battle. Fearing that the situation could deteriorate quickly if the South Koreans broke under the pressure of a renewed Chinese assault, Burke ordered the Middlesex forward to protect the New Zealand gunners. The hills of the Sudok San massif on 3 RAR's left flank were unoccupied, leaving the battalion's flank open and creating a four-kilometre gap between the Australians and the Canadians located further south. Burke probably took this risk because he thought there would be sufficient time for the Middlesex to occupy their allocated area later, even if the South Koreans withdrew. His intention likely would have been for the British and Australians to support each other with fire across the high ground and engage Chinese troops in a crossfire on the valley floor.

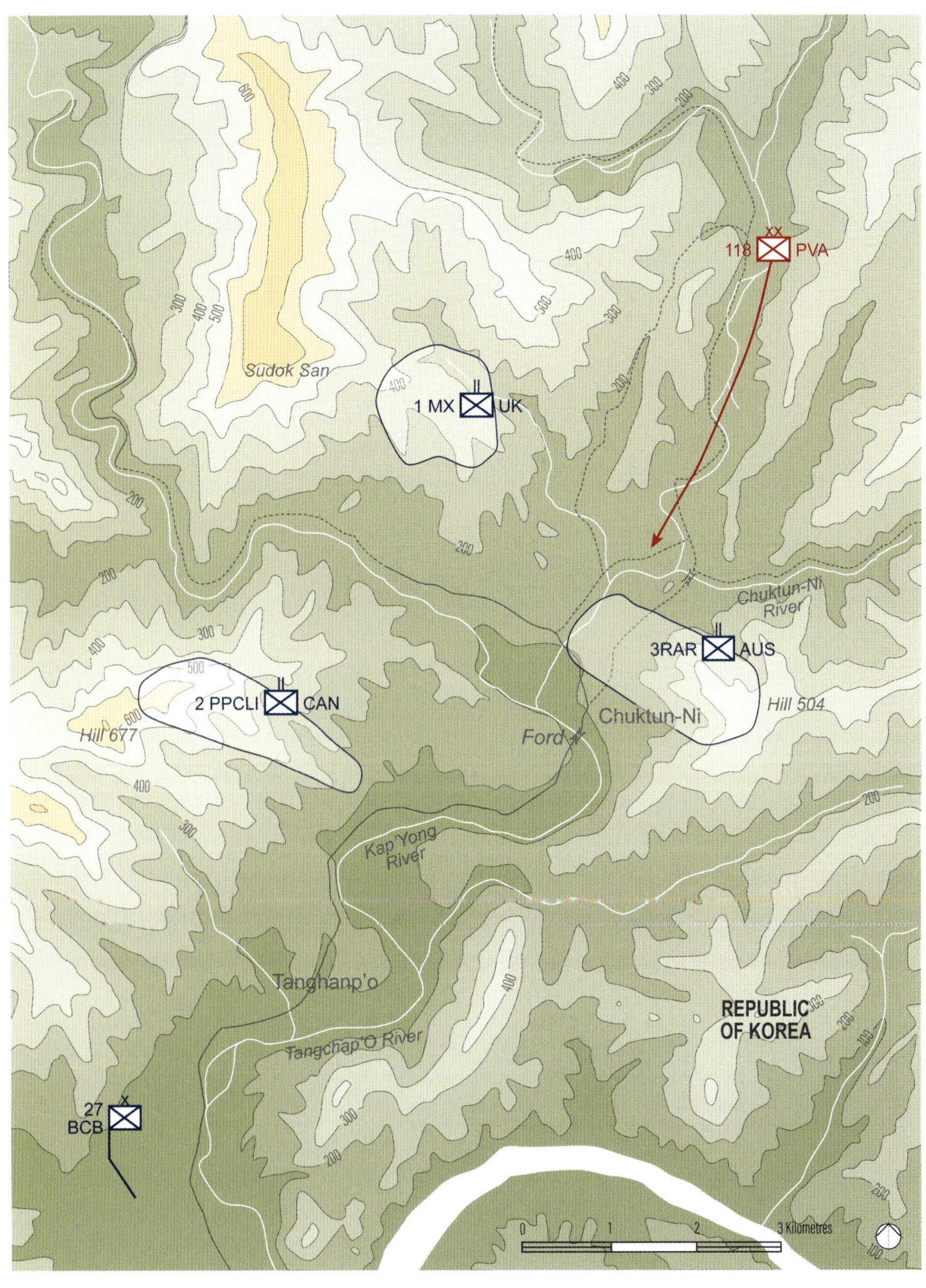

Map 2. Proposed blocking positions of 27 BCB on 23 April 1951 (based on a trace provided by LTCOL IB Ferguson, DSO, MC, in 1953)

Australian company positions

Burke directed 3 RAR to defend the approaches to Chuktun-ni.[36] Ferguson said later, 'my position orders were to hold that area for one day in preparation to recommence the advance. That's how vague the situation was'.[37] To achieve his mission, Ferguson ordered three companies forward and one company back. 'I'm a great exponent of "He who holds the high ground, holds the day". It was on that basis that I deployed my companies', he said.[38] He also had an additional task:

> *The area allotted to us was the equivalent of an area normally allotted to two battalions, side by side. So, when we got there, I had to decide which were the points to hold. I was given the extra task of holding the ford ... [across the] Kapyong [River]. As a deterrent, if you wish, to the withdrawing South Koreans. I had to hold that virtually as a fifth company in a four-company area, which is two battalions wide. My normal means of command was to tuck myself in between the companies. That way [I was] secure and better able to command. But having to hold this ford ... meant that I had to form a fifth company of my own [based on Support and HQ Company personnel].*[39]

Stan Walsh had ignored his brigade commander's order to detach a company for another task at Pakchon in November, but the primary reason for his removal was his directive to withdraw forward companies without consultation. Ferguson may have had Walsh's fate in mind when he discussed the 'fifth company' task with Burke and contemplated when and how he might withdraw if Chinese pressure became too great.

On the left, he ordered Darcy Laughlin's B Company to occupy a raised 1000-metre-long ridgeline west of, and overlooking, the north–south road running along the valley floor, and a ford near the junction of the Kapyong River and a tributary. This position had excellent fields of fire across all northern approaches to Chuktun-ni: 'In effect, B Company's position was a small natural fortress, flanked on both sides by paddy fields, standing in what was likely to be the main axis of the Chinese advance from the north'.[40]

Laughlin positioned his platoons on a knoll on the southern end of a ridgeline about forty metres above the flat valley floor that ran roughly north–south for about 1,000 metres. Laughlin could not occupy the ridgeline's northern knoll. It would have taken him too far away from supporting fire from O'Dowd's A Company, located across the valley on Hill 504's rising ridgeline. This positioning effectively changed Ferguson's defensive layout to 'one [company] up, two back and one further back'.

Laughlin positioned B Company's 4 Platoon, commanded by Lieutenant Len Montgomerie, on the north-eastern slope; 5 Platoon, commanded by Lieutenant Ken McGregor, on the north-western slope; and 6 Platoon, commanded by a Platoon Sergeant, probably Sergeant Ray Parry, in-depth on the southern slope. 6 Platoon's commander, Lieutenant Jim Young, was acting Company 2IC while Lieutenant Patrick 'Paddy' Outridge was away in Japan on leave.

An elevated view of the Kapyong Valley and surrounding hills where 3 RAR were in position during battle, Kapyong Valley, Korea, 16 April 1952. (PHOTOGRAPHER: CLAUDE HOLZHEIMER, AWM 147835)

The hills of the Kapyong Valley where 3 RAR was positioned during battle: A Company to the left, D Company on the crest of the centre hill, and C Company on the right, Kapyong Valley, Korea, 16 April 1952. (PHOTOGRAPHER: CLAUDE HOLZHEIMER, AWM 147841)

5/400049 LANCE CORPORAL (TECHNICAL SERGEANT) RAYMOND NORMAN PARRY

Raymond Norman Parry was awarded the Military Medal for his efforts during the first night of the Battle of Kapyong. It is not only through his award, but also the events themselves, that the nature and challenges of frontline leadership under pressure are revealed.

Raymond Norman Parry was born in Subiaco, Western Australia, in 1921 and was educated at Christian Brothers College in Perth.[41] His father was a veteran of the First World War, having been a member of the 11th Battalion and one of the first Anzacs ashore at Gallipoli. Growing up, Parry, alongside his mother and sister, would watch his father march on Anzac Day each year. This instilled in him a respect for the veterans and soldiers.[42]

At the age of 17, Parry attempted to enlist in the Army during the Second World War, but was turned away when he was recognised by a family friend who told him that he was too young and should 'get his tail home'.[43] Parry's father had always wanted him to join the Army to 'straighten him out'. In May 1941, Parry enlisted in the Second AIF and served in the 2/2nd Commando Squadron. Trained in guerrilla warfare at Wilsons Promontory in Victoria, Parry and his unit were then sent firstly to Timor and then Papua.[44] He was Mentioned in Despatches in 1943, after he and a comrade entered a Papuan town under Japanese control in an attempt to capture an enemy prisoner for interrogation.[45] Discharged in March 1946, at the end of the Second World War, Ray re-enlisted on 26 December 1950 for the Korean War.

Serving with 3 RAR in Korea, Parry was awarded the Military Medal for his efforts during the Battle of Kapyong. It was during operations in the Mokton-ni area on the first night of the battle that Lance Corporal Parry, with a light machine gun and three riflemen, was tasked with controlling a small knoll to the rear of B Company. Information was then received that the enemy had infiltrated the lines, and large numbers were forming up below the knoll to attack the company's position. Leaving his section under the command of his second-in-charge, Parry proceeded to the knoll alone. As he arrived at the outpost at approximately 0400hrs, fifty enemy soldiers launched their attack. Parry's citation reads:

> *By brilliant use of firepower under his command and inspiring leadership, the attack was thwarted; the enemy forced to withdraw leaving behind dead and wounded. Three further enemy attacks were made on the outpost in the next 20 minutes; all repulsed in the same determined manner as the first.*

Corporal Ray Parry (right), alongside Lance Corporal Mark Neyland, keeps an eye out for the enemy on Hill Sardine, 26 April 1951. (PHOTOGRAPHER: CLAUDE HOLZHEIMER, AWM 147348)

The knoll was to the rear of B Company's position, and had this fallen to the enemy, they could have dominated the company perimeter. There is no doubt that Lance Corporal Parry's quick appreciation of the situation and brilliant leadership, together with his determination to hold vital ground, was directly responsible for the company keeping its perimeter intact and at the same time thoroughly disorganising the enemy.

As a sergeant, Parry's platoon was instrumental in capturing the hinge during the Battle of Maryang San. After his tour of duty with 3 RAR, Ray received his discharge on 26 December 1951 and he returned to his job with the *Westralian* newspaper.

CAPTAIN REG SAUNDERS

Reg Saunders played a limited role in the Battle of Kapyong but remains one of Australia's best-known soldiers of the Second World War and Korean War, for his having been the first Indigenous Australian to gain a commission in the Army and for his status as a leader and role model for many who followed.

Reginald Walter Saunders (1920–90) was born on 7 August 1920 on the Bunyip Plain at Purnim, a rural village in western Victoria, 17km north-east of Warrnambool. He was a Gunditjmara man and a descendant of Framlingham Aboriginal Reserve residents.[46] His father, Chris, was an itinerant worker. Chris and Reg's uncle, Reginald Rawlings, for whom Reg was named, had both served on the Western Front during the First World War, where Reginald was killed.[47] Their mother, Mabel, died when Reg was 4 years old and his brother Harry was 2, and the boys were then raised by their maternal grandmother, Elizabeth, at Lake Condah Mission and Framlingham. Reg's education ended after primary school, and he went to work cutting logs.[48] As a teenager, he built a reputation as a skilled footballer, boxer and cricketer.

Saunders was working as a timber contractor with his father and brother when he enlisted in the 2nd AIF on 24 April 1940, at the age of 19, motivated by pride

Lieutenant Reg Saunders (with pipe), Officer Commanding C Company at the Battle of Kapyong, pictured in Korea in late 1950 before promotion and appointment. He is the most famous in a long line of Gunditjmara men and women from western Victoria who have served their nation in war. (PHOTOGRAPHER: ROBERT PARKER, AWM P01813.866)

and his patriotism for Australia.[49] His leadership qualities were soon evident. By August 1940, he was an acting sergeant in his training battalion. Then, after embarking as a private, he was quickly promoted temporarily again as a 'Saltwater' sergeant on the ship sailing to the Middle East.[50]

Saunders fought with the 2/7th Battalion in campaigns in North Africa (Bardia and Tobruk) and Greece. After a brief period of fighting, the battalion was evacuated and sent to Crete but had to abandon ship en-route. The 2/7th reached Crete 'with nothing except what we stood in – no guns, nothing, not a bloody thing', he remembered.[51] Most of the battalion was taken prisoner but Saunders evaded capture and remained on the island for about a year before making his escape. By the end of 1942, he had re-joined the 2/7th Battalion in New Guinea as a sergeant and had learnt of his brother Harry's death in action at Gona.[52]

Reg Saunders' father, Walter 'Chris' Saunders, served with the 10th Machine Gun Battalion on the Western Front in the First World War. (AWM P00889.012)

Saunders was commissioned as a lieutenant in November 1944 and served as a platoon commander and a company 2IC in the Aitape–Wewak campaign, during the closing months of the Pacific War.

He worked as a clerk in Melbourne before volunteering for K Force in 1950, leaving his wife, Dorothy, and three daughters behind. In November 1950, he joined 3 RAR in Korea and served as O'Dowd's 2IC after Pakchon. He took command of C Company in March 1951. He resigned his commission on 4 October 1954, after becoming disenchanted with peacetime military service.

In 1962, Saunders was elected president of the St Marys NSW RSL Sub-branch. The Federal government appointed him a liaison officer in the Office (later Department) of Aboriginal Affairs in 1969; after that, he lived in and around Canberra. He was appointed MBE in 1971 for his work in establishing communications between the government and Indigenous communities. In 1985, he joined the Australian War Memorial Council. Saunders died on 2 March 1990, survived by his ten children.[53]

3 RAR's defensive dilemmas

The brigade's tactical layout compromised 3 RAR and increased the risk. Gaps at the brigade level had to be accepted. But these then became gaps at both the battalion and company level. By occupying the summit of Hill 504, which was vital to his defence, Ferguson allowed a 600-metre gap, covered by artillery and mortars, between O'Dowd and Gravener's positions. If the Chinese found it, they could pour through.

The effect of tactical compromises continued down the chain of command. To cover the key terrain in his area, O'Dowd had to leave a 50-metre gap between Lieutenant 'Lou' Brumfield's 2 Platoon, located on a 'pimple' up the ridgeline, and Second Lieutenant Mulry's 3 Platoon, further down, closer to the road.

O'Dowd and Laughlin had to support each other across the valley floor, the central axis of the Chinese advance. To do so, O'Dowd located Lieutenant Frederick 'Freddy' Gardner's 1 Platoon close to the road, so it could sweep the valley floor with fire and be close enough to B Company positions to give Laughlin's platoons fire support – that is, within a maximum of 1,000 metres for light machine gun fire and 250 metres for effective rifle fire.

During the Battle of Kapyong, B Company, 3 RAR, held positions on the lower slopes above the road (centre), Kapyong Valley, Korea, 16 April 1952. (PHOTOGRAPHER: CLAUDE HOLZHEIMER, AWM 147843)

View from A Company's position on Hill 504, across the road and valley to where B Company was positioned during battle. (AWM 147836)

Depth was another compromise. The ridgeline leading up to the D Company summit position was too narrow to permit it. O'Dowd's dilemma was, he remembered, to 'occupy the lot and be weak everywhere or concentrate in strength at a vital point'. He located 1 Platoon at the lower end of the feature, to support B Company. He put 3 Platoon alongside 1 Platoon, where the ground began to rise sharply. 2 Platoon took up position on the knoll overlooking 1 Platoon and 3 Platoon. O'Dowd plugged the gap with CHQ and Sergeant 'Lennie' Lenoy's MMG Section, saying 'everything (was) in the "shop window" but there was an awful lot of territory to cover'.[54]

High on Hill 504, Captain Norm Gravener also faced dilemmas occupying key terrain. The summit was a narrow, steep-sided, kidney-shaped ridgeline about 600 metres long, running roughly north–south. A wooded feature at the northern end overlooked the enemy approaches from the north and the west. It was an ideal defensive location for a platoon, although fields of fire were limited by the convex slopes leading to the top.

Sergeant Stafford 'Lennie' Lenoy (left) and Sergeant James 'Jim' Stark share a stiff drink to keep out the cold. Sergeant Lenoy, an Aboriginal serviceman, was killed during the Battle of Kapyong while commanding his machine-gun section. (PHOTOGRAPHER: IAN ROBERTSON, AWM P01813.467)

If Gravener had a platoon occupy this position, there would be a 200-metre gap from there to the next one. If he did not occupy it in strength, the Chinese would have a secure foothold, covered from fire and from view, from which to launch their assaults along the axis of the ridgeline onto the summit of Hill 504. He said later:

> *Ferguson, who had an excellent eye for ground, drew my attention to the dilemma of whether to occupy this northern knoll or not. It was a classic problem for a defender – whether to go forward and open flanks or pull back tight and concede ground to the enemy unopposed. I decided to occupy the feature. I allotted the task to 12 Platoon, commanded by Lieutenant Johnny Ward. This was a critical decision that facilitated the effective defence of Hill 504.*[55]

Gravener located one platoon up, one back and one further back in depth on a reverse slope, to conform to the ground and to Ferguson's orders. Behind Ward's position, on the northern knoll at the southern end of a small saddle, Gravener positioned 11 Platoon, commanded by Lieutenant Russ McWilliam, and CHQ. McWilliam was a reinforcement who had served with the 1st Australian Parachute Battalion during the Second World War. He had recently arrived to assume his command, while the company was moving forward. He took over from Sergeant Len Opie, who went on leave to Japan earlier that morning, just before 3 RAR moved north to defend the approaches to Chuktun-ni.

Further back on the summit ridge of Hill 504, Gravener positioned 10 Platoon, commanded by Lieutenant David Mannett, MC. This layout was unconventional, but the steep-sided, narrow feature crowning the hill determined that a platoon stationed there had the best fields of fire and physical security.

The shape of the ground dictates the arrangement of a defensive position. The east–west ridgeline leading to Hill 504 compelled O'Dowd to adopt a broad layout facing north with no depth. The north–south ridgeline atop the Hill 504 feature constrained Gravener to a narrow, one-platoon frontage with significant physical depth, facing north towards the anticipated direction of the Chinese advance.

While his company commanders were considering how best to place their platoons, Ferguson was told by Burke to position his headquarters so as to 'give comfort and moral support to the withdrawing Korean forces'. This meant the ford over the Kapyong River from where he was to report on their withdrawal.[56]

Jack Gerke, OC Support Company, was one of several officers critical of Ferguson's tactics. He thought BHQ had been located for 'comfort and convenience' over 'safety and security', so Ferguson could have use of his truck and office.[57] Reg Saunders, OC C Company, went further in his comments on Ferguson, the location of his headquarters and the positioning of his companies. Saunders regarded Ferguson as a brave infantry officer but considered him an 'exhibitionist' who never carried a weapon but went around with a walking stick. In his view, Ferguson always isolated BHQ from the companies and did so again at Kapyong. Echoing Gerke, Saunders remarked on Ferguson's liking for a 'neatly signposted and well-laid out BHQ'. Locating B Company forward, said Saunders, was his CO's first mistake, as it would 'cop the lot' when the Chinese, whom Saunders felt Ferguson had underestimated, attacked.[58]

Ferguson had done his best to position 3 RAR on crucial terrain for Chuktun-ni's defence and to ensure companies could provide some mutual support. He had no illusions about the challenges that lay ahead, writing years later:

> *It soon became painfully obvious that the area to be occupied called for the deployment of at least two battalions so, no matter how our force was deployed, there would be gaps which could only lead to enemy infiltration.*
>
> *I planned to fill these gaps with enfiladed machine gun fire and mortar and artillery supporting fire. Little was I to know at the time that the majority of such support would not be available in the hours ahead. However, my greatest concern was that my headquarters, by virtue of the orders I had been given, had to be located almost two kilometres from our rifle companies.*[59]

In 1986, he said he put his headquarters where the South Korean 6th ROK Division commanding general was scheduled to locate his, intending to encourage the South Koreans to stay and hold ground. US officers, advisers to the 6th ROK Division, from the Korean Military Assistance Group (KMAG), were instructed to encourage South Korean commanders to consolidate their forces south of the ford, thereby giving depth to the Australian and Canadian positions.[60]

In effect, Burke gave Ferguson's headquarters a company protective task alongside the 6th ROK Division tactical headquarters, two kilometres behind the forward companies. O'Neill commented, '... Ferguson faced the prospect of having to control two battles, one involving the four companies and the other involving his own immediate headquarters area located directly beside the main enemy approach route and lightly defended'.[61] Thus, Ferguson's headquarters, comprising fifty-two personnel, along with the Assault Pioneer Platoon, the Anti-Tank Platoon and the light machine section of the Medium Machine Gun (MMG) Platoon, became responsible for its own defence, commanding and supporting 3 RAR's forward companies, and assisting KMAG officers in coordinating the 6th ROK Division's withdrawal.[62]

Saunders's and Gerke's criticism of Ferguson for not positioning himself and a tactical headquarters further north, closer to or even with his rifle companies, may have had some validity. Indeed, these two experienced officers verified that BHQ was in the wrong position to command the forward companies in a defensive battle. But these critiques and realities ignore Burke's orders. It is crucial to remember as well that when 3 RAR occupied their positions in the late afternoon of 23 April, no one could have foreseen the catastrophic events that would unfold later that night. The key lesson was that disobeying a brigade commander's orders to locate sub-units where he wanted them for additional tasks could result in a commanding officer's dismissal. Another lesson from the night withdrawal of battalion headquarters at Pakchon was that moving headquarters in the thick of battle is not an easy task. When the danger became apparent at Kapyong, it was too late, too dark and too dangerous for Ferguson and key headquarters staff to deploy forward closer to or among the forward rifle companies.

The Support Company – over 140 soldiers and up to twenty Bren guns, supplemented with US and British automatic weapons – was a formidable fifth fighting force when consolidated.[63] Its platoons operated in support of the rifle companies. The Mortar Platoon would set up a mortar line in the rear of BHQ and deploy Mortar Fire Controllers forward to 'call in' fire. The Medium Machine Gun Platoon would allocate sections of two Vickers MMGs to forward companies, to bolster their defences or support their attacks with sustained fire. The Anti-Tank platoon would assign teams of two 17-pounder Anti-Tank guns to forward companies. However, the absence of Chinese armour and problems with the operation of the 17-pounders meant that this platoon was often used to defend BHQ. The Assault Pioneer platoon sections were often deployed forward to assist with digging-in company headquarters positions and erecting barbed wire defences. On 23 April, with no attacks anticipated, this platoon occupied high ground overlooking BHQ, located in a re-entrant adjacent to the main road.

Usually, CHQ and the headquarters of each Support Company platoon would be co-located with BHQ and contribute to mutual defence. According to Alf Argent, the Support Company sub-units and functional sections of the BHQ occupied an area of 200 by 250 square metres.[64] Several interviewees recalled that the Anti-Tank Platoon, the Assault Pioneers and the Mortar Platoon made separate arrangements, as no one expected to be fighting that night.[65] Argent did not recall anyone at BHQ digging-in on 23 April.[66]

Sergeant Cecil 'Ces' Evans, OC MMG Platoon, sited the LMG Section (six men and two Bren Guns) to cover the ford. It was still light at 6pm when he posted soldiers to a vehicle checkpoint on the road north of BHQ.[67] The Anti-Tank platoon, commanded by Sergeant Frederick 'Fred' From, totalled over fifty men with seven Bren Guns and their anti-tank weapons, of which there were only two operational 17-pounders at Chuktun-ni. The remaining four were back with A Echelon. Lacking a particular lubricant for their recoil mechanisms, they were inoperable. The platoon also had several Projector Infantry Anti Tank (PIAT) weapons, which fired a round containing a 3.5-inch hollow charge, reputed to be capable of knocking out any tank then operational. Sergeant Jack Gallaway, the Battalion Signals Sergeant, spoke of the PIAT's 'only disadvantage', being that 'It could only be fired successfully by A Grade Front Row Forwards in robust health with nerves of steel. Best effective range? Approximately ten feet'.[68]

Sergeant From positioned his platoon just south of BHQ and the Kapyong River, covering the valley. Ferguson ordered From to provide a counter-penetration force for Laughlin's B Company. The Assault Pioneer Platoon – one NCO and twenty men with two Bren Guns – occupied the rising ground north of BHQ. Lieutenant Phil Bennett positioned the Mortar Platoon, comprising thirty soldiers who could fire mortars and defend themselves, south of BHQ, near Anti-Tank Platoon. He set up a mortar line with his six 3-inch mortars, each with an effective range of about 2,900 metres.[69]

Jack Gerke, OC Support Company, and the vehicles, stores and F Echelon personnel established their defensive position and accommodations at the rear of the Mortar and Anti-Tank platoons. F Echelon served as the immediate 'first line' source of resupply. It included the Support Company Headquarters; vehicles transporting rations, water and ammunition supplies; and approximately 150 Korean porters.

Further south-west of the Australian mortar positions was the mortar line of the US 2nd Chemical Heavy Mortar Company – a large, spread-out unit with over fifty vehicles. The US Army's Chemical Corps personnel were neither trained in, nor armed with, automatic weapons to protect themselves. They relied on infantry units for that.[70] The absence of US infantry suggested that no one expected a fight. Behind the US heavy mortars, 3 RAR's rearmost formation, the Administration Company and A Echelon, 3 RAR's 'second line' of supply were five kilometres south-west of BHQ.

ORDNANCE, SMOOTH-BORE, MUZZLE LOADING, 3-INCH MORTAR MKII

Mortars were introduced into Australian infantry battalions for the first time in 1934. Following newly adopted British organisations, a mortar platoon equipped with 3-inch mortars was added to battalions to provide the commanding officer with a readily available and responsive form of indirect fire support that he directly controlled – one that packed more punch than rifle-launched grenades but was cheaper and lighter, and thus more mobile, than a small artillery piece. At Kapyong, seventeen years later, the same model of mortar was filling this role for 3 RAR.

A development of the famous Stokes Mortar of the First World War, the 3-inch mortar Mk I was first employed by the British Army in 1917, and it was this variant that was introduced to Australian infantry battalions in 1934. In 1939, the improved Mk II, with a stronger barrel and baseplate and extended range ammunition,

A 3 RAR mortar crew lays down a mortar barrage to cover an attack by A and B Companies, Pakchon, Korea, 5 November 1950. (PHOTOGRAPHER: CLAUDE HOLZHEIMER, AWM 146949)

began entering service and would subsequently equip the Australian infantry battalions that served in both the Second World War and Korea.

3 RAR's mortar platoon in Korea was equipped with six 3-inch mortars, each with a detachment of three mortarmen. The doctrinal rate of fire for a 3-inch mortar was ten rounds per minute, but a well-trained detachment was capable of delivering up to fifteen rounds per minute. By the time of the Korean War, the 3-inch Mortar Mk II had reached the practical limits of its development but was still capable of projecting a 4.3kg (9.5lb) high explosive round out to 2,560m, with a blast radius of approximately 90m. Even though the minimum range was 250m, there are accounts of experienced detachments being able to fire much closer with careful calibration of elevation and the propellant charges of the round.

The 3-inch Mortar Mk II remained in service with the battalions of the Royal Australian Regiment until replaced with the US-designed M29 81mm in 1963. It continued to soldier-on with Citizen Military Force/Army Reserve battalions into the 1970s.

WEIGHT (COMPLETE)
56kg (125lb)

LENGTH
1.3m (51in)

CALIBRE
3.2in (81.5mm)

ELEVATION
45–80 degrees

TRAVERSE
11 degrees

MINIMUM RANGE
250m (275yd)

MAXIMUM RANGE
2,560m (2,800yd)

MUZZLE VELOCITY
189m/s (620ft/s)

RATE OF FIRE
10rpm

AMMUNITION
HE, Smoke, Illumination

Vickers machine gunners of 3 RAR await engagement with the enemy from the crest of a hill during their northward advance, c. 29 October 1950. (PHOTOGRAPHER: PHILLIP HOBSON, AWM HOBJ1649)

23 April – deployment

At about 3pm, 3 RAR began moving to its positions with, said the Official Historian, 'the practised efficiency which can only come from several months of operating as a team'.[71] There was no feeling of urgency nor of impending danger. Everyone expected to continue moving forward the next morning after a quiet night.[72] 27 BCB's units had done this many times before without firing a shot.

In most of their positions, the Australians found the ground so rocky that they could only dig shallow scrapes, with the B Company area an exception. Some soldiers built rock 'sangars', more as windbreaks than for cover from enemy fire. There was good-natured competition for the loose rocks in the area. Corporal 'Wally' Brown, a Section Commander with B Company, remembered: 'When we got onto the position, I thought we were like "shags on a rock". There was nothing to burrow into like we were used to burrowing'.[73]

Ben O'Dowd thought:

> *At this stage, the situation was a bit unreal. There was a division of infantry [6th ROK Division, approximately 10,000 personnel] in front of us, and the Divisional Headquarters was between us and Battalion Headquarters. In the infantry, if you can see Divisional Headquarters, you have got to be on leave. It was rather hard to take seriously that we would have to fight that night.*[74]

Tassie Long, a Machine Gun Platoon section commander, recalled occupying the positions at Kapyong. Each of the forward companies – A, B and D – had been allocated two .303 Vickers MMGs. As no one wished to carry their kit to the top of the highest features, the section sergeants drew matches. Long selected the shortest and felt himself fortunate to be allocated to B Company, on the low ridgeline beside the road. For reasons that he could not later explain, he brought all the ammunition he could unload from a truck and left it in a hole near his position, getting the driver to make another trip and bring more. As his section ate their evening meal, mail arrived – 'always a wonderful experience in Korea', said Long.[75]

VICKERS MEDIUM MACHINE GUN MK I

The Vickers MMG was among the oldest weapons to be employed on the battlefield at Kapyong. It first entered service with the British Army in 1912 and was employed by Australian forces in both world wars. Australian production at the government small-arms factory at Lithgow commenced in 1929 and ceased in 1945, by which time 12,344 Vickers MMGs had been produced.

The Vickers MMG operated with a short recoil system with a muzzle gas boost and was fed by 250-round fabric belts of .303-inch ammunition. This enabled a cyclic rate of fire of 500 rounds per minute. The barrel was cooled by a surrounding water-filled jacket. Designed before modern mass production techniques, the action of the Vickers MMG was composed of many expensively machined and precisely fitted components. Although its manual listed twenty-five different types of stoppages, the Vickers MMG had a reputation for being robust and reliable and able to maintain a high volume of fire over a prolonged period.

The Vickers MMG was operated by a crew of two – one to fire the weapon, and another to ensure the smooth feeding of its ammunition belts. It took four men, however, to move the gun, its tripod, ammunition, spare parts and tools, sights and water. The water in the cooling jacket – approximately four litres – would start to boil after about 600 rounds had been fired continuously, and evaporated at a rate of around one litre per 625 rounds, so needed to be kept filled to prevent the gun overheating and seizing up. There are accounts of soldiers filling the water casing with urine to keep their Vickers MMG firing once their supply of water was exhausted!

3 RAR's MMG Platoon was composed of three sections, each with two Vickers MMG. These sections were regularly split up and allocated to the battalion's rifle companies to bolster their firepower in defence – with a maximum range of 4,115m (indirect fire), the Vickers MMG was ideal for dominating the difficult terrain over which much of the fighting in Korea took place. Korea's harsh winters, however, caused difficulties with the Vickers' water cooling. In some instances, small fires were lit under the guns at night to stop the water from freezing and splitting the jacket open, and anti-freeze was also added to the water supply.

The Vickers remained the Australian Army's sustained fire machine gun until the early 1960s, when it was replaced by the 7.62mm M-60. Some quantities of the venerable old weapon, however, are believed to have been kept in Australia's ordnance stores until the 1980s.

Sergeant Henry Chaperlin, Support Company, 3 RAR, engages a Chinese patrol with a Vickers machine gun at Chipyon-Ni, February 1951. The bulbous shape on the muzzle of the machine gun is a flash suppressor. (AWM P01479.007)

LENGTH
1155mm (45.5in)

WEIGHT (COMPLETE)
38kg (84lb)

BARREL
721mm (28.5in)

CALIBRE
.303in (7.7mm)

FEED SYSTEM
250-round refillable fabric belts

MUZZLE VELOCITY
770m/s (2,525 ft/s)

RATE OF FIRE
500rpm

Letters meant so much to soldiers on active service thousands of miles from loved ones. They called out to each other with news of friends and family. Many a man's thoughts must have turned to home. The mail and a freshly cooked meal helped confirm their belief that 3 RAR was still in a reserve position.[76]

An elevated view from the hill in foreground occupied by A Company, 3 RAR, looking down to the hill occupied by C Company, 3 RAR (centre), during the Battle of Kapyong, Kapyong Valley, Korea, 16 April 1952. (PHOTOGRAPHER: CLAUDE HOLZHEIMER, AWM 147847)

US tanks deploy

First Lieutenant Kenneth Koch, Company A, 72nd US Tank Battalion, also deployed into the Chuktun-ni area in the late afternoon of 23 April. Koch's fifteen Sherman M4A3E8 tanks were formidable fighting machines. Each had one 76-millimetre cannon, and one .50 and two .30 calibre machine guns. The Chinese had no tanks and only a few anti-tank rockets among their infantry.

Koch had conducted a thorough ground and air reconnaissance of the brigade's defensive area and its enemy approaches in the previous week. This was a routine procedure when his tanks became part of the IX Corps Reserve, supporting 27 BCB. Infantry units can move over any terrain by day and night – armoured units do not. Koch and his platoon leaders, accompanied by the IX Corps Armour Officer, conducted a detailed tactical, terrain and traffic capability survey of the area on 16 April. They developed marked maps showing assembly areas, objectives, firing positions, routes and tank capacities.[77]

Koch deployed 4 Tank Platoon, under Second Lieutenant Di Martino, as a screening force north of Laughlin's B Company. Two tanks were on the northern slopes of the long ridge feature, just forward of Laughlin's standing patrol. Di Martino's three remaining tanks were further north.

1 Tank Platoon, under Second Lieutenant Wilfred Miller, was just west of Laughlin's men near the 6 Platoon position. Miller's five tank commanders deployed so they could fire rounds up the north-western and north-eastern areas of the valley. Koch located himself in his command tank with the four tanks of 2 Tank Platoon, back with BHQ. He positioned 3 Platoon to support 2 PPCLI.

Armed with only a few light anti-tank rockets, the Chinese infantry had limited options against US armour. Tanks could roam the valley floor, shoot infantry at will by day, and do the same at night with infantry protection and good natural and artificial light. During recent months, the Chinese had shown an understandable preference for attacking by night to offset the UN forces' air, armour and artillery superiority. Using darkness, vegetation and covered routes to get within range, Chinese infantry could use their rockets against the tanks and shoot tank commanders whose head protruded from the turret. Those with more appetite for risk and daring could climb onto the tank, lift the commander's hatch cover and throw a grenade or satchel charge down the opening, hoping that the tank commander did not have his pistol out ready to shoot them.

M4A3E8 'EASY EIGHT' SHERMAN MEDIUM TANK

Like much of the equipment and weapons employed by 3 RAR at Kapyong, its supporting armour was a vestige of the Second World War.

When the Korean War broke out, the United States' armoured forces were at a low ebb. Rapid demobilisation and deep budget cuts meant that tank design and production had been shut down, leaving the United States Army with only 6,000 serviceable tanks, down from 28,000 in 1945. Most of these tanks were concentrated with the US forces in Europe, leaving few immediately available for Korea. To equip armoured units for Korea, tanks were scraped together from training units, rebuilt from ordnance stores and even taken off plinths at the entrance to bases!

One of the models pressed into service was the M4A3E8, the final version of the famous M4 Sherman of the Second World War. Combat experience had resulted in multiple improvements from the early M4 variants. The M4A3E8 had a harder-hitting 76mm high velocity gun, and ammunition was stored in 'wet' boxes fitted with a fluid-filled jacket to prevent ammunition fires. The tracks were wider – 58.4cm (23 inches) – to reduce ground pressure and, combined with a new suspension system (Horizontal Volute Spring Suspension), made the tank more mobile in wet conditions. Due to the smoother overall ride, the crews nicknamed it the 'Easy Eight'.

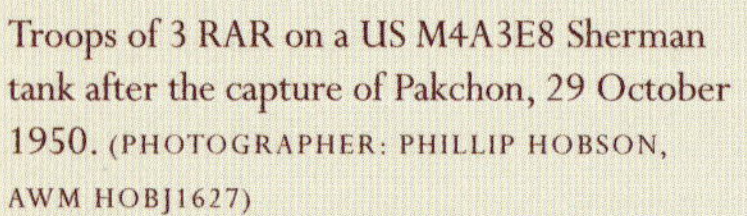

Troops of 3 RAR on a US M4A3E8 Sherman tank after the capture of Pakchon, 29 October 1950. (PHOTOGRAPHER: PHILLIP HOBSON, AWM HOBJ1627)

In Korea, the M4A3E8 was found to be mechanically reliable, easy to maintain, nimble to drive and, importantly, able to handle the hilly terrain. It was quite evenly matched with the T-34/85 tank that was the mainstay of North Korea's armoured forces. Although the T-34 had a heavier calibre (85mm) gun, the high velocity armour piercing (HVAP) ammunition used by the M4A3E8 could easily penetrate its armour. The superior crew training of the US tankers, however, proved the most critical factor in their success in several large tank-versus-tank battles in July and August 1950. Thereafter, encounters with enemy armour were rare, and the principal role of the M4A3E8 became the support of infantry operations, as at Kapyong in April 1951.

LENGTH
7.5 metres (24.6 ft) without gun

WIDTH
2.9 metres (9.5 ft)

HEIGHT
2.75 metres (9 ft)

WEIGHT
29,500kg (65,036lb)

POWERPLANT
Ford GAA V8 petrol engine – generating 525 horsepower

ROAD SPEED
40km/h (25mph)

RANGE
193km (120 miles)

CREW
5 – commander, driver, co-driver, gunner, loader

ARMAMENT
1 × 76mm main gun;
1 × .50 calibre AA machine gun;
2 × .30-06 calibre machine guns (coaxial and hull)

According to a record of Ferguson's orders taken by Alf Argent, Ferguson had allocated the platoons of Koch's tank company 'under command' of Laughlin's B Company and O'Dowd's A Company, enabling the Australian officers to control the tanks' actions.[78] If this was Ferguson's intention, then neither Laughlin nor O'Dowd established such a relationship. O'Dowd denied ever being assigned tanks 'under command'.[79] The subsequent conduct of the battle shows that Ferguson had no formal control over Koch's tanks. Koch had the task of fighting a separate battle to prevent the Chinese from advancing down the Kapyong Valley. He and his tanks were 'in location' with 3 RAR, free to fight the Chinese at will, and with his safety and that of his subordinates in mind. Ferguson had the job of stopping the Chinese from using the ridges on either side of the valley with the same purpose.

3 RAR dominated the northern approaches to the area from high ground on either side of the one- to two-kilometre-wide valley and the main north–south road running along its length. Telephone lines were laid from BHQ to each of the companies beside the road, and telephone communications within 3 RAR were excellent. Ferguson's headquarters was also in continuous communication with HQ 27 BCB through a British Rear Link signals detachment. Koch's tanks were on the valley floor astride the road. Artillery Forward Observers (FOs) and Mortar Fire Controllers (MFCs) were with the forward companies. The New Zealand guns were deployed north of the Australian positions in support of 6th ROK regiments. Normally the gunners would register defensive targets for 3 RAR's defensive positions with confirmation rounds to verify the 'fall of shot' from locations further south in the valley.

The Chinese Fifth Offensive had forced the 6th ROK Division south down the Kapyong Valley and mauled the 29 BCB defending the Imjin River valleys on the night of 22–23 April. Fortunately for 27 BCB, the 6th ROK Division north of them bore the brunt of the first night-time assaults in the Kapyong Valley. The South Koreans steadied after giving ground and waited for the next night's attacks. By then, the Middlesex were protecting the New Zealand artillery regiment assigned to support the South Koreans. Further south, Burke had deployed his battalions and a company of Sherman tanks into a blocking position resembling the spread of 29 BCB's positions, when the Chinese assaulted them on the night of the 22nd.

The lessons from this chapter focus on managing cascading risks during a crisis. General Van Fleet had to take risks to avoid the collapse of the 6th ROK Division. He ordered 27 BCB's artillery regiment fifteen kilometres north to support the South Koreans on 23 April, and Brigadier Burke tried to mitigate the risk to the gunners by sending the Middlesex to protect them. Further risk accrued when Van Fleet ordered 27 BCB to hold a front of approximately seven kilometres to control the valley – too great a distance for a continuous line of defence.[80] While commanders wisely recorded artillery and mortar targets in the gaps between battalions and companies, night-time afforded the Chinese the advantage of being able to infiltrate troops in the darkness. Robert O'Neill observed that had large numbers of Chinese reached the new 27 BCB position before the New Zealand

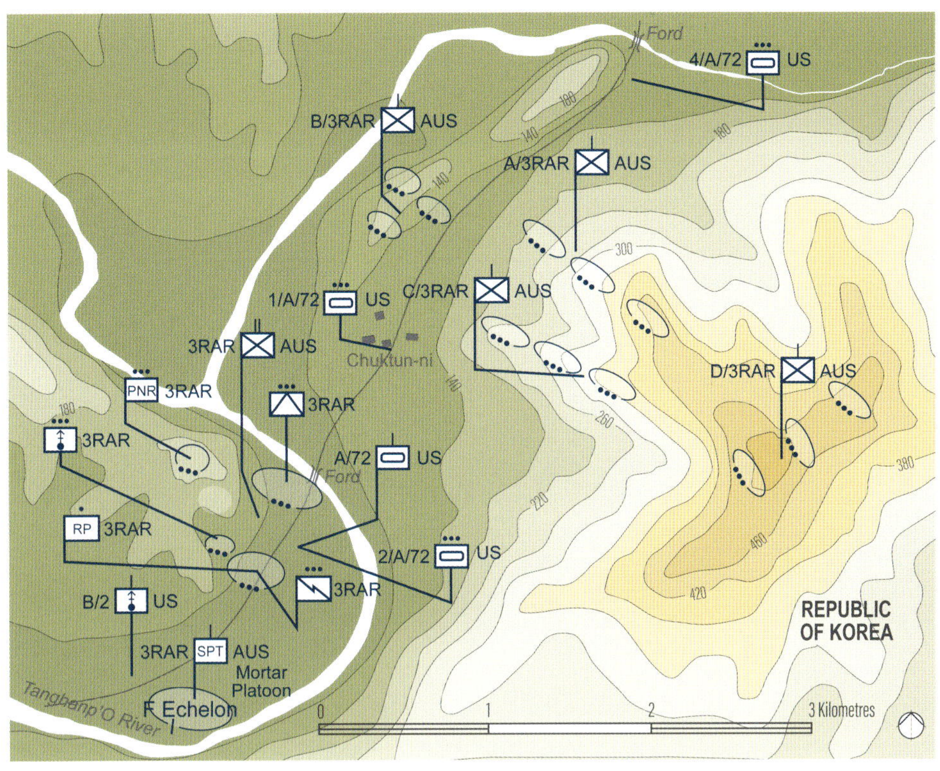

Map 3. Defensive layout of 3 RAR at 1900hrs, 23 April 1951

artillery and the Middlesex had reached theirs, during a 6th ROK Division withdrawal, the eight forward 27 BCB companies might have been cut off, likely sharing the Glosters' fate. This might have applied especially to 3 RAR, whose line of communication traversed the valley's exposed central sector.[81]

Risk management is fundamental to defensive operations because it is rare to have all the resources required, foreknowledge of enemy intentions and the time to establish sufficiently stout defensive positions to remove risk. 27 BCB did not have a complete understanding of what was about to happen on the night 23–24 April. The Argylls had left, so the brigade was down a battalion. 27 BCB followed orders, adapted to the terrain they had to defend and deployed into defensive positions efficiently and professionally.

While UN units defending the Kapyong and Imjin valleys were consolidating further south of their positions on 23 April, 29 BCB prepared for a second night of Chinese assaults. 27 BCB anticipated a quiet night, at least until the outcome of the continued attacks on the 6th ROK Division, after darkness fell on 23 April, was known.

CHAPTER 5

NIGHT BATTLE

23–24 APRIL 1951

THIS CHAPTER COVERS THE first night of the Battle of Kapyong, which began with Chinese forces pursuing retreating South Koreans amidst thousands of fleeing civilians. Fortunately for the 27 BCB defenders, the Chinese were on foot without tank support, had advanced beyond the range of their artillery and mortars, and were visible under a full moon and clear sky. US tanks on the valley floor were able to fire at them freely, but were not supported by infantry, a significant oversight in combined arms warfare, especially at night.

The night battle was crucial to blunting the Chinese offensive. There were several 'What ifs'. What if 3 RAR did not absorb and resist the initial shock of contact to allow the Canadians and British infantry located behind them more time to prepare, and optimise time for UN forces to consolidate further south in defence of Seoul? What if the Chinese exploited the gap on 3 RAR's left flank? Though Ferguson had located the battalion astride the Kapyong Valley, the Australians' left flank was exposed when the Middlesex did not occupy Sukon San, the position designated for them by Burke in his original orders specifying that his compatriots would join the Australians up front. There was no supporting unit on the Australian right flank either. What if the high ground occupied by A and D companies were lost? The Australians would most likely be overrun. What if B Company gave way on the long knoll on the valley floor? Most likely, the Chinese could launch an immediate assault on the Australian headquarters and the Canadians, leaving A, D and C companies isolated.

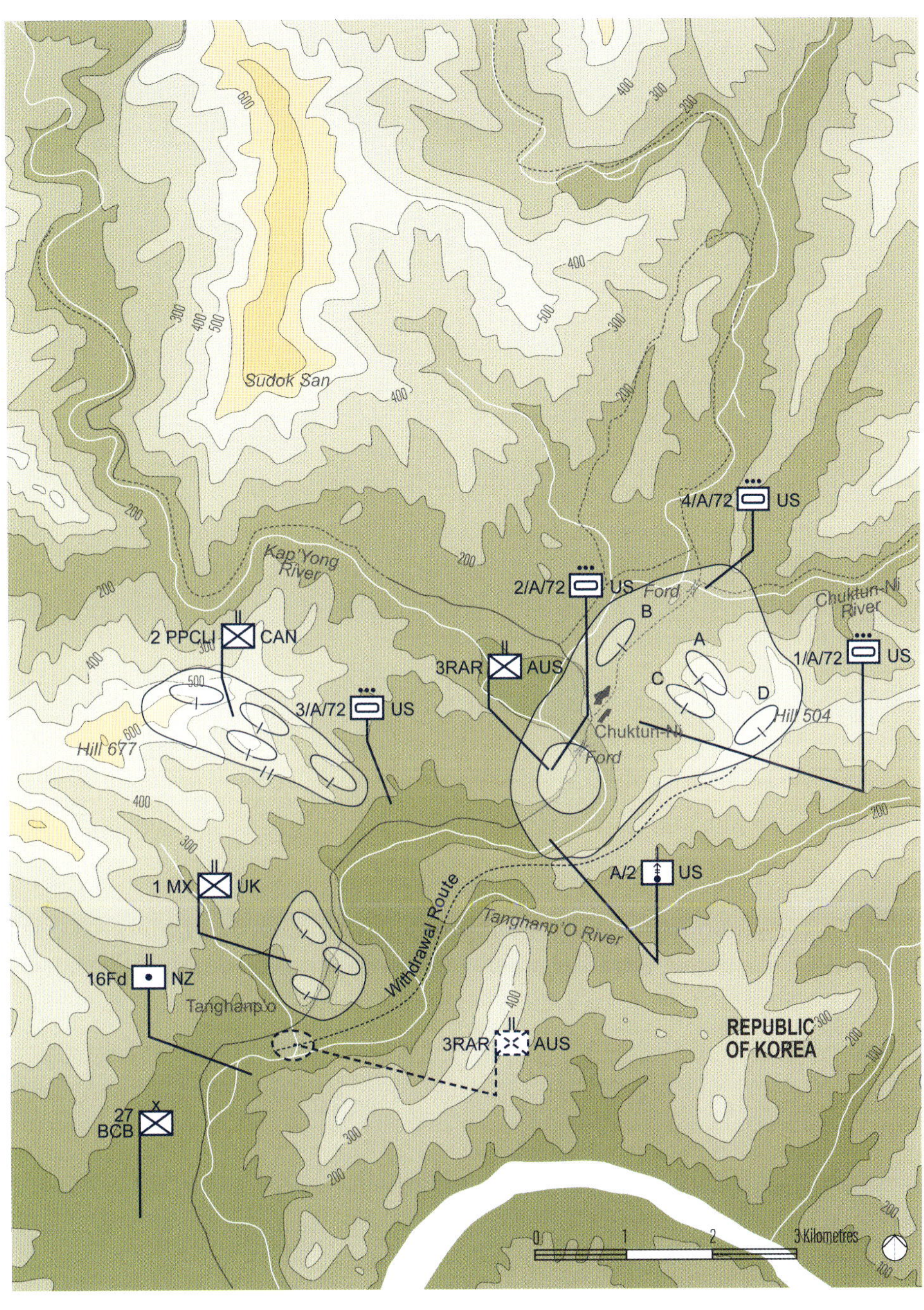

Map 4. Actual blocking positions occupied by 27 BCB on 23–24 April 1951 and 3 RAR withdrawal route (based on a trace provided by LTCOL LB Ferguson, DSO, MC in 1953)

What if the US tanks did not stop the advance along the valley floor? Most likely, 3 RAR could be bypassed, surrounded and mopped up later.

This chapter is more than just a description of events; it examines decision-making under pressure. It cross-references contemporary official records, along with O'Neill's Official History, accounts from other authors, and recollections of personal experiences and others' actions recorded in the early 1990s. The following twenty-four hours revealed the consequences of defensive compromises. More importantly, it shows how soldiers determined to hold their ground – despite being outnumbered, subjected to artillery and mortar fire, and aware they are isolated – can maintain their position against the odds. As O'Dowd would later say, officers can give orders, but they must command soldiers who are professionally competent and committed to carrying them out under pressure.

The Chinese planned to assault the Australian and Canadian positions on the ridges, as well as Koch's tanks on the valley floor that night. They could then push follow-on formations and supplies south for the thrust to Seoul. Ideally, they needed to get as far south as possible overnight before dawn exposed them to relentless UN firepower. They then had to overcome any UN troops still facing them and capture the city the following night. Any overnight delay on 23–24 April could be disastrous.

After resting, hiding and resupplying during daylight on 23 April, the Chinese attacked the South Korean positions approximately twelve kilometres north of 27 BCB in the early evening. Even with the light of a full moon and clear skies, it was dark enough to shield them from observed UN air and artillery support. By early evening, the South Koreans had faltered under the initial assaults, broken and begun a chaotic retreat. Capitalising on their success, the Chinese pushed fresh units through the attacking waves to continue the southern thrust.

The South Korean 6th ROK's divisional headquarters, located near the BHQ, gave Ferguson first warning of the calamity further north.[1] Sergeant Colin McGregor, 3 RAR's Intelligence Sergeant, visited the South Korean headquarters, where he found the commanding general, some staff officers, a KMAG colonel and some troops and equipment. There were two telephones in continuous use. As McGregor watched, staff moved arrows on a map indicating the progress of the Chinese advance. His last glimpse before he reported what he saw to Ferguson showed two enemy brigades about ten kilometres north of 3 RAR. 'The ROK Division HQ', said McGregor, 'did not remain in position for very long'.[2] Soon, the South Korean general's staff struck their tents, packed up, got in their vehicles and joined the surge of humanity heading south.

Signs that momentous events were occurring further up the valley became apparent at around 7pm. Ben O'Dowd, who had a 'grandstand' view of the road, said later, 'As daylight began to fade, a trickle of ROK soldiers appeared heading south along the road. There was nothing disturbing about this at first, but shortly, the procession developed into a disorganised, shouting, panic-ridden rabble'.[3] South Koreans were streaming through the Australian position. Much of their equipment – rifles, machine guns, uniforms, belts of ammunition, and soldiers' webbing equipment – was abandoned by the roadside. He witnessed, '... men, women, children and animals, all bunched together in a confusing melee; screaming, shouting, crying children, with their cattle, with their goods on their back'.[4]

Experience had taught O'Dowd that Chinese soldiers, some wearing civilian clothes and others in uniform, would mingle with the refugees to penetrate to the rear in numbers. 'I wanted to test out the situation by firing a few bursts of MMG fire over the heads of the throng moving south', said O'Dowd. 'This would send the civilians scurrying off the road, leaving any Chinese around the place to reveal their hand.'[5] Ferguson refused permission because O'Dowd had no identified enemy to shoot at.

Amidst this torrent of South Korean soldiers and civilians were the vehicles and guns of the 16th Field Regiment, RNZA, and trucks and other vehicles carrying the Middlesex battalion. Their move south was a mixed blessing. It was comforting to see the New Zealand 25-pounder guns. They would establish battery gunlines to support 3 RAR's forward companies as soon as they could, unless the Chinese following the South Koreans attacked the gunners in numbers further south.[6] Setting up gunlines in the dark under the pressure of fire from infiltrating Chinese troops would challenge the New Zealand gunners.

A stream of Korean refugees fleeing the fighting some weeks before the Battle of Kapyong.
(PHOTOGRAPHER: IAN ROBERTSON, AWM P01813.422)

The Middlesex would also find consolidating a defensive position in the dark under similar pressure difficult. The challenge for the Chinese was to maintain momentum now that the South Koreans had broken, and get past the tanks and infantry that had deployed astride the valley in sufficient numbers to continue their advance on Seoul.

Ferguson must have been disappointed to see the Middlesex stream past his headquarters without occupying their assigned positions on his forward companies' left flank. This meant that the Chinese could infiltrate west of B Company's position and not strike any opposition further south until they met the Canadians occupying Hill 677. The Middlesex's movement to the south and the New Zealand gunners' late arrival meant that Burke's defensive layout was weakened before a shot was fired. It went from a risky, over-stretched 'two up and one back' layout to a tactically dangerous 'one-up and two-a-long-way-back', with no artillery support for the forward battalion, which was about to face multiple Chinese assaults. Arguably, 3 RAR was on its own on another Gloster Hill.

Some braver South Korean soldiers abandoned the retreat near the Australians in the BHQ area. Sergeant Fred From, commanding the Anti-Tank Platoon, recalled a South Korean warrant officer bellowing instructions at retreating soldiers to stop and take up positions near From's platoon. Other NCOs joined him, gathering about a hundred soldiers near the ford. From thought the South Koreans probably feared the warrant officer more than the Chinese. He wielded a long, thick stick to persuade any soldier who hesitated that he meant business.[7]

For the diggers in 3 RAR's forward companies, the sounds and silhouetted sights of a division of 10,000 South Korean troops retreating among thousands of desperate civilians jolted them from their leisurely occupation of the hills around Chuktun-ni into well-practised preparations for combat. They checked weapons and clips of ammunition, placing grenades and spare magazines within easy reach. Bren and Vickers gunners carefully arranged their ammunition to ensure they could maintain high rates of suppressive fire.

Waiting for combat, especially at night, is a nerve-wracking and tense experience. Many of the Australians had experienced Chinese night attacks and counterattacks in earlier defensive battles, particularly at Pakchon. Most had been in brutal close-quarter fighting. They relied on the instinct for self-preservation and a desire to protect their mates to fuel their fighting spirit. Few were motivated by a desire to kill. Their world was the stretch of dark ground directly before them. They anticipated the moment of intense excitement and fear when their attackers would close in on them, and they would open fire.[8]

Shortly after Ferguson prevented O'Dowd from firing over the refugees' heads to expose enemy troops hidden among them, firing broke out at BHQ. The Chinese had got behind the forward companies. A Company was now isolated, and an attack was only a matter of how long it would take for the Chinese to find O'Dowd and his diggers in the dark and get organised.[9]

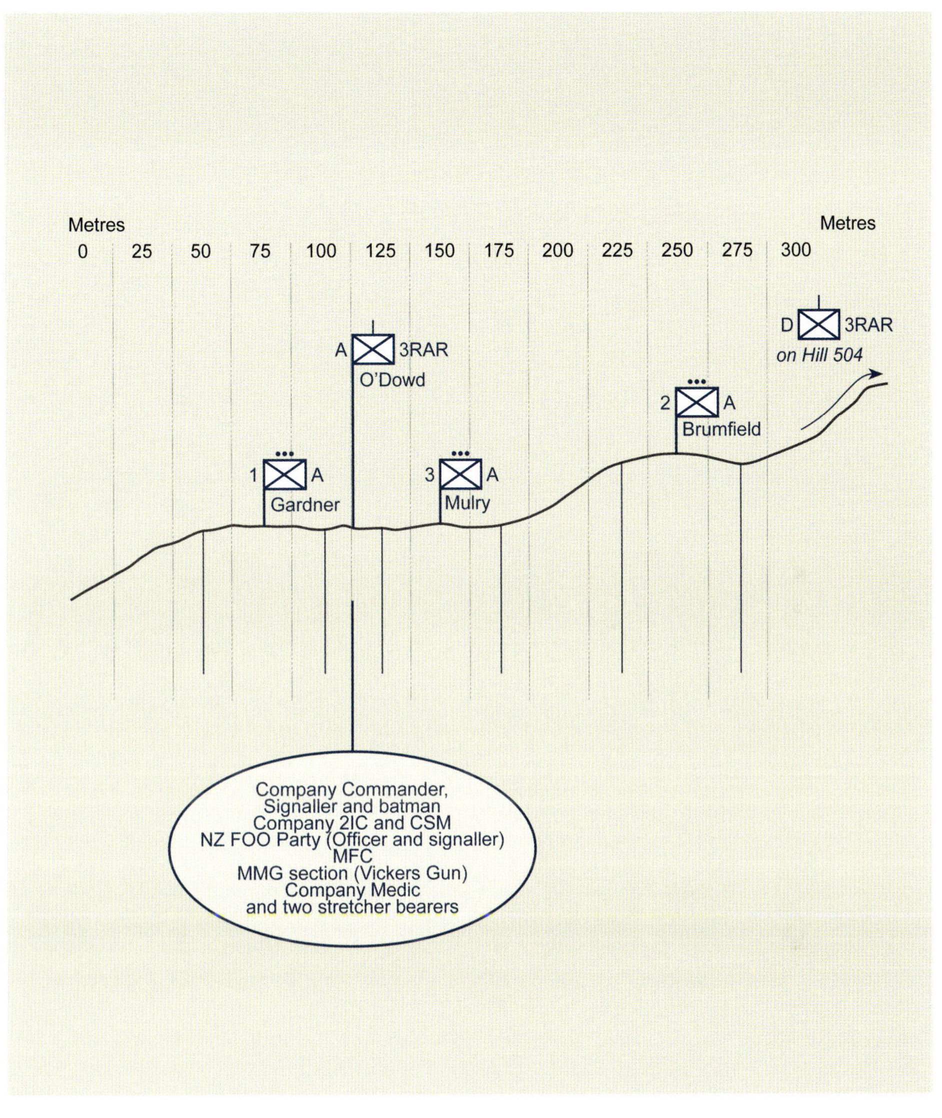

Figure 1. Layout of A Company positions at 1900hrs, 23 April 1951 (based on a trace provided by LTCOL BS O'Dowd, MBE (RL) in 1992)

MAJOR BERNARD 'BEN' O'DOWD

Captain Ben O'Dowd accompanies Lieutenant General Sir William Birdwood CB, CBE, MC as he inspects members of 3 RAR forming a guard of honour at Kure, Japan, in March 1949. (PHOTOGRAPHER: IAN ROBERTSON, AWM P01813.274)

Bruce Ferguson, Ben O'Dowd, the legacy of Charlie Green and the experience and grit of corporals and diggers substantially impacted how and why the Australians fought the way they did at Kapyong. O'Dowd's outstanding leadership under fire during a stubborn A Company defence overnight on 23–24 April, and a night withdrawal of the forward companies under fire overnight 24–25 April, begs the questions, 'What made him?', 'What was exceptional about him?' and 'What can the contemporary Army learn from him?'

Bernard 'Ben' O'Dowd was born in Perth in 1918. At the age of 10, he became a ward of the State of Western Australia, and he left school at 14. After holding several low-paid jobs in Perth, he found work as an underground miner – a bogger – near Kalgoorlie, before joining the 2nd/11th Battalion in 1939, aged 21. He was wounded at Derna in Libya, in January 1941, returning to duty as a newly promoted corporal that June. The battalion fought in New Guinea from 1944 to 1945. O'Dowd received a commendation for the Member of the British Empire (MBE) award for his leadership under fire. He had led his men through a swamp and into an area with large numbers of Japanese to drive off an enemy patrol and prevent his company from being surrounded.[10]

O'Dowd was commissioned in the field and volunteered to serve with the occupation forces in Japan, arriving in February 1946. In October 1948, he completed a four-week commissioning course in Japan. The following year, he was promoted to captain, assuming duty as a company commander in 3 RAR.

When the Korean War broke out, O'Dowd joined K Force, becoming Charlie Green's 'Battle 2IC' four weeks after arriving in South Korea. O'Dowd kept a photo of his former CO for the rest of his life.[11] He was wounded in March 1951 and returned to duty a month later. The following week, he and his men faced the Chinese onslaught at Kapyong.

First assaults

The rapidity of the Chinese advance, despite their difficulties in communicating and observing at night, and their scarcity of radios and maps below battalion level, gave them the initiative at the start of the Battle of Kapyong – as did their achieving surprise by attacking three separate places within thirty minutes from 9.30pm.

The first was against Lieutenant Di Martino's tanks, positioned north of B Company. A Chinese company attacked without pausing for reconnaissance right off their line of march at 9.30pm. Fortunately for the US tankers, their vulnerability to night attacks by infantry was mitigated by the clear night. But visibility was still inadequate for tank commanders to operate with their hatches closed. They bravely directed fire and manoeuvred their tanks with their heads above the turrets. The shock from the tank gun and machine-gun fire broke the Chinese momentum, pushing them back. They had 'bumped' the tanks and would attack them more astutely next time. The failure to coordinate the tanks and infantry in defence led to unnecessary casualties later that evening.

Even before Di Martino began dealing with assaults on his tanks, there were warning signs that many Chinese had bypassed them and were pressing up against A Company. Private Pat Knowles and another digger were in a listening post on A Company's left flank, about twenty metres further down the ridgeline towards the valley floor from Freddie Gardner's 1 Platoon. At about 8.30pm, they heard voices below their post. Knowles reported them to Gardner. On returning to his position, he heard more voices and weapons being cocked. Knowles crept up to 1 Platoon again, informing Gardner and going from post to post to warn everyone. An hour later, a runner found him with a message from O'Dowd: 'Shut up and stop panicking. There is no one down there'.[12]

Within minutes, a Chinese probing attack on Gardner's 1 Platoon proved Knowles right. Gardner, a recent enlistment to the Australian Army from the British Army, told O'Dowd that he had beaten off the attack but could hear more Chinese lining up in the valley below, preparing to have another go. Presumably, O'Dowd told him to hold his position, and Gardner and his diggers strained to hear and see when and where their opponents would attack next.

Meanwhile, while the Chinese were attacking Gardner's platoon and Di Martino's tanks, a more ominous attack intensified two kilometres behind them in Ferguson's headquarters area. Soon after firing erupted from the probing attacks on Gardner's platoon, groups of Chinese began shooting at close range on the BHQ, anti-tank, mortar and assault pioneer positions. A 3.5-inch anti-tank rocket smashed into a Sherman tank near the headquarters, mortally wounding its commander. Refugees scattered everywhere and made it difficult to identify attackers, though muzzle flashes allowed defenders to return some aimed fire.[13]

At BHQ, Sergeant 'Doc' Tampling, 3 RAR's Medical Sergeant, saw bullet holes appearing halfway up the RAP tent and, worried that the six-foot-six doctor might get 'his head blown off', told Don Beard to get down as more bullets tore through the canvas. 'We definitely knew that it was "on" in our area', said Tampling.[14]

Soldiers of 3 Platoon, A Company, 3 RAR, 1951. (AWM 044746)

Unhelpfully for Ferguson, withdrawing vehicles and tank movements had cut the telephone lines to three of the forward companies, leaving only one open to Laughlin's B Company.[15] To make Ferguson's coordination of the defensive battle even more difficult, his headquarters signallers could not raise the forward companies on the battalion command net frequency except through C Company, the closest company.

It was an unlikely coincidence for four rifle companies to have damaged radios simultaneously. A more likely reason for the radio communications breakdown was BHQ's low ground location two kilometres down the road, and the characteristics of the recently issued US Type 31 VHF radio sets. There had been no time for training on them, and some Australian operators may not have been aware of the line-of-sight requirement to ensure effective communication, or of other requirements for efficiently operating these radios. According to Jack Gallaway, the Signals Sergeant, who was on leave during the battle but examined the area decades later, BHQ was not on a line-of-sight to the forward companies except B and C companies. Signallers in A and D could communicate with each other and C Company, but not BHQ.[16] According to Corporal Lindsay Beeck, Ferguson's signaller,

Ferguson did not direct him to turn his radio on and join the battalion command net after the telephone lines were cut. Beeck does not remember Ferguson using the radio overnight, but he did resume radio communications the next day when moving to the forward companies.[17] Ferguson said later that he did have radio communications with D Company when he came forward the next day, and presumably would have connected to the other companies as he came closer.[18]

Guns or no guns?

Personal accounts and official records provide a contradictory picture of the artillery support available on the night of 23–24 April. O'Dowd recalled it would have 'been comforting to have artillery registered ... so that defensive tasks could smash up the enemy in their assembly areas', but that his attached Kiwi Forward Observation Officer informed him the guns were not available because 'the guns had moved into position after dark and were not surveyed in'.[19] Darcy Laughlin wrote in 1952 that B Company did have close artillery support. O'Dowd, citing a subsequent investigation, disputes this.[20] Regarding his own company and what he could hear, he wrote:

> *I was well experienced in recognising incoming and outgoing artillery fire, and I know we had no such support on the first night of Kapyong. Furthermore, I can find no other soldier who experienced it that night ... I understand that ... [New Zealand gunners] fired a tremendous number of shells ... but these must have been in support of the Canadians or somewhere well out of hearing from our location.*[21]

The gunners had decided to 'leapfrog' their batteries further back to a location south of the Middlesex position, disrupting but not stopping the artillery support. One battery was always available to the Australians that night.[22] But the gunners couldn't provide optimal support. They could not survey all their guns in, having moved into position after dark. The 27 BCB War Diary states that the Middlesex and two New Zealand batteries were back in position by 11pm on 23 April, leaving one battery available for tasks. It also mentions that two US batteries of Self-Propelled 105mm howitzers, previously supporting the 6th ROK Division, were placed under the command of 27 BCB. Presumably, this additional firepower was available on the night of 23–24 April, at least in the early hours of 24 April.[23]

A possible explanation for the lack of support for A Company is that O'Dowd's NZ FOO, Lieutenant Dennis Fielden, and his signaller were killed by Chinese small-arms fire during the initial assaults on O'Dowd's headquarters. They would have done everything possible to call down artillery fire if they had not been killed, and it had been available.[24] But this assumes that no one else in the company could call and adjust the fall of shellfire, which seems unlikely. The conflicting accounts suggest both the difference in individual companies' experiences and how chaotic the situation was that night.

A pause

The Australians were being surrounded. By 11pm on 23 April, after probing attacks on Di Martino's northern tank platoon, 1 Platoon and BHQ, the Chinese had closed up on A and B companies closest to the valley floor and infiltrated further south, despite the tanks inflicting heavy casualties. There was a pause while they regrouped, but the situation was dire. Ferguson's headquarters was cut off from his forward companies. Laughlin was the only company commander Ferguson could speak to by telephone; he could only communicate with his other company commanders by radio on the battalion net via C Company. He chose not to interrupt artillery radio communications to speak to them through the artillery forward observers, located with each company. The mortar fire control net was closed too. The 3-inch mortar crews, commanded by Captain Phillip Bennett, who would go on to serve as Chief of the Australian Defence Force (1984–87) and Governor of Tasmania (1987–95), were busy fighting a small-arms battle in defence of their mortar line.

US mortar support was about to disappear. After completing several fire missions forward of Laughlin's B Company in support of Di Martino's tanks, the men of the US 4.2-inch heavy mortar company abandoned their vehicles and mortars and withdrew south-east.[25] Chinese attacks in the BHQ area, and the fear of being cut off by others who had infiltrated further south, appeared to have been sufficient justification for the US commander to decide to save his soldiers by withdrawing on foot.

The second wave of assaults

The Chinese assaulted Di Martino's tanks north of B Company again at about 10.30pm, an hour after the first attack. This time, they were prepared. In quick succession, bullets hit each tank commander. Di Martino slumped down into his hatch, mortally wounded. His wounded subordinates decided to pull their tanks further south along the valley to receive treatment.[26]

At the sound of them leaving, Lieutenant Jim Young, B Company's acting 2IC, ran out to try and stop them. In his haste, he ran down the side of the hill and onto the valley floor without a weapon. A tank driver told Young he was moving to the rear to get medical attention for his crew commander and reload. Young persuaded him to stay and support B Company for a while longer, on condition that the crew commander be evacuated to the Australian RAP in a B Company jeep. He also promised that B Company vehicles would bring tank ammunition up from A Echelon. As Young guided the tank into position, he spotted movement to the right of the road. Thinking it was ROK troops, he called out and was answered with a Chinese grenade. He dived for cover, as did a US heavy mortar FOO and his signaller, who had been looking for A Company. The tank driver reversed, and the grenade exploded harmlessly on the road. As Young lay in a ditch, Chinese troops chasing the tank ran over him, throwing several grenades in his direction without effect. After lying low for a while, he made his way back to B Company.[27]

16TH FIELD REGIMENT, ROYAL NEW ZEALAND ARTILLERY

The 16th Field Regiment, Royal New Zealand Artillery, was the mainstay of New Zealand's commitment to the Korean War. It was raised on 27 October 1950 specially for service in Korea and made up of volunteers from New Zealand's own 'Kayforce', who had begun training two months earlier. Prior to volunteering, only one in ten of these men had experience with artillery, and only one in three had undergone any form of military service. Composed of three gun batteries – 161, 162 and 163 – each equipped with eight 25-pounder field guns, the 16th Field Regiment joined the 27th Commonwealth Brigade in Korea on 26 January 1951.

Deployed forward in support of Republic of Korea forces, the 16th Field Regiment was the first 27th Brigade unit into action as Chinese forces advanced along the Kapyong Valley. The extent and effects of its fire at various points in the battle have been debated by veterans and historians, but there is no doubt as to its critical overall role. From 23 to 25 April, the 16th Field Regiment's own guns fired around 10,000 rounds at ranges from 2,700 to 9,000 metres. By the evening of 24 April, it was controlling the fire of seven United States batteries in addition to its own guns.

For its actions at Kapyong, the 16th Regiment was awarded a South Korean Presidential Citation, which it noted merited the 'highest praise':

> *Two Batteries were initially forward in support of 6 Republic of Korea Division and these were skilfully withdrawn to join the balance of the Regiment in a new position which 27th British Commonwealth Brigade had been ordered to hold at all costs. Throughout the battle during the nights of 23rd and 24th April and all day of 24th April it operated its guns ceaselessly and efficiently and played an important part in holding the position.*

After Kapyong, the 16th Field Regiment operated as part of the 28th British Commonwealth Brigade, and later alongside British and Canadian regiments to comprise the divisional artillery to the 1st British Commonwealth Division. Its last rounds of the Korean War were fired at 0530hrs on 2 July 1953, just four-and-a-half hours before the ceasefire came into being. Since its guns first came into action on 29 January 1951, the 16th Field Regiment had fired more than 800,000 rounds.

The 16th Field Regiment was disbanded following the end of the Korean War but was re-raised in 1958 as part of the New Zealand Army's regular brigade group. The Anzac links forged throughout the Korean War were subsequently renewed when 161 Battery supported Australian forces in South Vietnam between 1965 and 1971, including as the Direct Support Battery for 3 RAR during its 1967–68 deployment.

A battery of New Zealand 25-pounder (Mark II) guns gives artillery support to a 3 RAR reconnaissance, in force across the Imjin River, June 1951. (PHOTOGRAPHER: PHILLIP HOBSON, AWM HOBJ2238)

He was not the only officer walking about in the dark that night, worrying about the tactical situation. Lieutenant Wilfred Miller, a young West Point graduate commanding the other tank platoon assigned to the valley floor near B Company's area, heard Di Martino's tanks withdrawing. Like Young, he was keen for them to stay and fight. In a letter written in 1978, Miller recalled stopping a platoon of tanks that were coming back, and saw Di Martino's body with a bullet wound between the eyes. He walked forward to find out what was happening, sensing soldiers to his left, right and in front, just three yards away. Thinking they were South Korean, Miller called out as they approached. They immediately dispersed, hit the ground and fired at him as he threw all the grenades he had, fired his pistol till it was empty and then ran until he came to some Australian infantry positions, grateful that they did not shoot him.[28]

Miller had directed the tanks of the late Di Martino's platoon to hold in the rear of his own platoon, but they continued back past BHQ and their company headquarters to obtain medical assistance and replenish ammunition. For the next hour, groups of Chinese probed around B Company's position. One group got into the headquarters area, took casualties and withdrew.

Miller's tanks continued to fire on the long columns of Chinese they saw marching down the road in the distance. Unlike Di Martino, he had plenty of infantry support on either side from the A and B Company ridges, preventing the Chinese from getting close enough to pick off his tank commanders.

Continuing Chinese assaults

Corporal Clem Kealy, commanding the B Company standing patrol further north on the tip of the low ridgeline, was in a dilemma: 'How long can I do my job before I have to withdraw?' At 11pm, he reported to Laughlin by telephone that the Chinese were massing on the valley floor below him and on his flanks. Soon after, Laughlin ordered him to withdraw to the main B Company position.[29]

Thirty minutes later, at least two Chinese companies assaulted Lieutenant Len Montgomerie's 4 Platoon. Australian machine guns and rifles, and US tank fire from the valley floor, repulsed them. The Chinese had no answer for the Australians' resolve to hold ground, or for the firepower they and the Americans brought to bear. By 1.30am, after taking heavy casualties in several more assaults, the Chinese withdrew. All was silent again around B Company's perimeter.

There were no Australian casualties, mainly because they had good fields of fire from higher ground. Accurate shooting from experienced Australian infantry soldiers cut down the attackers before they could return effective fire or get within grenade range. Defenders lying down low to the ground and taking aimed shots can inflict more casualties than attackers running forward, firing from the hip, or pausing to fire from a kneeling position. Tanks using both their main armaments and heavy machine guns on one flank compounded the Chinese soldiers' ordeal.

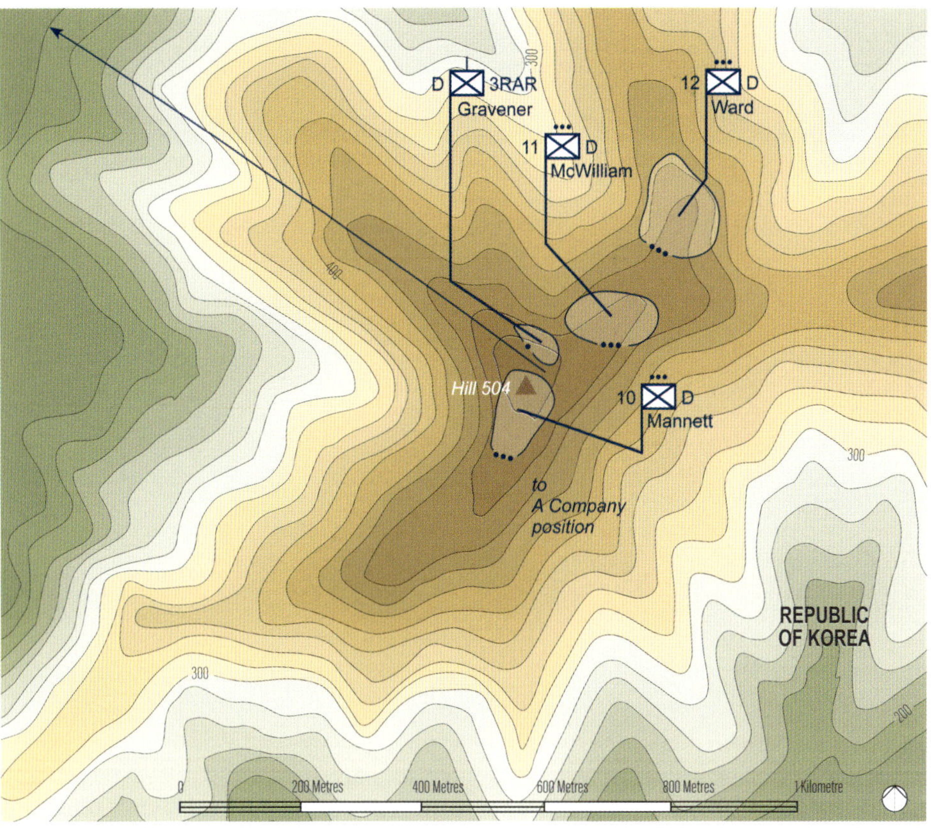

Map 5. Layout of D Company positions at 1900hrs, 23 April 1951 (based on a trace provided by MAJ WN Gravener, MBE (RL) in 1992)

Unable to dislodge B Company, and after heavy losses, the Chinese changed their axis of attack to A Company, possibly realising that they needed to capture the high ground held by O'Dowd (A Company) and Gravener (D Company) before dawn. After sunrise, they would be prey for US tank and Australian small-arms fire, as well as New Zealand and US artillery. Worst of all, aircraft carrying bombs, napalm, rockets and cannons would seek them out.

US ARMOUR AT KAPYONG

The experience of the Second World War had demonstrated to the United States Army, as it emphasised in the 1949 edition of its *Field Service Regulations*, that 'no one arm wins battles'. Thus, a tank battalion was added to the establishment of each infantry regiment (in the United States Army this was a three-battalion organisation), and a heavy tank battalion to each infantry division. Formed in October 1948, the 72nd Heavy Tank Battalion was the divisional tank battalion of the United States 2nd Infantry Division in Korea. Despite its title, only one of its three companies were equipped with a 'heavy' tank – the M26 Pershing with a 90mm gun – and the other two were equipped with M4A3E8 Sherman medium tanks.

The M4A3E8 tanks of Company A were, nonetheless, fundamental to the success of the defensive action at Kapyong. They occupied blocking positions early in the battle, closely supported the infantry defence, evacuated casualties and brought forward ammunition, and mounted several counterattacks. By the time the battle was over, Company A had expended 32,000 rounds of .30-in calibre machine-gun, 11,830 rounds of .50-in calibre machine-gun and 162 rounds of 76 mm high explosive. No tanks were lost in the battle, although two were damaged by hits from 3.5-in rockets. Three tankers were killed and twelve wounded.

An assessment of the battle by the Armor Officer of US IX Corps, Lieutenant Colonel George B Pickett, attributed the successful employment of the tanks at Kapyong to detailed tactical, terrain and trafficability reconnaissance that had been conducted by First Lieutenant Kenneth Koch, the Company Commander, and several other armoured officers in the days prior to the battle. This allowed the identification of routes, objectives, fighting positions and likely enemy concentration areas, which facilitated rapid movement and action.

The battle, however, highlighted that inherent vulnerabilities of armour needed to be managed. Reflecting on the need for Koch's tanks to sally back and forth during the battle, Pickett noted that tanks are incapable of continuous action and must have a protected area in which to refuel, rearm and be maintained. He also reminded that tanks occupying a combat outpost at night needed to be closely protected by dismounted troops. Many of Pickett's observations reflected the chaotic nature of the battle that swirled around the tanks: the imperative for tank commanders to fight with their tank and crew rather than becoming fixated on firing the external machine gun; the loss of situational awareness if a tank commander 'buttoned down' his hatch; and the potential to lose control if armour officers dismount to direct their tanks on foot.

These points aside, Pickett lauded the 'aggressive determination and outstanding leadership' of Company A's officers, which was reflected in the award of a Distinguished Service Cross (US) and a Military Cross (UK) to First Lieutenant Koch, and a Distinguished Service Cross to First Lieutenant Wilfred Miller, the commander of a tank platoon.

Members of 3 RAR riding on a US M4A3E8 Sherman tank. (PHOTOGRAPHER: PHILLIP HOBSON, AWM HOBJ1521)

Battle of Kapyong diorama, by Dean Colls and Louise Skacej, 2007. The night-time scene shows four Australian soldiers gallantly protecting the rear of B Company, located on an island feature of the Kapyong Valley. (MIXED MEDIA, 1940 × 5300 × 2650MM, AWM ART93183)

By midnight, even after the setback against B Company, the Chinese were still capable of aggressive assaults. O'Dowd later wrote that A Company's initial contacts came via enemy probing patrols searching for soft spots and coming upon forward weapons pits. The Australians, said O'Dowd, 'shot them off the ridge'. Then things became more serious:

> *... the fight for our ridge line started in earnest with the Chinese blowing bugles and whistles ... to assemble their men. When the bugles and whistles stopped, we knew that they were on their way. Some ... did not carry weapons – just bucketfuls of grenades. Our next indication of an assault was the showers of grenades ... exploding all around us. The Chinese grenadiers had the job of keeping my diggers' heads down so the riflemen and machine gunners could rush in and get amongst us.*[30]

Sergeant George Harris, A Company's acting CSM, remembered Gardner's 1 Platoon also repulsing a series of assaults, each one preceded by bugles and whistles. The dead and wounded were carried out during the lulls between attacks, and fit men moved forward. CHQ and 3 Platoon also came under attack. A Company was in danger of being overrun.[31]

By midnight, 1 Platoon was desperately hanging on. All the Bren gunners had been killed or wounded. Gardner's fighting strength had been reduced from about thirty men to thirteen; some of this group were also wounded. He knew the next Chinese attack might be strong enough to overrun the remnants of his platoon. He moved back to confer with O'Dowd, who ordered him to withdraw back into the company headquarters area. He did so, and the Chinese quickly occupied the vacated 1 Platoon position.

A Company stared out into the darkness in the early hours of 24 April, awaiting the next Chinese assault. O'Dowd wrote later, 'I now had the ludicrous situation of three platoons on the feature, one of them being Chinese and definitely not under command'. The perimeter was thinly manned, and he feared that an enemy attack on the left flank, combined with a frontal assault, could have succeeded. But the Chinese didn't press their advantage. O'Dowd guessed that there was no officer or anyone with authority to organise them.[32]

From 2am to 3am, the attacks grew sporadic. O'Dowd thought Chinese casualties 'must have been tremendous, for they poured themselves into the defenders' fire'.[33] They had had enough of A Company and began dropping mortar and incendiary bombs on them, setting alight the low heather that ran through the area: 'a thick blanket of smoke and exploding ammunition adding to the distress of the casualties' lying on the cold ground in the open.[34]

CO 3 RAR's movements overnight 23–24 April

While Laughlin and O'Dowd had been fighting defensive battles from about 10.30pm to 1am, neither Gravener's D Company nor Saunders' C Company had come under attack. Private Stan Bombell, a C Company rifleman, remembered feeling uneasy when firing broke out, and remained awake for the entire night. A young reinforcement with him slept soundly until the morning.[35] From 10pm to 1am, the BHQ position came under intermittent fire from groups of Chinese infiltrators. The noise and lack of landline or radio communications made it tough for Ferguson to control his forward companies' defensive battle. However, he managed to speak with his old Second World War comrade, Darcy Laughlin, by telephone. Laughlin informed Ferguson of B Company's relatively secure situation and of the sounds of combat coming from A Company's ridgeline.[36]

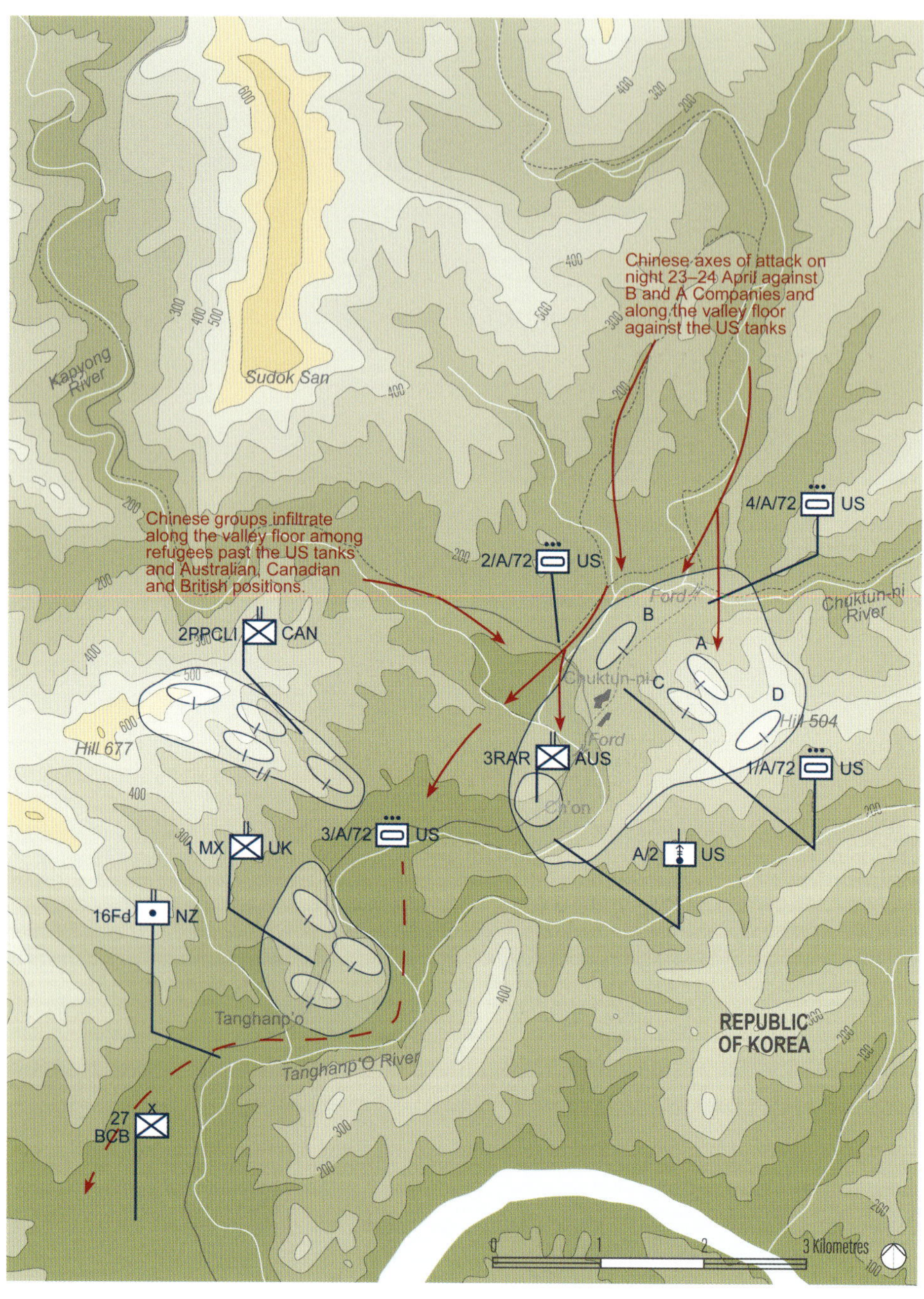

Map 6. 27 BCB situation at 2200hrs, 23 April 1951 (based on a trace provided by MAJ J Gerke, DSO in 1952)

Ferguson decided to visit the Middlesex position and report to Brigadier Burke at HQ 27 BCB, located further south. The brigade's war diary records that communications with 3 RAR failed at 1.40am on 24 April, suggesting something had happened to the British signals detachment responsible for maintaining a rear link from 3 RAR to Brigade Headquarters. However, there is no record of the activities of this group, and none appear to have become casualties. Ferguson drove to the Middlesex HQ and used the Middlesex rear-link radio set to Burke's headquarters to report 3 RAR's situation. According to the 27 BCB diary, Ferguson said that the Chinese had assaulted his forward companies and his headquarters simultaneously, resulting in two battles. He knew little of the forward companies' situation due to the poor communications.[37] While Ferguson was away, neither O'Dowd nor Gravener could recall anyone from BHQ speaking to them in the early hours of 24 April.[38]

To have reported back to Brigade HQ from the Middlesex Headquarters at 1.40am meant that Ferguson had left BHQ at about 1.15am. Jack Gallaway, the Signals Sergeant at the time, believed that a breakdown in communications between 3 RAR BHQ and Brigade HQ is unlikely to have been the reason for Ferguson going to the Middlesex HQ. He explained that communications to BHQ was by WS19 or WS19 HP, of which there were two sets, operated by Royal Corps of Signallers personnel, in the rear-link signallers' purpose-built vehicle. The HP set was capable of broadcasting voice communications as far as Tokyo. Gallaway believed that either one could have reached Brigade HQ on low power with a single length of aerial.[39] This technical explanation does not remove the possibility that this detachment was not operating or available for other reasons.

Ferguson explained to an interviewer in 1986 that his HQ was overrun and had sustained heavy casualties. Unable to exercise command in that rapidly deteriorating situation and with communications restricted to one company, he explained, 'you can't command anything if you can't tell them what to do'. Ferguson said he withdrew in the middle of the night because the obvious place from which to command was the Middlesex HQ, where he could speak to the gunners, UN aircraft and the brigade.[40] Missing from this explanation was how to communicate with and command the forward companies. Ferguson seemed to be saying that his priority when forward companies were under fire and trying to hold ground was to marshal fire support and organise reinforcements.

Eyewitnesses suggest Ferguson was compelled to seek the security of the Middlesex position because of Laughlin's report of A and B companies being under heavy attack, and his headquarters receiving harassing fire from infiltrators. Len Eyles, his adjutant, remembered that before he departed, Ferguson issued a warning order to withdraw the remainder of BHQ at first light. Eyles told the author that Ferguson inexplicably also took the battalion's rear-link radio set, the only means for 3 RAR to communicate with HQ 27 BCB if the British signallers were out of action.[41]

Alf Argent told the author that Ferguson directed him to go about a kilometre down the road towards the Middlesex to prepare for 'stepping back' a tactical headquarters to maintain radio communications before main headquarters' withdrawal at first light. He did so, taking up a position about a kilometre south of the primary BHQ position in anticipation of Ferguson and a tactical headquarters team arriving. Much to his dismay, he saw Ferguson drive past him towards the Middlesex. Argent waited, wondering why Ferguson had changed his mind and gone back without him.[42]

Gallaway also spoke with Argent and interviewed Ferguson's signaller, Lindsay Beeck, who was equally puzzled. Beeck remembered Ferguson leaving him behind, rendering the CO unable to communicate with his fighting units. Stranger still, said Gallaway, was that Ferguson took the rear-link radio with him, making it impossible for staff at BHQ to communicate with him or Brigade HQ. He remained out of communication until he returned, and Beeck rejoined him the following morning.[43]

Could a perception of his headquarters being overrun have prompted Ferguson to move back to the Middlesex position? With tongue in cheek, Argent told the author in 1992 that the only real danger he saw at BHQ that night was Len Eyles striding down the road with his pistol drawn. However, he does recall a cacophony of battle sounds: tanks and bazookas firing, grenades exploding, and small arms firing in the BHQ area.[44] He and others deny that the headquarters area was overrun or that there were 'casualties everywhere' as Ferguson told Kit Denton in 1986.[45]

The number of casualties in the BHQ area is one indicator of the fighting's intensity. The Assault Pioneers had one soldier killed; the Anti-Tank Platoon's platoon sergeant was seriously wounded and died later. The Signals Platoon lost two soldiers.[46] At least four more soldiers were killed in the BHQ area – two from the LMG Section, and two Regimental Police who died when a Chinese infiltrator threw a grenade into their jeep. Captain Phil Bennett reported later that the Mortar Platoon had to fight off several Chinese attacks of about squad size during the night, suffering three wounded.[47]

The Official History, possibly informed by Ferguson, describes a desperate battle around Ferguson's HQ from before 10pm as Chinese troops, mingling with retreating South Koreans, bypassed BHQ and the US tanks, surrounded the headquarters and set up a roadblock to the south. O'Neill wrote that a section of light machine guns, the whole of the Assault Pioneer Platoon and the Regimental Police section were hit by waves of Chinese assaults and forced back. Intensified Chinese attacks on the HQ's perimeter at dawn, and fire from Chinese positions on the BHQ area from high ground previously held by the light machine-gun section and Assault Pioneer Platoon, led to Ferguson's decision to withdraw.[48]

Interviews conducted with veterans more than three decades after the battle suggest that the situation at BHQ was not as critical as depicted in the Official History. Sergeant Fred From, the Anti-Tank Platoon Commander, and the Assault Pioneer Platoon Commander, Lieutenant Ces Evans, reported that after initial contacts with groups of Chinese infiltrators and some furious exchanges of fire, the BHQ area was relatively quiet for several hours.[49] Most casualties occurred in these opening encounters.

Ferguson told Kit Denton how he feared that his headquarters was, or would soon be, overrun, and of his imperative to clear his supply and casualty evacuation route along the road. He requested a Middlesex company to clear the high ground and take the pressure off his headquarters and the soldiers defending the area, and possibly cover this flank when BHQ withdrew.[50] It is unclear where Ferguson was between 1.40am – when he radioed from the Middlesex HQ, advising Brigade Headquarters of 3 RAR's situation – and about 4am, when Argent met him at the tactical headquarters location that Argent had selected south of the main headquarters. The Brigade War Diary records Ferguson's presence at the Middlesex HQ and his requests for a Middlesex company to clear the route north to BHQ.[51] A British veteran remembered Ferguson briefing his company commander before they moved north up the road, just before dawn. The author could not find anyone who recalls seeing Ferguson at BHQ during the hours after 01.30am. According to Lyndsay Beeck, Ferguson appears to have moved forward from the Middlesex position and met with Argent south of BHQ, just before first light.[52] It is probable that Ferguson briefed the Middlesex company near the Middlesex position around 3.30am, then went forward behind them for personal security.

Ferguson likely joined Argent about a kilometre south of BHQ before first light, which was at 5.15am. Argent saw linesmen bringing telephones and cable back from the main headquarters to establish a Tactical Headquarters. Soon after the group assembled there, it was hit by mortar fire, wounding one of the signallers. Argent wondered if this mortar blast was what temporarily deafened Ferguson. He and Ferguson returned to the Middlesex who, said Argent, 'were very thin on the ground'. By then, the sun had begun to rise, and Argent felt that withdrawing with Ferguson after the mortars had fallen near them was 'very undignified'.[53]

Help from the Middlesex

The relief force, D Company, 1st Battalion, the Middlesex Regiment, made their way up the road to relieve pressure on BHQ just before dawn. Argent met the British company commander on the road south of the abandoned US mortar company's vehicles and directed him to high ground west of BHQ. The Middlesex assaulted up the slope at approximately 4.40am and drove the Chinese from their positions, suffering six casualties. Second Lieutenant Barry Reed, the Middlesex assault platoon commander, received the Military Cross for this action.[54]

Another pause

Meanwhile, while Ferguson and BHQ were sorting themselves out in the early hours of 24 April, the Chinese assaulted A and B companies for the last time under the cover of darkness. At 2am, the Chinese assaulted O'Dowd's headquarters and Harold Mulry's co-located 3 Platoon. A Company repelled their attackers, who had the added advantage of launching their assaults from 1 Platoon's former position. At 2.15am, they assaulted B Company but were also thwarted.

SECOND LIEUTENANT BARRY ST GEORGE AUSTIN REED, D COMPANY, 1ST BATTALION, THE MIDDLESEX REGIMENT

Second Lieutenant Barry Reed's Military Cross citation verifies the intensity of fighting near 3 RAR's BHQ. It shows that the Chinese had occupied the high ground overlooking the BHQ area. Indeed, the volume of fire prompted the British CO to order the OC of D Company to withdraw, carrying four wounded soldiers, and to later award a Military Cross to Reed, the platoon commander who led the attack on the Chinese positions. Interestingly, after dawn, the Australians could move around the BHQ area untroubled by Chinese fire.

Born in Hertfordshire, England, on 5 May 1931, Barry St George Austin Reed was the eldest son of Douglas Austin Reed and Mary Ellen Philpott.[55] He was educated at Rugby School before being commissioned into the 1st Battalion, Middlesex Regiment, in 1950 for national service. Serving in Korea, Reed commanded a platoon without a break from November 1950 until May 1951.

It was during the Battle of Kapyong that Reed demonstrated the power of his leadership as a platoon commander. During the battle, Reed's company was ordered to seize a small ridge and protect the left flank of the Australian Command Post, which was in danger of being overrun. Coming under fire from the left flank, Reed led his soldiers along the road. In the darkness and confusion throughout the action that followed, Reed maintained complete command of his platoon. When four of the six men in his left-hand section were wounded and began to falter, Reed rallied the group and drove off the attack, saving his company from almost certain encirclement and making their withdrawal with the wounded possible. His citation stated, '[Reed] showed great dash and determination, leading his men with exceptional skill, never hesitating to get to grips with the enemy'.

After his time in Korea, Reed remained a territorial officer with the British Army until 1960, when he retired at the rank of major.

On leaving the army, Reed sought employment at Harrods department store in London to gain experience in menswear, which was the family trade.[56] In 1953, he joined the family business – the Austin Reed Company – which was a menswear company founded in 1900 by his grandfather. The company had seen success with 'off-the-peg' suits and men's formalwear throughout the 1920s, made Winston Churchill's wartime 'siren suits' during the 1940s, and had acquired a Royal Warrant as hosier to King George VI. In 1958, Reed became the Managing Director and brought a new focus to the company's fashion line, bringing it relevance into the 1960s. Barry married first in 1956 to Patricia Bristow, who died in 2002, and found love again in 2005 with Mary Rose Farquharson.[57] Reed died in October 2020, survived by Mary Rose, and a son and daughter from his first marriage.[58]

There was now a welcome respite for the Australians until dawn. The heavy casualties caused by A and B companies and the US tanks appeared to persuade Chinese commanders to break contact and regroup during the remaining hours of darkness. They had not pushed the Australians off their positions with hasty attacks off the line of march down the valley overnight. They had not troubled D Company, located on top of Hill 504, and C Company, located behind A and D companies. A Company had borne the brunt of the Chinese attacks overnight and had lost 50 per cent of its fighting strength. Despite heavy exchanges of fire during assaults, B Company had not sustained any casualties. Laughlin and his men were still dominating the valley floor and the north–south road from high ground and had the comfort of hearing tanks operating below them and to the north.

The ordeal for A Company was about to resume as the sun began to rise. Chinese mortars and mountain guns had caught up with their infantry. Observers could now locate the Australians in the growing light and call fire down onto them.[59] Chinese mortar bombs began to fall behind O'Dowd's forward positions, where over fifty casualties lay. O'Dowd had no way of evacuating the wounded with the enemy in control of the ground behind his company down the valley. They were moved to the reverse slope of the ridgeline, away from direct enemy fire. Corporal Nobby Clarke, the company medic, and his orderlies worked on them with what meagre resources they had in their medical bags. They had no morphine – there was no way to treat pain.[60] 'The blokes just had to suffer', remembered O'Dowd.[61] Wound dressings soon ran out; water, too. There was no way of properly treating the wounded for shock by keeping them warm. O'Dowd recalled:

> *We could only lay them on the cold ground and cover them in any blankets or sleeping bags we could get our hands on and wait for the morning. Had we been able to keep them warm and treat them for the shock and pain, perhaps some of them that died would have lived.*[62]

West of Kapyong, the second night of attacks on 29 BCB near the Imjin River on 23–24 April demonstrated the risk of trying to hold ground without reinforcement. Between 11pm and dawn, waves of Chinese attempted to force a 29 BCB retreat by overrunning the Glosters. Tank, artillery and mortar fire slaughtered hundreds of attackers, but the Chinese failed to annihilate the Glosters. 29 BCB had been mauled for a second night, but held its ground. The surviving Glosters consolidated on Gloster Hill to await their fate.[63] The Chinese had also mauled 27 BCB's forward battalion, 3 RAR, but 27 BCB held its ground.

As the sun rose on 24 April after a night of fighting, the commanders of 27 BCB and 29 BCB and their US divisional commander had to decide what to do next. The fate of nearly 3,000 British, Australian, Canadian and New Zealand soldiers lay in their hands. Their choices were to counterattack the Chinese with fresh troops, assaulting through the 27 BCB and 29 BCB positions; reinforce each brigade and direct them to fight on; or withdraw them and hope that UN formations further south had had sufficient time to consolidate.

This chapter explains decision-making under pressure and resilience under fire. Bruce Ferguson, as mentioned earlier, was aware that he was solely responsible for his men's survival. He might have been angry that his headquarters was located two kilometres south of his forward companies on his brigade commander's orders. When he saw the Middlesex drive south and the 6th ROK Division Headquarters depart, he could have decided to set up a tactical headquarters and push forward. Instead, under pressure from Chinese infiltrators and to improve communications, he withdrew to the Middlesex position to confer with his brigade commander, having ordered his headquarters staff to join him there after first light. His forward company commanders would have appreciated knowing what he was doing and what he planned to do next.

The first night's battle highlights the determination of A and B companies to hold their ground under fire. A Company's defence was exemplary, and the number of casualties demonstrates their tenacity. B Company may have been tempted to join the withdrawing tanks but chose to hold their positions, aware that the Chinese were on the valley floor in substantial numbers and advancing to cut them off. The forward two platoons of the US tank company performed admirably in the face of hundreds of attacking infantry. One platoon remained in position despite being tempted to withdraw after witnessing another platoon sustain casualties.

In contrast, Bruce Ferguson's overnight movements were puzzling, and his recollections years later were uneven. This chapter focuses on his actions because they were unusual, controversial among veterans, and significant for educating contemporary commanders on what to do and what not to do in similar high-pressure circumstances. Charlie Green had understood a commanding officer's responsibilities to direct a battle and to plan future manoeuvres, and that logistic support is also a function of command. Green appointed a Battle 2IC [now known as an Operations Officer] to direct operations following his plan and to report to him if something occurred requiring further decisions and directions. This arrangement left Green to think about 3 RAR's future moves and activities.

Concerning resupply, the author could not find documents or information from interviews on the whereabouts or activities of OC Administration Company, who would have been responsible for resupply; and the RSM, who should have overseen ammunition resupply. Both might have been on leave. Nevertheless, Ferguson was still responsible for resupply and casualty evacuation for two of his companies after an intense overnight battle. He was also responsible for directing 3 RAR's overnight operations and for conferring with his brigade commander about the battalion's next moves and activities on 24 April. He now faced some critical decisions after his return to 3 RAR's position in the morning.

CHAPTER 6

DAY BATTLE

24 APRIL 1951

THIS CHAPTER COVERS THE period from first light on 24 April until 3 RAR's withdrawal later that evening. While the defenders had a daylight advantage, decisions had to be made about preparing for another night's defensive battle. Brigadier Burke had to develop a plan to impede the Chinese advance. Ferguson, who consulted with Burke in the early hours of 24 April, had to follow his commander's orders for 3 RAR's part in the coming battle, which did not appear to have changed, despite A Company's casualties and the battalion's isolated location. Both commanders had options. This chapter discusses what they were and describes the consequences of command decisions.

One of Burke's options after the fighting on the night of 23–24 April was to reinforce the Australian position by deploying the Middlesex to Sudok San, following his original plan – but the Middlesex would have to clear the Chinese from this objective. Another was to leave the Australians without reinforcement or flank protection, hoping they could withstand another night of Chinese attacks after replenishment and casualty evacuation. A third was to request reinforcement from his US divisional commander. A fourth was to withdraw the Australians and rely on the Canadians and UN firepower to delay the Chinese, while readying the Middlesex to counterattack. The Australians would be in reserve to cover any additional withdrawal or launch counterattack contingencies.

The first moves after dawn were to adjust 3 RAR's layout, replenish the forward companies and evacuate casualties. Presumably, in his overnight discussion with Burke, Ferguson spoke of tightening his defensive layout by withdrawing B Company across the valley to take up a depth position behind A and D companies on Hill 504. He also asked Burke for a Middlesex company to accompany him to his main headquarters to cover its withdrawal. Later events suggest that he planned to visit the forward companies on the Sherman tanks, resupplying them with ammunition and evacuating casualties. When the promised reinforcement of 3 RAR's position for another night's fighting was cancelled, Ferguson directed O'Dowd to withdraw the forward companies. Let's review these decisions, follow the action on Hill 504 when the Chinese had another crack at dislodging a company position and outflanking the remainder of the battalion, and describe what happened.

Withdrawing battalion headquarters

Ferguson's decision to withdraw his main headquarters had some logic, but his subsequent decision not to establish a tactical headquarters to command the battalion withdrawal that evening did not. Before he left for the Middlesex position after midnight, Ferguson had decided that his headquarters was in an untenable location. He assessed that he and his staff were unable to perform their command functions while under Chinese fire and with unreliable communications between the BHQ and the forward companies. Don Beard wrote later that he was informed of these intentions, confirming the pressure on the main headquarters position.[1] Ferguson wrote later:

> *Just before dawn, I decided that the position of my headquarters would not enable it to regain control of the battle and that I should withdraw to the higher ground occupied by the Middlesex Regiment. Hopefully, with better communications there, I could regain control and thus provide the full weight of supporting fire, including aircraft and artillery support, which were vital if the forward companies were to receive the relief they so urgently needed.*[2]

Positioning himself further away from his forward companies, instead of establishing a tactical headquarters to command the bulk of the battalion from a forward position, is puzzling. Infantry battalion commanders usually direct the actions of company commanders from a forward position nearby, as Charlie Green had done. Specialist officers who accompany a commanding officer's tactical headquarters, and forward observers stationed with each company, ensure the timely use of artillery and mortar support. Forward air controllers in spotter aircraft coordinate close air support. Although responsible for providing fire support for battalion operations, commanding officers rely on these specialists who communicate on separate radio frequencies, employing well-practised procedures to execute fire support plans.

Based on subsequent events, Burke approved Ferguson's decision to consolidate his defensive layout after dawn by withdrawing BHQ to the Middlesex position and directing B Company to cross the valley floor and occupy a position adjacent to C Company, behind A and D companies on Hill 504. Stan Walsh's dismissal after ordering 3 RAR's premature withdrawal at Pakchon five months earlier suggests that Ferguson would not have given up the B Company position without approval. He would have discussed 3 RAR's dangerous situation with Burke by radio and/or in person from the Middlesex position sometime between his arrival at 1.30am and 4am, when he returned to his proposed tactical headquarters.[3] Australia's Official Historian appears to have accepted Ferguson's account. Citing intensified Chinese attacks on BHQ's perimeter at dawn, the casualties among some of the headquarters platoons and direct Chinese fire coming from recently won high ground, O'Neill concludes that Ferguson had no option but withdrawal.[4]

Ferguson's accompanying the Middlesex company sent to secure the high ground on his headquarters' western flank just before dawn suggests he was intent on withdrawing his headquarters and support company elements as planned. Both O'Dowd and Gravener reported later that they were unaware of Ferguson's intentions or of the B Company withdrawal order before Laughlin and his men set out across the valley floor. Ferguson had not communicated with either officer overnight.[5]

After Chinese troops occupied the high ground along the sides of the valley behind Ferguson's headquarters, 3 RAR's forward companies were four kilometres behind enemy lines. Burke had the option to withdraw them to where they could form part of a tighter brigade defensive line with the Middlesex, leaving 2 PPCLI forward to confront the Chinese. This was compelling because the Middlesex had not occupied their previously planned positions on 3 RAR's western flank. Based on his discussions with Ferguson in the early hours of 24 April, Burke likely assessed that the Australians were surrounded and cut off. His order for the Middlesex to send a company to clear the route north to 3 RAR suggests he endorsed Ferguson's adjustments. He may also have been aware of the fate of the Glosters on the Imjin River and was contemplating withdrawing 3 RAR.

The withdrawal of BHQ and attached elements shortly after dawn was a credit to the initiative and steadiness of Captain Len Eyles, the Adjutant, and Lieutenant Phil Bennett, OC Mortar Platoon. Both were later Mentioned in Despatches for their efforts and leadership that morning.[6] When the fighting in his area died down an hour before dawn, Bennett sent a party to link up with BHQ and learned that Ferguson had moved part of his headquarters during the night. He then spoke to Eyles, who was organising BHQ's withdrawal and told Bennett that the forward companies would likely also be withdrawn during the day.[7]

Eyles and Bennett then set about organising personnel and vehicles into a convoy. US tanks supported the withdrawal as small groups of vehicles departed on a schedule. The tanks proved very useful further south, engaging groups of Chinese who fired on the moving vehicles speculatively at long range from hiding places on the high ground.

Early that same morning, Jack Gerke noticed that all was quiet. His Support Company group and F Echelon personnel had kept their heads down during the night. Marauding Chinese infiltrators had not discovered them. He heard, from a passing Mortar Platoon driver, that BHQ was withdrawing and that he should 'Bug out! Battalion headquarters is back down the road. Watch out for "Gooks" on the road: they hold the high ground over there!'[8] This brief exchange was a quick but effective set of orders by military standards: Mission, Situation, Own Troops, Enemy! Get out!

Gerke wasted no time. He called his soldiers together and sent them down the road to run the gauntlet of sporadic long-range Chinese rifle and machine-gun fire without tank support. Fortunately, there were plenty of vehicles left by the US mortar company for the task and no casualties.[9] His group also picked up several Australian stragglers, probably from BHQ, withdrawing on foot.[10]

Meanwhile, after dawn, while the Chinese retired to the north to regroup and hide from observation, Koch decided to withdraw his tanks back down the valley to replenish their fuel and ammunition. He claimed later that his men had killed 500 Chinese during the night and in the pre-dawn crossfire created by B Company and his forward platoon. He was confident that the Chinese would not advance south along the valley floor for the time being, especially by day.[11]

Becoming prisoners of war

One casualty of the BHQ withdrawal on the morning of 24 April was Private Bob Parker, Ferguson's dispatch rider.[12] Parker came under fire, crashing his motorbike when the front wheel broke and landing on the side of his head and right shoulder before tumbling into a roadside ditch. Above him, the bike's engine was roaring. When he climbed up to turn it off a .50 calibre machine gun bullet blew a hole in the seat next to his head. He dived back into the ditch and realised he was wounded in the hip. When a bugle sounded down the road and he saw about thirty Chinese running towards him, Parker felt 'horribly alone and bloody scared'.[13] He fired several rounds from his Owen gun but ran out of ammunition. Unable to offer further resistance, he raised his hands and stood up. His memory of the next few moments remained vivid years later:

> *They came at me firing from the hip, led by a young squad leader ... I don't think there was a more frightened person in all the world. I said 'Arrr, shit' and gave them a big grin, and suddenly I was not frightened anymore. Then ... up they came and patted me on the back, and all crowded around me. All I could do was give a sickly grin.*[14]

Parker was led away and found himself among hundreds of Chinese. His recollections offer some insight into how the Chinese had been able to infiltrate so effectively and maintain a steady supply of supplies.

He was taken up a hill overlooking BHQ and handed over to an officer who took his hand to guide him through the dark. Around him were hundreds of heavily armed Chinese, each holding pieces of vegetation. When they moved, he said, 'it was like a whole forest moving'. On the hill's reverse slope, he saw dozens of mules carrying mountain guns and ammunition. Parker worried for his battalion.[15]

UN prisoners of war in Korea are marched along a road by their Chinese captors, April 1951. (AWM P02758.006)

Another casualty of BHQ's withdrawal was Private Horace 'Slim' Madden, a signaller who was concussed by a Chinese mortar bomb explosion. In the dark and confusion, no one noticed that he had been left behind. The Chinese captured him when they swept into the area after BHQ had moved out.[16]

Later that day, Parker and Madden met. They remained together as the Chinese moved them north to a prison camp. They eventually joined Private Keith Gwyther of D Company, left behind after also being concussed by a mortar blast, at Camp 5 after a gruelling forced march that contributed to the deaths of scores of UN POWs.[17]

Parker and Gwyther survived, but Madden died six months later. He was awarded a posthumous George Cross.

2/400030 (NX204932) PRIVATE ROBERT PARKER

The Australian Army formally recognised the character and resilience of several of its prisoners of war in Korea. Why? The story of Bob Parker's capture and subsequent resilience during the imprisonment ordeal epitomises the character that the Australian Army cherishes.

Parker was born a shearer's son in Bundarra, in the New England region of New South Wales, in 1926. He left school to work at the Standard Telephones and Cables Company in a radio laboratory, where he learnt to be a radio operator – but his passion was for racing motorcycles.

Private Robert 'Bob' Parker, sitting on his Harley Davidson motorcycle, takes a brief rest as Lieutenant Colonel Ferguson's personal dispatch rider. (AWM P03874.004)

During the Second World War he joined the naval cadets and gained further experience as a signaller. In 1944, at the age of 18, he enlisted in the Army and continued his work in signals. At the end of the Second World War, Parker was sent to Japan for service with the British Commonwealth Occupation Force. He was discharged from the Army in 1947 and returned to Australia, where he joined the Commonwealth Militia Force while working as a linesman for the Postmaster General. However, upon hearing about the call for experienced re-enforcements for Korea, he immediately signed up.

Parker was a garrulous, competent and fearless soldier whom Ferguson selected to be his personal dispatch rider. As the Chinese forces attacked at Kapyong and forced the withdrawal of 3 RAR, Parker rode his motorcycle in the withdrawal of the Signal Platoon position. He was then taken prisoner on 24 April 1951 after his motorcycle received damage from a fifty-calibre machine gun, with ricochet fragments wounding him in the hip as he crashed into a ditch. He was captured by Chinese soldiers and was later marched for fourteen days to 'Bean Camp', without medical attention and with only meagre rations. At the same time, he was dodging repeated aerial attacks from allied aircraft.

On the night of 5 June 1951, Parker set out with a party of 350 prisoners of war on the 'death march' to Pyoktong, on the Yalu River. The next night, Parker escaped with a fellow Australian prisoner of war, Corporal Donald Pattison Buck. Parker and Buck survived for eleven days on raw vegetables, bran and salt, while hiding from the enemy. They were then sighted by enemy troops and, after a long chase in which their bare feet suffered considerably, they were recaptured. Sent to an indoctrination school (Camp 12), Parker and his fellow Australian prisoners of war organised resistance to indoctrination and collaboration. They planned escape groups, and on 25 June 1952 Parker was again successful in escaping from his captors. However, he was recaptured after just four days and sent to the infamous 'Sweat Box' punishment cell at Camp 5, and subjected to extreme ill-treatment.

Mentioned in Despatches, Parker's citation reads:

Private Parker recorded valuable information on Communist methods of interrogation, together with information concerning escape methods. His indomitable courage in the face of terrible hardship and steadfast refusal to give in to his captors was an inspiring example of loyalty and devotion to duty.

Parker was one of the prisoners released at the end of hostilities during the 'big switch' in August 1953. He was twice Mentioned in Despatches during the Korean War. Robert Parker died on 20 January 2015, aged 88 years.

2/400186 PRIVATE HORACE WILLIAM MADDEN

The character and resilience of Private Horace 'Slim' Madden, who was one of three members of 3 RAR taken prisoner at the Battle of Kapyong, warranted recognition. In an unusual process, he received a posthumous George Cross for his resilience and inspiration as a prisoner of war. He was an ordinary Australian who displayed extraordinary character.

Private Horace William 'Slim' Madden GC, Japan, 1947. (AWM P02580.001)

Madden was born at Cronulla, New South Wales, on 14 February 1924, to Charles Bernard Madden and Pearl Ellen Clemson.[18] He was educated at Sutherland Intermediate High School and then worked as a labourer before following his father's footsteps to become a railway porter. He gave his occupation as 'fruiterer's assistant' on enlistment.

On 26 May 1942, Madden began his service with the Australian Army. Initially serving in the Militia, he was posted to the 114th Australian General Hospital at Goulburn, New South Wales. He then transferred to the Second AIF in August 1943 and served with field ambulance and supply units in New Guinea, Bougainville and Morotai before being sent to Japan as part of the British Commonwealth Occupation Force. Having returned home to Sydney, Madden was discharged from the Army in December 1947. He re-enlisted in August 1950, and served with 3 RAR in Korea. He was employed as a driver with the battalion at first, and then became a linesman with the signals company. The job of the linesmen was tough, working in below-zero temperatures to maintain communications with the forward companies during operations.

On the evening of 23 April 1951, during the Chinese attack at Kapyong, Madden was concussed by enemy fire. The battle left him disorientated, and the following morning Madden found himself surrounded by the enemy. Forced to surrender, Madden began a harrowing journey into captivity with several other members of the battalion. They were beaten and abused by the enemy, and subjected to other forms of punishment and mistreatment. Nevertheless, Madden's demeanour was still a show of defiance and selflessness – he refused to collaborate with the enemy and was determined to support his struggling comrades. For his efforts, Slim Madden's name and example became widely known through the various groups of prisoners.

Madden's health declined and he was moved to 'the Caves' at Kandong. He was then forced to march 225 kilometres to Pingchong-Ni, along with other sick and wounded prisoners, in October 1951. Collapsing en route, Madden was transported by cart and survived the journey. However, captivity had taken its toll, and he soon died.

After the war, testimonials were provided by officers and men from many units of the Commonwealth and Allied Forces of the heroism Slim Madden displayed. He was posthumously awarded the George Cross, with part of his citation reading:

> *Despite repeated beatings and many other forms of ill-treatment inflicted because of his defiance to his captors, Private Madden remained cheerful and optimistic. Although deprived of food because of his behaviour, resulting in severe malnutrition, he was known to share his meagre supplies purchased from Koreans with other prisoners who he was of the opinion were worse off than himself. It would have been apparent to Private Madden that to pursue this course must eventually result in his death. This did not deter him, and for over six months, although becoming progressively weaker, he remained undaunted in his resistance. He would in no way cooperate with the enemy.*

Slim Madden died of malnutrition and as a result of ill-treatment while a prisoner of war in Korea on 6 November 1951, aged 27 years. His remains were recovered after the war and are buried at Busan, in the United Nations Memorial Cemetery in Korea. In 1955, Madden was awarded a posthumous George Cross for the courage he showed in the face of terrible hardships and threats of death, sustained by an indomitable spirit.

Situation with the forward companies

As dawn broke on 24 April, the forward company commanders faced tactical challenges, threats and decisions. Some had been in tough fights; others had not come under attack. Still, it was clear that the Chinese were going to try again. The question was whether 3 RAR would withdraw that day – when UN firepower could cover them and the Chinese were not a threat because they were regrouping for night attacks – or try to hold their ground for another night. Unbeknownst to Ferguson or his commanders, plans for reinforcement were being made. What happened next illustrates the challenges defenders face when given orders to hold for as long as possible. When do the number of casualties, immediate pressure and signs of further enemy action combine to warrant withdrawal?

A Company

Although it had suffered 50 per cent casualties, with daylight and expanded fields of fire, A Company had the upper hand over its attackers. If they had to fight again that night, there were insufficient soldiers and ammunition to survive. After the dawn, Chinese soldiers were caught out in the open, lying in small hollows or behind tufts of heather. The Australians opened fire on them when they broke cover in search of better protection or to try and get away. O'Dowd recalled, 'They were potting them like rabbits all over the place, having a great time killing them in front of us until I had to spoil this sport and call a cease-fire because we had already used a lot of ammunition: resupply was by no means assured, and development of the tactical situation from then on left no room for optimism'.[19] His first order of business was consolidating his defensive position. He had fewer soldiers to occupy perimeter positions, to create an all-round defence. He set out to regain the initiative, tighten up his layout and determine how to evacuate the casualties.

After first light revealed the Australian positions, a Chinese machine gun, whose crew had set up on the rise between 2 Platoon and 3 Platoon during the night, opened fire. CHQ and the remnants of 1 Platoon and 3 Platoon were at its mercy. Then the crew commander began blowing a whistle, presumably to signal others hiding further down the slope to join them. Brumfield ordered his 2 Platoon machine gunners to engage the Chinese crew. Unfortunately, they had to cease fire when their bullets fell in the CHQ position. When the Chinese gun opened up again, Brumfield sent down a fighting patrol to eliminate it. In what O'Dowd described as 'a sharp, neat little action', 6 Section wiped out the post but had one man killed.[20]

O'Dowd then needed to regain the position further down the slope from which 1 Platoon had withdrawn during the night. He gave 3 Platoon this task. Lieutenant Harold Mulry, described by O'Dowd as 'an old warhorse', '... gathered a bunch of fellows together, lined them up, and they went in'.[21] Sergeant George Harris, the Acting CSM, and a few others from company headquarters joined the assault. They charged down the hill, yelling and firing from the hip. The Australians were outnumbered, but the speed and ferocity of their attack drove the Chinese from the position. Harris said, 'They didn't feel like fighting us anymore'.[22] 3 Platoon's attack soon became a turkey shoot. The Chinese tried to hide in thickets or any low ground they could find down towards the creek bed running along the valley floor. 'We began to pick them off while they lay on the ground or when they broke cover like darting rabbits', remembered Harris. 'We were enjoying ourselves until our dear old Major [O'Dowd] decided to stop us firing because ammunition was very scarce.'[23] It was the second time that O'Dowd had had to order a ceasefire to preserve ammunition that morning. After they regained the position, Mulry discovered a wounded member of 1 Platoon. The Chinese had captured him, but moved him to a safer spot when 3 Platoon began its assault. O'Dowd stated years later, 'We were indebted to our enemy'.[24]

Other Australians were also finding plenty of Chinese soldiers to shoot that morning. Tassie Long, positioned with his MMG Section in B Company, across the valley floor, fired on the Chinese fleeing from A Company's assault. When he got to forty, he stopped counting the number of men falling to his section's guns.[25] A Company was now secure but still hurting, with half its soldiers either dead or wounded and dwindling supplies of ammunition, food and water. Most soldiers stayed above ground because the rocky ridgeline did not permit digging below ground level.

In summary, A Company had spent a harrowing night fighting for their lives. The wounded were in dire condition. Many were in agony and needed pain relief, stabilisation and evacuation to medical facilities. Some had suffered painful burns from the heather set alight by Chinese mortar bombs. Though he had good fields of fire on all approaches to his position after dawn, O'Dowd did not have enough able-bodied soldiers to occupy the entire ridgeline. It might only be a matter of time before the Chinese realised this and attacked again. To O'Dowd's amazement, morale and confidence remained high.[26]

B Company

Darcy Laughlin had prepared B Company for withdrawal at 7am to consolidate with the other three companies across the valley. D Company, high on the hill, had not been attacked overnight. Still, there were signs of the Chinese creeping forward in numbers and assembling in the undergrowth on the lower slopes, readying themselves for an assault despite the inevitability of coming under intense artillery and mortar fire. C Company had had a quiet night, listening to the sounds of battle elsewhere.

A surprised O'Dowd had known nothing of B Company's withdrawal until his radio operator told him that Laughlin's men were about to abandon their position. Despite being located at the Middlesex location several kilometres away, Ferguson should have understood the risk this move posed for the forward companies. It was obvious, said O'Dowd, that the Chinese would occupy B Company's knoll overlooking A Company's exposed left flank. He urged Ferguson to turn B Company around over the radio, but received no response.[27] After a challenging and exhausting night, Ferguson was in no mood to have O'Dowd questioning his decision. Equally, having also endured a dangerous and demanding night, O'Dowd was angry about having his left flank opened to the Chinese without a good reason. According to O'Dowd, Ferguson did not discuss his decision or provide reasons.[28]

The Battalion War Diary explains that the decision to withdraw B Company from its uncontested position dominating the valley floor at 8am was due to its separation from the other companies across the road.[29] However, the timing is off; the withdrawal began an hour earlier, and the justification of being 'separated' is weak without the context of an initial withdrawal. It would have made no sense to abandon the B Company position if the Australians were to continue their task of 'defending the approaches to Chuktun-ni'.

Ferguson most likely ordered B Company off its knoll as a preliminary move before directing O'Dowd, Gravener and Saunders to withdraw when, and if, Burke ordered it. Ferguson's early morning consultations suggest he was deeply concerned about the viability of continuing to defend Chuktun-ni and sought, and received, permission to plan and prepare for a withdrawal. The deployment of a Middlesex company to support the BHQ withdrawal and the abandonment of B Company's position were preliminary adjustments to facilitate withdrawal, not continued defence.

In his 1952 report on the battle, Laughlin supported Ferguson's rationale for adjusting the 3 RAR position:

> *The BHQ had been overrun and had been forced to withdraw, and we were, therefore, ordered to withdraw from our present position through C Company. We were to take up a position between C and D Company, thus forming a complete battalion perimeter on the high ground.*[30]

After dawn, B Company's CSM, WO2 Eric Bradley, began supervising groups of men moving around the company position, counting dead Chinese: the total was 173. Much to Bradley's surprise, he found groups of Chinese hiding in the low paddy field areas of the valley. There was one dramatic incident before one group surrendered when Bradley sent some men to check a nearby paddy. When a digger fired his Owen gun over the field, fifty or sixty Chinese stood up. One threw a grenade at a soldier, and he went down. Other soldiers who thought their mate had been killed or severely wounded immediately opened fire, killing as many as twenty Chinese before Bradley stopped them when the supposedly killed soldier stood up almost unscathed. The survivors, some thirty-nine men, were taken prisoner.[31] Bradley's intervention demonstrated the importance of strong moral leadership in a situation where angry, perhaps nervous, soldiers reacted in a heated and uncertain moment. For saving their lives, he was followed closely by the prisoners, who feared leaving his protection for the rest of the day. Laughlin began the withdrawal soon after this incident.

B Company crossed the road and valley floor to the C Company position, suffering two wounded from random long-range Chinese gunfire, and moved up behind D Company to strengthen its position and cover its withdrawal if ordered.[32] Logically, C Company was positioned to support A Company and would have covered its withdrawal. Positioning companies to cover the movements of other companies, thereby achieving a clean break with the enemy during withdrawal, is a sound tactic.

CO visits the front line

After dawn, Ferguson decided to visit the forward companies to assess the situation, bring up much-needed ammunition and evacuate the wounded. He spoke with Wilfred Miller, the US tank platoon commander, who, with Koch's concurrence, agreed to take Ferguson forward with his tanks. The Australians strapped ammunition to the sides of each one. Miller also agreed to evacuate critically wounded Australians. These negotiations with Ferguson, described in US sources, confirm that the US tank company was not 'under command' of 3 RAR.[33] Furthermore, their early morning preoccupation with evacuating US vehicles abandoned by the US Chemical Mortar Company rather than supporting the forward companies suggests that Ferguson had no control over them.

Ferguson decided to take Don Beard, the RMO, and Alf Argent, his Intelligence Officer, to operate his radio. Because there was so little room for passengers on Sherman tanks, Miller ordered his ammunition loader out to make room for Ferguson. Argent sat inside, bringing Ferguson's radio set with him. Beard travelled on another tank. As they moved forward of the Middlesex position up the road, Beard recalled that the tanks came under sporadic, inaccurate small-arms fire from the high ground to the east.

Ferguson, Beard and Argent arrived between A and C Companies while B Company was in the final stages of its withdrawal across the valley, probably around 8am. Ferguson later commented that, after dawn on 24 April, his main concern was assessing the situation and discussing with his company commanders whether they could hold their positions for another night. By this time, Burke had informed Ferguson that a US Regimental Combat Team, the 5th Cavalry Regiment, was about to reinforce 27 BCB. This formation comprised three motorised infantry battalions and was roughly equivalent to a British mechanised brigade. Though there is no record of their communications that morning in diaries, Burke appears to have ordered Ferguson to hold the line, awaiting the cavalry's arrival.[34]

Ferguson's discussions were now about whether the forward companies could hold until the 5th Cavalry occupied positions west of the road on Sukon San and deployed armoured vehicles onto the valley floor. The Americans would clear the Chinese from the rear areas, plug the gap left when the Middlesex continued south the evening before, and secure 3 RAR's western flank.[35] Burke had the option of sending the Middlesex to relieve 3 RAR's forward companies after the Americans had established themselves in the area. Their enthusiasm to return to the front line might have been tempered by knowing that 28 Brigade would relieve 27 Brigade in the next few days.

As soon as Ferguson arrived with the tanks, work parties from A Company began unloading the ammunition and strapping seriously wounded men to the sides. Wounded men able to sit upright sat inside while the US gunners rode on top, holding onto and comforting the men on the stretchers. Don Beard remembered Ferguson's 'extraordinary bravery and compassion' when he made at least two round trips to the Middlesex position alongside wounded men whose stretchers were strapped on Miller's tank.[36] The same could be said of Miller's men, whose comfort of the wounded and exposure to enemy fire on the outside of their tanks was admirable and deeply appreciated by the Australians.[37]

Much to O'Dowd's and the other forward company commanders' dismay, the only type of ammunition brought forward on the tanks was .303 Vickers MMG ammunition (Mk 8Z Belt).[38] The rounds had to be stripped from belts before being loaded into rifle and Bren gun magazines. Fortunately, there were no Chinese attacks while this transfer of ammunition took place. However, the Chinese occupying B Company's old positions fired on the ammunition-carrying parties. Aside from extra handling, the other disadvantage of loading ammunition intended for the Vickers MMG into rifles and Bren guns was that the rounds damaged the inside rifling of their barrels because of their increased charge. Those men who carried Owen Machine Carbines that needed 9mm ammunition borrowed .303 rifles from the wounded, and loaded magazines with Vickers ammunition.

There seems to have been a breakdown in the 3 RAR resupply system. The sources are inconclusive about why only one type of ammunition was delivered and why medical supplies, food or water were not sent to the forward companies on 24 April. Veterans from the forward companies were critical – some very critical – of the situation. O'Dowd later wrote, '... soft-skinned vehicles could get through without drawing [accurate] fire, and I can now see no excuse for Battalion HQ not conducting normal resupply'.[39]

One of the most crucial meetings during the Battle of Kapyong occurred after Ferguson arrived. The only eyewitness account is O'Dowd's. He remembered being told to meet the CO and Intelligence Officer. Expecting that Ferguson had brought a small tactical HQ to take command in the forward area, O'Dowd learned instead that Van Fleet wanted to move 5 Regiment of the Cavalry Division to occupy the features on his left. Doing so hinged on 3 RAR holding the road from their overnight positions. Burke wanted B Company to re-occupy their recently vacated position. Ferguson wanted to know if O'Dowd would hold for another night. He agreed if B Company was back in its original position and the cavalry on the high ground to the west. Otherwise, said O'Dowd, the rifle companies would have to be withdrawn. Ferguson agreed to get back to him before leaving to observe B Company's return to the ridge.[40]

B Company and the Honeycomb

On arrival at B Company, Ferguson must have ordered Laughlin to return to his former position across the valley on the knoll, but there is no record. It is unlikely he spoke with Gravener in person, because Gravener was busy atop Hill 504. Assuming he had come to reassess the situation in anticipation of relief by the 5th Cavalry Regiment,

Ferguson's thinking may have been to have Laughlin's men reoccupy their old position to cover the arrival of the Americans. Darcy Laughlin said in 1952 that at 9.30am on 24 April, B Company was ordered to secure the ground from which it had withdrawn, as reinforcements were expected. In the meantime, Chinese troops had occupied their former position.[41]

Laughlin ordered Lieutenant Ken McGregor, 5 Platoon commander, and last in the order of march for B Company's withdrawal, to turn around and move straight back to the company's former position. He had begun moving through C Company to occupy positions behind D Company by this time.[42] McGregor said B Company came off its old position at about 7am in single file and made its way across the valley floor to the lower slopes of the spur occupied by C Company. Aside from one soldier who was shot in the arm, and another shot in the hip by stray bullets, the withdrawal was uneventful.[43]

On the way over, the line of soldiers had passed a small knoll on the valley floor known among the Australians as 'the Honeycomb'. It was a derelict defensive position studded with several bunkers and protected by a trench system. From a distance, these constructions looked like the cavities of a honeycomb.

During the Second World War, McGregor and Laughlin were sergeants in the 2/3rd Battalion. They had much in common and knew each other well.[44] When Laughlin told McGregor to turn his platoon around and move back to the positions they had vacated, McGregor was not happy. Infantry soldiers rarely enjoy walking back over the ground they have just traversed to enemy-occupied ground they had just abandoned. More importantly, McGregor felt that the order for him to turn his men around and attack a position the company had given to the Chinese, and which favoured defenders was, in Australian vernacular, 'A big ask'. McGregor recalls Laughlin's one-sentence direction, 'I want you to go back straight away', to which he replied sarcastically, 'How expensive do you want it to be?'[45]

His question left unanswered, McGregor turned his platoon around with some urgency, needing to reoccupy the area before the Chinese consolidated in large numbers. There was no time to support McGregor with flanking fire from other platoons, tanks, mortars or artillery. With several groans of disappointment and audible curses, the diggers followed orders.[46] As they did so, they detected movement in the Honeycomb. McGregor decided that a small group of Chinese had hidden in one of the old trenches. He and his platoon sergeant, Sergeant Doug Frazer, moved up to the forward section and ordered them to line up and assault the Honeycomb.[47] After clearing these trenches, McGregor planned to move his other two sections forward and assault back onto B Company's old position. The section occupying the Honeycomb would provide fire support for this attack.[48]

Private Stan Connelly was a Bren gunner in the section detailed for the assault. They formed a line and fired as they ran close to the position, believing there were eight to ten Chinese in the trench, only to find that there were many more returning their fire.

Men fell to Connelly's left and right before he was struck in the thigh by a 30-calibre round, which blew off much of his buttock. He collapsed within five yards of the trench.[49] Chinese fire cut down eight men in McGregor's assault. The remainder went to ground and fired back. McGregor was shot through the jaw and lay on his side, stunned and bleeding heavily. Someone tended to him and called out to others to find out who was wounded and who was able to assist.[50]

For the remainder of the company, the orderly movement through C Company became a rescue mission after the shock of realising that McGregor and his diggers were under heavy fire and had been cut to pieces. There were urgent calls for medical assistance and fire support. Soldiers rushed forward, firing at the Chinese to keep their heads down, while the diggers lying in the line of fire in front of the trenches dragged themselves away.

It was a dramatic sight. Over eighty Chinese soldiers held the Honeycomb. They had probably hidden before dawn, knowing that daylight would expose them to small-arms fire from the men defending the ridges. McGregor's assault had spurred them into opening fire. Other Chinese, in B Company's former position, joined in shooting at the Australians on the valley floor.

Scores of Chinese were now firing at the twelve Australians who had attacked the Honeycomb, and diggers were rushing forward to help their mates. Several men lay still, either unconscious or too afraid to move for fear of being shot again. Others were trying to drag themselves into better cover. The unwounded were firing back. Thinking quickly, Tassie Long had the MMGs attached to B Company set up where they were. Their fire kept the Chinese heads on the knoll down.[51]

Stan Connelly remembered lying in front of the Chinese trenches, hearing enemy voices just a few metres away and thinking, 'How in the hell am I going to get out of this?' He didn't know if he could stand up, but didn't want to wait to be shot. 'As fast as I could', said Connelly, 'I threw off my gear and jumped to my feet and hopped, limped, hobbled and staggered over the longest 20 yards I have ever travelled ... I heard a few shots go over my shoulder, but I made it safely'.[52]

All the Australians in the assault on the Honeycomb survived. Several who were seriously wounded were evacuated home. McGregor had his jaw wired shut and took nutrition through a straw for fourteen months after returning to Australia. He never discussed the circumstances of that day with anyone until the author interviewed him in 1992. He realised that he and his men had been victims of a poor tactical decision, but he believed that the consequences were the misfortunes of war: something best kept to oneself.[53]

After McGregor's assault failed to clear the Chinese from the Honeycomb, Laughlin mounted a deliberate company attack. He ordered Lieutenant Len Montgomerie to lead the assault with 4 Platoon, while the other platoons provided flanking fire support. In 1952, Laughlin wrote that the platoon moved in from the right flank. Twenty-five yards out, they charged, taking the first trench at bayonet point. In the 'fierce hand to hand combat that followed, Montgomerie's men cleared the position – trench by trench'. The Chinese fought courageously, but the Australians were methodical and fierce, clearing their way with rifle fire, butts and bayonets, supplemented with grenades, Bren gun bursts and Owen guns. When the forward-most elements came under fire from a nearby knoll, Montgomerie's aggressive attack on this second position with his lead section caused some enemy to flee; the rest were killed.[54] The use of bayonets lent extra ferocity to the assault and had a psychological effect on the enemy. Many took their chances, running through small-arms fire to get away.[55]

Ferguson told Kit Denton in 1986 that he arrived in time for the attack on the Honeycomb. In a draft manuscript, he wrote of loading and firing the .76 mm gun on Miller's tank to support Montgomerie's assault.[56] Miller recalls Ferguson sitting in his ammunition handler's seat during the trip to Chuktun-ni, but does not mention him loading ammunition to support an Australian attack.[57] Aside from Laughlin's mention of tanks arriving from the south, there is little evidence to support Ferguson's recollection. He arrived after Montgomerie had completed his assault, probably on his second run up to the forward companies. Although he occasionally slept, Alf Argent, who travelled in Ferguson's tank, does not remember it firing in support of Montgomerie's attack. He recalls arriving in Chuktun-ni and Montgomerie proudly taking him on a tour of the area where the attack had occurred and showing him the bodies of Chinese soldiers his men had killed.[58] According to Laughlin, the attack and occupation of the Honeycomb lasted until 12.30pm. The Australians counted fifty-seven bodies in the trenches and a further twenty-four near a second knoll.

Montgomerie lost two NCOs in the attack, Corporal Bill Murphy and Lance Corporal Eric Devine, and one private, Ken Matchett, and two others were wounded. His leadership and courage under fire earned Montgomerie the Military Cross. His leading Section Commander, Corporal Don Davie, received the Military Medal.[59]

Assessing that the Chinese had occupied B Company's old position in strength, Laughlin sought and received permission to resume his withdrawal to a position up behind D Company, now engaged in a fierce defensive battle. Laughlin may have decided that his fellow company commander and mate, Norm Gravener, needed him and his men. With the benefit of hindsight, it is surprising that Ferguson did not see the tanks as a solution to recapturing the B Company position, had he wanted to reclaim an advantage. At that time, at least one platoon of four tanks was available to support the Australians. The Chinese were in the open and unable to defend themselves by day against armour. Tanks had previously been used successfully with 3 RAR at Chongju, where David Mannett had earned the Military Cross.

In one regard, however, speculation about Ferguson's decision-making is moot – and action to recapture the Honeycomb was going to result in the death and wounding of more Australians. Ferguson was not the type of officer to have risked Australian lives unless capturing the B Company position was vital to the success of the US relief force.

4/400059 (SX15503) LIEUTENANT LEONARD MONTAGUE MONTGOMERIE MBE, MC

Lieutenant Leonard Montague Montgomerie was recognised for his leadership during the Battle of Kapyong. His platoon bore the brunt of the Chinese attacks on B Company overnight on 23–24 April, and he led them in a spirited assault on over eighty Chinese defenders at the Honeycomb mid-morning on 24 April. He was an example of the quality of K Force volunteers who joined 3 RAR before deployment to Korea in September 1950.

Lieutenant Leonard Montgomerie, Officer Commanding 4 Platoon, 3 RAR. Kapyong, Korea, 26 April 1951. (PHOTOGRAPHER: CLAUDE HOLZHEIMER, AWM 147354)

Montgomerie was born at Port Clinton, South Australia, on 28 November 1921, and raised near Ardrossan. He enlisted in the Second AIF on 16 December 1941, and served with 2/7th Commando Squadron, 2/6 Cavalry (Commando) Regiment, in Papua and New Guinea, including the Aitape–Wewak campaign. He was wounded in action on 23 February 1945 and discharged on 5 March 1946 as a lieutenant.

On 11 November 1950, Montgomerie re-enlisted as a K Force volunteer and joined 3 RAR in Japan just before the battalion's deployment to Korea in September 1950. As platoon commander of 4 Platoon, B Company, Lieutenant Montgomerie was said to have displayed outstanding qualities of leadership, courage and daring during the Battle of Kapyong. As an inspiration to his soldiers, cheering and urging them on against a dug-in enemy that was stronger in numbers and fire power, Montgomerie was awarded the Military Cross. The citation read:

> *The enemy was entrenched in well dug in positions, well armed and had repulsed previous attacks on their position and were continuing to defend the position with stubborn resistance. Lieutenant L. M. Montgomerie leading 4 Platoon advanced across open ground towards the enemy strong point. During the advance his platoon came under fire from the objective and from the right flank. Despite casualties he pressed on with the attack. When his platoon was approximately thirty yards from the objective they came under intense fire from LMG, rifle, submachine and hand grenades. Showing complete disregard for his personal safety and although outnumbered by approximately two to one he led a bayonet charge against the first line of trenches. After bitter hand to hand fighting the first trench was secured. The enemy continued to stubbornly resist from dugouts within the position and from trenches on the other side.*
>
> *Lieutenant Montgomerie, displaying outstanding initiative, manoeuvred his sections into positions from which these positions could be grenaded and finally assaulted by bayonet. Later, when his platoon again came under fire from the retreating enemy he again led an assault and killed 20 enemy and captured four prisoners. After this action a total of 67 enemy dead were counted in and around this position.*

Montgomerie married Patricia Phyliss Hicks, a Canadian supervisor for the Red Cross contingent in Japan and Korea, on 28 May 1955 at St Peter's Garrison Church in Kure, Japan. That same year, Montgomerie was presented with his Military Cross on Anzac Day in Japan, and was then appointed Member of the Order of the British Empire in the Queen's Birthday Honours of 1955. After leaving the Army having attained the rank of major, he lived in Canberra, working as a public servant. He died there in 1976, aged 54. His funeral, with full military honours, was held at the Duntroon Chapel.

4/158 (SX19733) PRIVATE (TEMPORARY CORPORAL) DONALD BREYNARD DAVIE MM

Don 'Pete' Davie was an example of a young man who volunteered for a three-year contract with K Force because he was too young to have experienced the Second World War in full. He was a man of character and strength, with leadership and tenacity. He was a soldier.

Davie was born at Rose Park, South Australia, in 1925 and grew up during the Great Depression years in rural areas, following the missionary work of his father, Reverend Leslie Davie. On 25 May 1943, he enlisted in the Second AIF. Serving with B Troop, 2/7th Field Regiment, Davie saw action at Tarakan during operation OBOE

in 1945. After the unit was disbanded in January 1946, he transferred to the British Commonwealth Occupation Force in Japan. In 1949, Davie transferred to the newly formed 3rd Battalion, Royal Australian Regiment, and was deployed to Pusan in Korea on 28 September 1950.

At the Battle of Kapyong, Corporal Davie commanded No. 1 Section of 4 Platoon. On the afternoon of 24 April 1951, 4 Platoon were ordered to attack a position on which the enemy were entrenched. While forming up, Davie observed a party of enemy run from their position in an endeavour to outflank 4 Platoon. He immediately moved his section to a position from which they destroyed the entire enemy party. The attack then proceeded, and Davie's section task was to clear the right-hand enemy defences. As he advanced, his section came under intense machine-gun, rifle and grenade fire from its objective, and from a knoll beyond. Davie demonstrated strong leadership as he tasked one of his soldiers to engage the knoll, while he led the remainder of the section with fixed bayonets in an assault on the objective. Through this attack, Davie's section cleared the first line of defences, while suffering the loss of just three casualties. The section then came under heavy machine-gun fire from further trenches to the rear, but Davie pressed the attack with his remaining men and completely cleared his objective. For his efforts, Davie was awarded the Military Medal for having 'displayed outstanding leadership and courage, showing complete disregard for personal safety, and [being] an inspiration to his own section and the remainder of his platoon'.

Davie's deployment to Korea ended on 29 October 1951, but he then went on to serve in Malaya from May 1953 as a Sergeant with the Australian Observer Unit. He was discharged on 30 June 1959. In 1999, Davie completed a study at Charles Darwin University on 'Military aspects of the opening phase of the Indonesian struggle for independence, August 1945 to April 1946', demonstrating a lifelong commitment to the professional knowledge of soldiering. Davie died on 17 October 2013, aged 88 years.

Corporal Don Davie MM (standing, back row, fourth from left), and 4 Platoon, B Company, 3 RAR, at Kapyong, Korea, 26 April 1951. (PHOTOGRAPHER: CLAUDE HOLZHEIMER, AWM 147350)

Attacks on D Company

Chinese commanders decided to shift their axis of attack from A Company to further up the ridgeline to D Company, occupying the kidney-shaped summit. The decision to do so in broad daylight under artillery and mortar fire demonstrated the Chinese determination to seize the position and continue their advance to Seoul. If D Company did not hold, the Chinese could bypass 3 RAR's forward companies and push on to assault the Canadian position that night or maintain momentum and assault down Hill 504's ridgelines in an attempt to overrun A, B and C companies.

Overnight, the Chinese had probed D Company intermittently. After dawn, Gravener saw a reconnaissance party moving a long way forward of A Company, up a spur line leading to 12 Platoon. The platoon engaged the enemy group, who withdrew. At about 7am, as B Company began their withdrawal across the valley floor, Gravener recalled:

> *12 Platoon was hit hard, and they had a few people wounded – about seven to eight casualties, which was not too bad considering the strength of the attack. Johnny Ward, the Platoon Commander, and his men were well outnumbered and had a difficult position to hold.*[60]

The terrain favoured the defenders. To attack, the Chinese had a long, hard climb to get to the lip of the tree-covered summit area. The Australians were well camouflaged and difficult to detect as the assault waves made a 50-metre dash to close with them. Despite accurate artillery fire hitting them on the way up the slopes, the Chinese persisted, taking heavy casualties. Gravener remembered Ward saying to him on the phone, 'I think you should come down here, Boss. The bastards are all over the place. I think perhaps we should be moved. I remember quite distinctly my reply … "Johnny, all we have to do is sit tight, and it will be all right"'.[61]

Each assault followed the same sequence. The main attack was launched in-depth on a narrow frontage of four to five soldiers after preparatory mortar fire. A platoon-sized group fired in support and threw grenades. 12 Platoon met these attacks with machine-gun and rifle fire and grenades in the final stages of the attack as enemy 'sprinters' crested the convex slope, giving the Australians just seconds to engage. It was frightening close-range shooting, said Gravener.[62] The enemy suffered heavy casualties in each of the six attacks launched up until about 10.30am. Gravener estimated that Ward and his soldiers had killed a platoon and wounded scores of others. Australian casualties were light. Subject to ammunition resupply, 12 Platoon could hold its ground.[63]

Artillery support was the game-changer for D Company's defence of Hill 504. Gravener did not have a New Zealand artillery forward observer in location. Still, having done the job in the Second World War, he took it on, directing shellfire onto the Chinese assaulting Ward's position, and onto the approaches and the enemy's forming-up places, from 7am until a mid-morning pause in attacks.[64]

When the Chinese battalion commander decided to change his axis of attack further to D Company's west, Ward saw infantry forming up, and Gravener called in artillery fire, forcing the Chinese to withdraw and resume their original axis.[65] Sergeant Ray McKenzie, Gravener's Mortar Fire Controller, attempted to contact the mortar platoon, but they were out of range and not communicating on the mortar net frequency. Like A Company earlier that morning, D Company was enduring a steady bombardment from Chinese mortars, which intensified before assaults on Ward's platoon.

McKenzie remembered making his way between 10 Platoon's position and CHQ, along a small saddle. He heard and then observed machine-gun fire impacting in front of him, but made it back to CHQ safely, and after a change of orders, returned to 10 Platoon:

> *When I arrived back at my old position, one of the diggers said, 'Gee, you were lucky when you were going to CHQ. That burst of machine gunfire nearly got you!' I said, 'Not lucky, he was firing high. I saw the fall of shot in front'. He said, 'It did not all fall in front. There was a lot falling behind you'. So it would appear that I had been caught in the centre of a machine gun burst and had not been touched. 24th April 1951 was not my day to die.*[66]

At about 11.30am, the Chinese resumed attacking 12 Platoon. In what Gravener described as 'a very much practised drill', they repeated the same tactics.[67] This predictability enabled the Australians to inflict numerous casualties, both as the enemy formed up and during their assaults. The speed with which each Chinese attack was prepared, launched, and then repelled by 12 Platoon created a terrifying tempo of close combat.

Corporal Bill Rowlinson DCM

Much of 12 Platoon's success in defending the wooded knoll was due to the determination and fighting qualities of Ward's left-forward section commander, Corporal Bill Rowlinson. His men were the first to engage because they faced the narrow Chinese axis of assault. On 24 April, Rowlinson's section withstood over six hours of 'hard fighting' through some twelve separate attacks.[68]

Chinese assault groups often carried Russian-designed submachine guns nicknamed 'burp guns' because of their sound. The 'burp' was a burst of automatic fire from a 73-round circular magazine. Burp guns were able to generate a lethal cone of fire. The Chinese attackers could literally 'hose down' Rowlinson's section at close quarters with automatic fire.[69]

Six diggers from Rowlinson's section were wounded in these assaults and evacuated. Ward sent men from the depth sections to replace them. The depth sections did a fine job supporting the forward section with covering fire and reinforcements. Every weapon pit in Rowlinson's area had to bring fire to bear on the next assault.

Rowlinson was wounded in the leg but remained in charge, refusing evacuation. Hard at work during this period, tending to the wounded and supervising their evacuation, was the D Company medical orderly, Private Ron 'Nugget' Dunque. He moved about under fire to answer the call, 'Medic! Medic!', treating the wounded and staunching the flow of blood from Rowlinson's leg. He, helped by men from the depth sections, also assisted wounded to the rear. Sometimes this meant rigging up a stretcher and carrying a man out, which would expose four stretcher-bearers to Chinese machine-gun fire. Nugget Dunque, acting as a bearer, was wounded across the forehead during this time but remained on duty. For his courage under fire and care for the wounded on 24 April, Dunque was awarded the Military Medal.[70] Another of the men risking their lives to help the wounded was Lance Corporal Harry Richey. He carried one wounded digger from Rowlinson's section and returned for another, losing his life trying to rescue the second man under fire. Richey was Mentioned in Despatches for his selfless courage.[71]

TYPE 50 'BURP GUN'

Known as the 'Burp Gun' to both Commonwealth and United States forces in Korea because of the distinctive noise it made when firing, the Type 50 submachine gun was one of the mainstay weapons of the Chinese People's Volunteer Army.

Sergeant Brian Charles Cooper MM of 2 RAR displays a Russian PPSh M1941 or ChiCom Type 50 ('burp gun') and ammunition pouches he captured during the Battle of Maryang San, 24 July 1953. Cooper earned an immediate award of the Military Medal for his conduct in action in the battle. (PHOTOGRAPHER: PHILLIP HOBSON, AWM HOBJ4564)

A Chinese-manufactured version of the Soviet PPSh-41, the Type 50 was a straightforward and reliable weapon that could be easily stripped and maintained in the field. It featured a simple blowback action and fired using a fixed firing pin set in an open bolt, fed from either a 35-round box or a 71-round drum magazine (some sources state the Type 50 could only accept box magazines, but extant examples with drum magazines contradict this). The Type 50's most notable characteristic was its high rate of fire – 900 rounds per minute – although it was a selective fire weapon which could fire both single shots and automatic bursts.

With a maximum effective range of 150–200 metres, the Type 50 was most useful in close combat and suited Chinese offensive tactics of engaging at short range with high volumes of fire from infantry weapons to compensate for a relative lack of artillery support. Routinely, the eleven-man assault squads leading Chinese offensive operations would carry four Type 50s. Whole squads of Type 50s were also formed for special tasks, such as providing close-in fire support groups for assaults on hill-top positions.

Despite its high rate of fire, the Type 50 was a reasonably accurate weapon, but its capabilities were often wasted due to poor tactics and the limited training of VPA soldiers. It was commonly employed to generate marching fire by advancing infantry, and large volumes of fire were often used to compensate for a lack of accuracy. Nevertheless, in ambushes and patrol clashes the firepower of the Type 50 could prove decisive.

Members of 3 RAR take part in a course in enemy weapons identification in preparation for the battalion's imminent move to Korea from Japan. Here, Lieutenant Alf Argent holds a Russian 7.62mm PPSh M1941 submachine gun ('burp gun') with its magazine removed. (PHOTOGRAPHER: IAN ROBERTSON, AWM P01813.354)

LENGTH
858mm (33.75in)

WEIGHT
3.63kg (8lb)

BARREL
273mm (10.75in)

CALIBRE
7.62 × 25mm

FEED SYSTEM
35-round detachable box magazine or 71 round drum

RATE OF FIRE
900rpm

MUZZLE VELOCITY
473m/s (1,400ft/s)

3/2196 PRIVATE RONALD EDWARD 'NUGGET' DUNQUE MM

Too young to serve during the Second World War, Dunque's troubled childhood and propensity for adventure led him to Korea. While he gave a lot to the Army, the Army in return gave him the discipline and opportunity that he had lacked as a child.

Dunque was born at Lismore, New South Wales, on 2 April 1931 but soon found himself in Victoria. As a child, Dunque was orphaned and spent a number of years circling through orphanages and foster care, where he found life difficult.[72] At the age of 6, he had even attempted to run away from his foster care, deciding that living on the street with a little black dog he had befriended was a better option. He was later taken in full-time by Ivy McLean, who became a constant and reliable foster mother for Dunque. Leaving school at 13, he took up itinerant work on cattle and sheep farms before being inspired by a movie about crocodile hunting in north Queensland.[73] Dunque and a mate were on their way to Queensland when they were turned around and sent home by the Sydney police.

Influenced by his foster sister's boyfriend, who was a veteran of the 9th Division from the Second World War, Dunque enlisted in the Army in Melbourne in 1949.[74] After completing his training at Puckapunyal, Victoria, Dunque was posted to the 67th Battalion, in the British Commonwealth Occupation Force in Japan. The unit became 3 RAR prior to deployment to Korea. Dunque was appointed to Battalion Headquarters as a bandsman, then served in Korea with D Company as a stretcher-bearer from 28 September 1950.

Private Ronald Edward 'Nugget' Dunque looks through the sights of a Russian 7.62mm Degtyarev (DP) light machine gun during enemy weapons identification training in Japan, in preparation for 3 RAR's imminent move to Korea, August 1950. (PHOTOGRAPHER: IAN ROBERTSON, AWM P01813.347)

During the Battle of Kapyong on 24 April 1951, Dunque found himself attending to casualties of 8 Section, 12 Platoon, who were under heavy enemy attacks. There were six casualties within the Section, and Dunque made six separate trips to attend to and evacuate them all as the battle raged. During his attempt to retrieve the last of his injured comrades, Dunque was wounded in the temple by an enemy grenade but still carried on, regardless of his own injury. Later the same day, while attending the casualties of 10 Platoon after a mistaken napalm bombing on the company position, Dunque was wounded again – this time in the leg by an exploding grenade set off by the flames racing through the position. Refusing to be evacuated, he continued his work before trekking the six-hour route withdrawal with the rest of his company. He was one of the last two Australians to withdraw from the Kapyong position. For his actions during the battle, he was awarded the Military Medal.

With his deployment ending on 11 October 1951, Dunque later returned to Korea for a second tour from 29 September 1953 until 8 October 1954. After then serving in the Malayan Emergency, Dunque was discharged from the Army in October 1956. During his discharge, Dunque was handed his birth certificate, which he had never known existed but was evidently given to the Army by his foster mother.[75] Later, he would find he had a number of siblings from his birth mother. Ron died at the Repatriation General Hospital in Adelaide, South Australia, on 3 July 2004, aged 73 years.

2/400239 (NX37487) CORPORAL WILLIAM 'BILL' JOSIAH ROWLINSON DCM AND BAR

A soldier since 1938, Rowlinson's ambitions to serve were not fulfilled during the Second World War as he had never been deployed overseas. Eager to serve and 'do his bit', Rowlinson re-enlisted for service during the Korean War. His strength and leadership during the Battle of Kapyong was recognised with the award of a Distinguished Conduct Medal (DCM), and were followed by further acts of bravery at the Battle of Maryang San, for which he was awarded a Bar to his DCM.

Sergeant William 'Bill' Josiah Rowlinson DCM, Korea, 1951.
(PHOTOGRAPHER: PHILLIP HOBSON, AWM HOBJ2676)

Born on 22 July 1920 at Manly, New South Wales, Rowlinson was the third of six children of Gilbert Douglas Rowlinson, a carpenter, and Pearl May Gates.[76] After leaving North Sydney Boys' High School, having achieved sub-intermediate level, Rowlinson became a wireless mechanic. At age 18, Rowlinson joined the Militia and began his career as a soldier. When the Second World War commenced, Rowlinson transferred to the Second AIF, joining the 2/7th Armoured Regiment. In December 1943, he chose to take a demotion from Sergeant to Private in order to serve with the 1st Australian Parachute Battalion, hoping to see combat. However, he was never deployed overseas. On 27 March 1946, he was discharged from the Army.

On the outbreak of the Korean War, Rowlinson re-enlisted. He was deployed with 3 RAR on 16 December 1950. During the Battle of Kapyong, Rowlinson was a section leader of 12 Platoon, D Company. With D Company assigned the role of right-flank protection on feature 504 and the ridgeline to the north-east, Rowlinson was tasked with leading the left-forward section. During the night of 23 April 1951, enemy probing patrols endeavoured to penetrate his section position and were repulsed. On the morning of 24 April 1951, enemy forces of platoon strength maintained continuous attacks against this section position for a period of five to six hours and were again driven back, sustaining heavy casualties. During these attacks, Rowlinson and six members of his section were wounded. While his wounded soldiers were evacuated, Rowlinson remained on duty and continued to lead his section until he was ordered to withdraw. Rowlinson was evacuated to Japan in order to recover from his injuries, but returned to Korea on 17 June 1951, where he was promoted to Temporary Sergeant. At the Battle of Maryang San, the casualties that had been inflicted required Rowlinson to take command of 12 Platoon. Again wounded in battle, he continued to lead his men, and his quick thinking and inspired leadership assisted in them capturing the hill. For this action, he was awarded a Bar to his DCM.

Rowlinson remained in the Army after he returned from Korea, and he was commissioned as a Lieutenant on 5 April 1952. However, he failed to pass promotion exams for the rank of captain in 1955 and 1956, largely due to his limited education. On 19 July 1957, Rowlinson resigned his commission, and he was subsequently employed by the New South Wales Department of Education, becoming caretaker and house services officer at the Wagga Wagga Teachers' College. He married Melba May Smith in April 1950, and they had a son. Rowlinson died on 17 November 1998 of ischaemic heart disease in the RSL War Veteran's Home, Caboolture, Queensland.

Cancelled reinforcement

After visiting the forward companies and returning to his new BHQ location near the Middlesex, Ferguson received word that the 5th Cavalry had been postponed and would not arrive in time to bolster 3 RAR's western flank to participate in another overnight battle.[77] The US Official History reveals that the 5th Cavalry Regiment had been hit hard on the first night of the Chinese offensive further north, and had withdrawn to reorganise in rear areas south of 27 BCB. The cavalrymen needed more time to reconstitute for combat. The regiment was rescheduled to reinforce the Kapyong Valley in twenty-four hours, not on 24 April.[78] This delay required Brigadier Burke to reconsider leaving 3 RAR on Hill 504.

With no prospect of US reinforcement, Burke decided to withdraw the Australians on the evening of 24 April, after D Company held their ground. He still had the Canadians on the high ground covering the Kapyong Valley to the south, to further delay the Chinese overnight; and had aircraft, artillery, mortars and tanks to support them.

To illustrate and compare different circumstances and different decisions, 29 BCB's experience west of Kapyong on 24 April is instructive. During the previous night, the Glosters had been under relentless attack. The Chinese had infiltrated the brigade and bypassed it with regimental-sized forces. 29 BCB's four battalions had been reinforced with a US and a Filippino battalion, and had been allocated more US tanks and medium artillery in support. Nonetheless, 29 BCB's position was dire, and the Glosters were in great peril. Though he was authorised to withdraw at 9am on 24 April, Brodie launched one last attempt to relieve the beleaguered battalion using the Philippine 10 Battalion Combat Team, supported by Centurion and light tanks. In Farrar-Hockley's opinion, this was insufficient: 'A reinforced brigade or regimental combat team was the minimum force required to effect a relief'.[79]

After the Filipinos and tanks failed to reach the Glosters and withdrew under fire, just after 3pm, General Soule, the US Divisional commander, informed Brodie that he was moving a task force of two battalions of the 65th Infantry Regiment, most of the 64th Tank Battalion, and the 10th Field Artillery Battalion, to relieve the Glosters early on 25 April. He scheduled this task force to deploy behind 29 BCB by 5.30pm on 24 April.[80] On receiving orders at 3.15pm to hold overnight until reinforcement in the morning, Lieutenant Colonel Carne, CO 1st Glosters, replied, 'My command is no longer an effective fighting force. If it is required that we shall stay here, in spite of this, we shall continue to hold. But I wish to make known the nature of my position'.[81] In the hours to come, in Farrar-Hockley's words, 'The run of these events lay along that narrow line between tragedy and farce'.[82]

Summation

The night-time battle on 23–24 April was a tale of slaughter and survival. B Company and the US tanks by night, supported by artillery and air power during the day, had killed and wounded hundreds of enemy troops. On Hill 504's ridgeline, the Chinese attempted to bypass the slaughter on the valley floor and break through A Company, but multiple night-time assaults had failed. O'Dowd and his diggers held their ground at high cost and with much suffering.

After daybreak, the Chinese rolled the dice again on Hill 504 and attempted to drive D Company from the high ground and bypass the tanks on the valley floor, despite the danger from artillery fire. The Australians endured six hours of attacks, killing scores of their assailants with direct small-arms and indirect artillery fire, forcing them to give up and regroup for further attacks under the cover of darkness.

As the late afternoon began turning into night on 24 April, 27 BCB and 29 BCB braced for battle. The Glosters were pessimistic about their chances of holding overnight. Brodie hoped that they could hang on against the odds, and the morning counterattack with two fresh battalions would save them. Burke was in a stronger position. Unlike Brodie, who had to rescue the Glosters with a counterattack and then see if 29 BCB could hold the line with reinforcements, A and D Company on Hill 504 had done their job and repelled night-and-day assaults respectively. B and C companies were now located in all-round defence behind A and D companies, to give depth and counterattack options. C Company could have reinforced A Company with fresh troops, but at the cost of compromising all-round defence and sacrificing depth. However, when Burke ordered Ferguson to withdraw B Company, he had opened 3 RAR's left flank and left the US tanks without infantry support on their western flank. Burke decided not to counterattack on the afternoon of 24 April with the Middlesex and US tanks to reoccupy B Company's old commanding position and possibly push the Chinese off Sukon San – the Middlesex's intended defensive position – to cover A Company's flank for another night fight, when the 5th Cavalry Regiment reinforcement was postponed. Burke directed Ferguson to withdraw the Australians intact to give depth to his position back with the Middlesex. It would be the Canadians' turn to repel the Chinese overnight with optimal tank, artillery and mortar support after the Australians withdrew under fire.

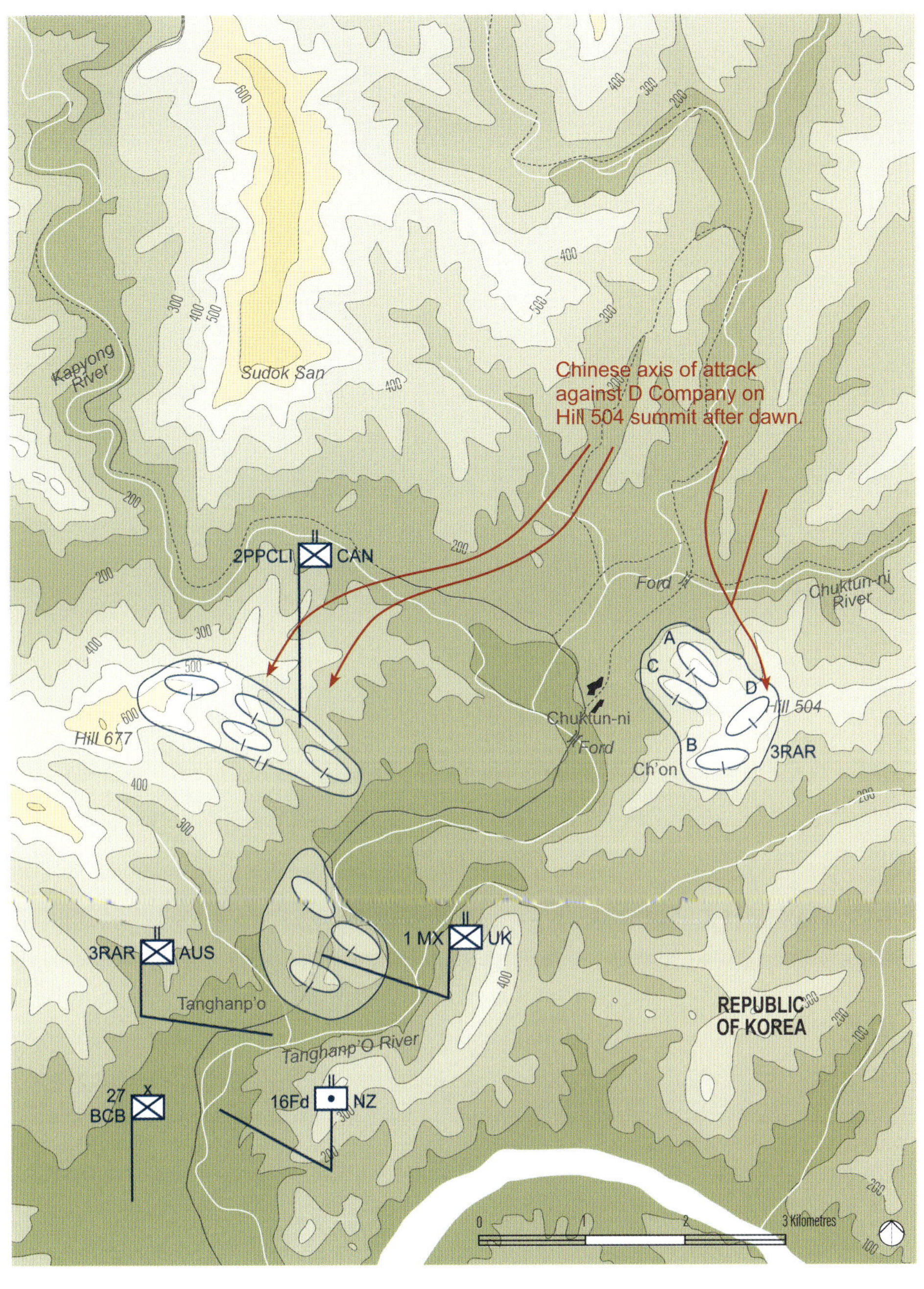

Map 7. 27 BCB situation at 1530hrs, 24 April 1951

CHAPTER 7

WITHDRAWAL

24–25 APRIL 1951

THIS CHAPTER DETAILS THE planning and execution of the Australian withdrawal that ended 3 RAR's participation in the Battle of Kapyong. Preparations had begun early on 24 April with BHQ's move to the rear and B Company's crossing the valley to the main battalion position. B Company's attempted reoccupation of its old position in anticipation of reinforcement from the 5th Cavalry Regiment was a mistake. When Burke learned that the 5th Cavalry was not going to arrive by nightfall, he correctly assessed, according to Australia's Official Historian, that the forward companies would not be able to survive another night of heavy attacks in exposed, isolated positions.[1] He directed Ferguson to resume preparations for a withdrawal. Fortunately, there was a withdrawal route along the shoulder and to the rear of Hill 504, down to the Kapyong River, adjacent to the Canadian position. When the Australians got there, the Canadians could engage any following Chinese troops to allow the Australians to achieve a clean break, and to move to and occupy positions near the Middlesex.

There is some disagreement about when and how the orders to withdraw the forward companies came about. The Official History says that Ferguson ordered his companies to 'withdraw along a ridge running three kilometres to the south-west from Hill 504, some 500 metres east of the Kapyong River' after he arrived at the forward company locations on the tanks.[2] Ferguson later told interviewers that he issued orders for a withdrawal to the company commanders and then delegated responsibility for carrying it out to O'Dowd, who was senior.[3]

The conventional doctrine for withdrawal, especially when an enemy is expected to follow up aggressively, is that the commanding officer has the responsibility to issue orders and command a battalion withdrawal from a forward-positioned tactical headquarters, with communications to each company on a battalion command net, and accompanied by an artillery battery commander and his forward observation party to direct fire, and a forward air controller to direct close air support. The key to the success of a withdrawal is to achieve a clean break from the enemy through surprise and speed, as well as leapfrogging – a tactic in which one sub-unit covers another from a fixed position while it moves; then when the moving unit is on the ground and ready, the supporting unit moves under its cover. Bringing artillery and mortar fire onto the following enemy groups also assists in achieving a clean break.

Interviews recorded decades after the battle appear to be closer to the truth of when and how orders were issued.[4] O'Dowd recalled that while Ferguson was with the forward companies that morning, he spoke only of the requirement for them to hold their positions until the 5th Cavalry arrived. Years later, O'Dowd said he had emphasised to Ferguson that his company could not hold unless the Americans occupied the high ground to the rear and to the west. He believed any new attacks on his position would be better planned and stronger than those of the previous night, and that he could not stay without US support. Later in the day, after lunch, Ferguson informed O'Dowd that the Americans were not coming and told him to try and get the rifle companies out.[5]

Gravener said that O'Dowd told him, after Ferguson had left in the late morning, to return to the Middlesex position, and that the forward companies were required to do a 'Mafeking', by which he meant holding on until a relief force arrived.[6] Saunders said that he did not receive orders from Ferguson that morning. He learned he was required to withdraw his company when he monitored a radio transmission from Ferguson to O'Dowd in the early afternoon.[7]

Alf Argent, who accompanied Ferguson and was by his side when he returned to the Middlesex position that morning, did not recall Ferguson issuing orders for a withdrawal to any of the company commanders. He did remember that after they returned to the Middlesex position and it became clear that the 5th Cavalry could not relieve the forward companies by nightfall, Ferguson took the radio from him, set it down and spoke conversationally with O'Dowd about withdrawing the forward companies, not in the format of orders for a withdrawal.[8] The 27 BCB War Diary does not specify when Burke ordered Ferguson to withdraw the forward companies, but agrees with O'Neill on the reason: that it was clear 3 RAR would be unable to hold on against Chinese attacks for another night.[9]

The withdrawal plan

O'Dowd and Ferguson discussed a withdrawal plan over the radio early in the afternoon. Ferguson had decided not to go forward and command in person with a tactical headquarters group, but to have O'Dowd develop the plan, deliver orders to the other company commanders and control the withdrawal. He seemed to want to revert to his former role as Battalion 2IC, ensuring that O'Dowd, commanding the withdrawal, received the support he needed to make a clean break from the Chinese and to count the battalion through the main rear checkpoint.

He and O'Dowd agreed on the withdrawal route and on locating the Battalion Check Point on the ford east of the Middlesex position, where companies could be counted through and, if necessary, pick up guides to lead them to their new position. After talking with O'Dowd over the radio, Ferguson directed Len Eyles, his Adjutant, to have Jack Gerke take a Support Company group to secure the 3 RAR Check Point.[10]

After an exhausting night and morning, O'Dowd had to summon the energy and his faculties to plan and conduct a battalion fighting withdrawal. He had been at Pakchon in November 1950 and knew that such manoeuvres, especially at night, could quickly turn into a catastrophe unless everyone knew their role. He recognised that there were two ways out. One, to fight back down the road, and the other to get behind D Company and 'beat our way' down the ridgeline leading to the Middlesex, two miles distant. Laughlin could see the valley to the south from his position and made it clear that fighting down the road was impossible, leaving the ridgeline as the only option. But the enemy was on the other side of the road in B Company's former position, and would see the Australians moving up the ridge behind D Company, which was then engaged in a fight on the summit. The Chinese attacking D Company's position would follow any withdrawal, and O'Dowd hoped Gravener would be able to get his men out when the other companies were able to support them. Compounding his worries, O'Dowd expected that the Chinese would have also established a blocking position on the withdrawal route.[11] In effect, he expected a breakout fight and close combat during the withdrawal.

To improve command and control, O'Dowd assigned Corporal Ron Perkins, his Mortar Fire Controller, as his signaller, creating a two-person tactical headquarters and freeing himself to concentrate on the withdrawal. Perkins came onto the battalion command radio net as the control station, and each company understood that Perkins represented O'Dowd. O'Dowd delegated command of his company to Captain Bob Murdoch, his second-in-command, for the withdrawal. Essentially, O'Dowd was acting CO 3 RAR for the withdrawal.

The withdrawal's timing was critical to its success. O'Dowd knew that in daylight the Chinese would see what was happening. However, the diggers would have good fields of fire and high ground to keep the enemy at bay in the early stages. He would also be able to use observed artillery fire to slow the Chinese down. O'Dowd hoped that when night fell, he would be well on his way to the Middlesex position, and the last company would be able to achieve a clean break. He wrote that the withdrawal was to commence at 4pm.[12] Other sources give differing times.[13] 3 RAR's Unit Diary notes that the withdrawal was complete at 10.30pm and had taken seven hours, which would have meant a 3.30pm start.[14]

O'Dowd's challenge was to protect the withdrawing platoons when D Company broke contact. He wanted to avoid what had happened to A Company at Pakchon. His plan, communicated to his fellow company commanders by 2.30pm, was to drop High Explosive (HE) shell fire and smoke on B Company's old position when A Company started moving. B Company were to move in behind D Company, evacuate the wounded and clear a path down the ridgeline, dealing with any Chinese blocking forces or waiting for O'Dowd to bring up another company if they could not. If B Company got through, it was to secure both sides of the ford near the Middlesex position. C and A Companies were to get between D Company and the enemy as D Company withdrew, leapfrogging, holding up the Chinese and keeping them at a distance until the Australians could make a clean break. If O'Dowd was successful, the enemy could not come to close quarters during the withdrawal.[15]

The news that the forward companies were to withdraw brought mixed reactions. Most of the diggers did not like the idea because withdrawals were tricky, and they symbolised defeat. They wanted to escape the danger, but many thought they had fought hard to remain in position and were angry that the promised relief from the 5th Cavalry would not be forthcoming. George Harris, A Company's Acting CSM, summed it up:

> *We all knew quite well that they had to do something with A Company. I thought that one of the other companies would come up and relieve us ... But with all our casualties and how we were exposed on the ridge, we could not have held for another night.*
>
> *We had to leave our dead behind, which was a bit painful. We lined them all up; we could not carry them. We even had to destroy some of our own weapons because we did not have sufficient men to carry them all.*[16]

For Harris, leaving their dead in the A Company position was more than 'a bit painful'. Among them was a close friend who had fought alongside him in the Second World War, Private Roy 'Padre' Ingram. They had saved each other's lives on several occasions and shared many hardships. Ingram died trying to rescue a wounded man, while wounded himself.[17]

There was a lull in the fighting around D Company from about 1.30pm until 3pm. The Chinese may have decided to wait until the light faded before renewing their attacks. O'Dowd thought that his luck was holding and, as the time for withdrawal approached, that the companies would be able to achieve a clean break without enemy contact. Gravener skilfully withdrew Ward's 12 Platoon back to his company headquarters area without any casualties, despite running a gauntlet of Chinese automatic fire.[18] He was pleased to watch Chinese mortar bombs fall on Ward's vacant position soon after.

Gravener called in artillery on Ward's old position as Chinese troops went in at 3pm and occupied the area.[19]

Napalm incident

Just when O'Dowd and Gravener might have felt that it was only a matter of waiting another forty minutes before A Company started moving and a massive artillery barrage signalled the withdrawal, tragedy struck, demonstrating the need for robust procedures for the control and coordination of close air support. A spotter aircraft fired a targeting rocket into D Company's position, despite a brightly coloured panel identifying it as a UN unit.[20] The origins of the attack that followed remain unclear. Neither Gravener nor O'Dowd had requested air support that afternoon. Ferguson or Brigade Headquarters may have provided poor instructions, or attack aircraft and their spotters may have been prowling the skies for targets of opportunity. Whatever the case, Sergeant Ray McKenzie saw what happened next:

> *As I was leaving to return to my original position near the MMGs, I saw a US Marine Corsair line up and start a run in on our position. I was angry about this because our marker panels were clearly visible. I saw the big silver bomb leave the plane and watched it fall in the D Company area, on 10 Platoon, where I had been two minutes before. The napalm exploded and took all the oxygen out of the air. I felt like I was just breathing heat.*[21]

Eight Australians were burnt and one killed.[22] Private 'Nugget' Dunque, D Company's Medical Orderly, who had a large white bandage covering a head wound at the time, recalled:

> *Napalm is a pretty ferocious sort of weapon … I then saw the most appalling apparition. A man with no flesh – his hands were dripping flesh – completely naked. As he walked, I saw these huge bloated feet. The sticks and the stones came up through his feet. He sat down next to me. I didn't know who he was. He looked at me and said, 'Jesus, Nuggett, [noticing the bandage on Dunque's head] you're having a bad day'. Harry Giddens! I recognised his voice.*[23]

The companies couldn't communicate directly with aircraft; it was only frantic radio messages from Australian signallers and US tank commanders, who watched the accident from further down the valley, that warned off a second Corsair about to make its run to drop more napalm on D Company. Lance Corporal Harold Giddens survived the six-hour withdrawal from Kapyong and died in Ballarat, Victoria, in 1992, aged 73.[24]

The Chinese took advantage of the napalm strike and attacked while D Company was still stunned. This time, they assaulted 11 Platoon, commanded by Lieutenant Russ McWilliam, from the east. Fortunately, McWilliam's platoon had not been splashed with napalm and were able to cut the Chinese attackers down.[25] McWilliam was a reinforcement officer who had moved forward to take over his assigned platoon from Sergeant Len Opie on the afternoon of 23 April, after Opie went on leave to Japan. He now had the opportunity to lead his men under fire, quickly establishing his command after this successful action. Unfortunately, he was killed on 7 October 1951 by a Chinese mortar bomb, after leading his platoon during the Battle of Maryang San.[26]

Solving a casualty evacuation problem

The napalm attack on D Company killed one soldier and left eight with serious burns, who needed to be stretchered out, as did six others suffering from gunshot wounds sustained during the Chinese assaults on 12 Platoon earlier that day. Miller's tanks had evacuated A and B Companies' casualties earlier that morning. Each stretcher required six fit men – four carriers and two to rotate with them. The problem was finding about eighty men to take the stretcher cases, and twenty more to assist the walking wounded.

The solution lay in Eric Bradley's Chinese prisoners, about whom O'Dowd had forgotten.[27] As B Company moved up the slope past the rear of D Company's position,

A group of 3 RAR soldiers stand over Chinese prisoners captured during the Battle of Kapyong, Korea, 24 April 1951. (PHOTOGRAPHER: RAYMOND PARRY, AWM P04953.007)

most of the stretcher cases were picked up, and many of the walking wounded were assisted. But the likelihood of having to fight through a Chinese blocking position meant Laughlin could spare no more men. His CSM, Eric Bradley, took the initiative and ordered the prisoners to carry the wounded and, in some cases, spare weapons and ammunition, solving half the casualty evacuation problem. The other half was solved when A Company's men, passing D Company's rear, answered the call to help carry the wounded from the napalm strike. None were left behind.[28]

One bearer, Private Pat Knowles, helped carry one stretcher and, for half an hour, resisted the wounded man's pleas for water. Knowles had been told not to give the wounded water, and he had none in any case. He told the soldier to be quiet because he did not have any water, and heard no more.[29] Later the blanket fell, exposing the soldier's terribly burnt, disfigured face. Recognising the agony that man was enduring in silence remained Knowles' most vivid recollection of Kapyong and haunted him for years.[30]

While Laughlin and his CSM found a use for the Chinese prisoners, O'Dowd waited for the artillery to neutralise B Company's old position so C Company could move, but the gunners did not open fire. He got Ferguson on the radio and asked why the guns were late. Ferguson responded that the wind had changed, so the guns were re-registering the impact point for smoke rounds. Mindful that he had to be well on the way before nightfall, O'Dowd did not wait, and ordered Saunders' C Company to move.[31]

The 16th Field Regiment War Diary does not explain why there was a delay in beginning the fire plan for the withdrawal. The changed emission point for smoke should not have affected the use of HE shell fire, also requested by O'Dowd, but the many calls for fire support from 2 PPCLI during the afternoon may have. So too might the fact that in the four hours since Burke ordered the withdrawal, neither the New Zealand Regiment nor Ferguson sent a FOO party to replace the New Zealand gunners killed in A Company's position the night before and to assist O'Dowd with artillery support for the withdrawal. Indeed, now that he was the acting commanding officer for the withdrawal, he was entitled to have a battery commander and his FOO party assist him. As the last company to be withdrawn according to O'Dowd's plan, Norm Gravener had time to continue to call in accurate artillery fire while other companies thinned out and withdrew.

Fortunately, as the time for A Company to withdraw drew near, Koch's company of tanks provided covering fire, sending round after round into the Chinese positions on the knoll previously occupied by B Company.[32] Reg Saunders and his company had moved back in support, following O'Dowd's order. This 'foot on the ground' and the shells smashing into the Chinese on B Company's old position cued Bob Murdoch to move A Company up the ridge towards D Company, with less risk of being chased. B Company was on its way, clearing the withdrawal route. The New Zealand artillery fire plan did increase some risk when some rounds narrowly missed one of the US tanks, causing it to back off quickly. Overall, the withdrawal had begun according to plan.

Achieving clean breaks

O'Dowd achieved a clean break from the Chinese occupying B Company's old position after it was clouded in smoke and rocked with the impact of HE rounds. C and A Companies were on their way, following B Company, while D Company was still fending off Chinese assaults. Gravener told O'Dowd that he couldn't withdraw because he was under attack, and it would be 'a bad time to go'.[33] When there was a lull, D Company began 'thinning out'. In well-practised drills, individuals, sections and platoons covered each other's rearward movement in bounds. McWilliam's 11 Platoon was last out. Its final clearance gave D Company the break it needed. Gravener marched the guns down the ridgeline behind his withdrawing soldiers, and his expertise covered the absence of forward observers. He recalled:

It was possible to bring the guns down the ridgeline [after 11 Platoon had come down from the summit]. I did this and gave the following orders to the guns as we went: 'Drop 50. Go on'. 'Drop 50. Go on'.[34]

O'Dowd had already reconnoitred D Company's next position on its first bound. When Gravener's men were clear of C and A companies, he stopped them and ordered C Company back. The Chinese followed up immediately, but artillery fire forced them to take cover, and C Company got away without casualties.

This leapfrogging of companies continued until late at night. The Chinese were hard on the heels of each one, despite suffering heavy casualties from shellfire. The Australians' battle discipline was impressive. No one moved until ordered. Everyone remained composed and kept the Chinese at bay until it was time to go. No one panicked and ran. Each digger moved back, covered by his mates, and his mates covered him as he moved until they were all clear of the Chinese pursuing them. Disciplined fire control by the diggers and accurate artillery support were the key to each company achieving a clean break without sustaining casualties.

Commanding under pressure

O'Dowd was a steadying influence during the withdrawal. He was going back and locating positions for each company on the move, guiding them into position and, once they were down, ordering the next one to make its break. Any hint of panic or fear on O'Dowd's face might have caused others to lose confidence. He remembered one incident momentarily shaking his own:

In the dark, I got a hell of a shock ... looking for positions to put companies down. All of a sudden, I found myself in the middle of a bunch of Chinese soldiers, which frightened the hell out of me until I realised that they were our prisoners. What really worried me was that they were carrying arms.

I got hold of one of the escorts and said, 'What the hell do you mean allowing these prisoners to carry arms'. He said, 'You do not expect the bloody wounded to carry them, do you?' By the time I had digested this piece of logic, they had disappeared into the dark. He knew what he was doing, and I had to get on with my job.[35]

O'Dowd received welcome news over the radio from Darcy Laughlin – there was no blocking position along the route or at the ford. Now the challenge was to stay ahead of Chinese forces chasing the leapfrogging companies. Gravener could only estimate roughly how to adjust artillery support in the dark.

After rolling back the companies, O'Dowd met up with Jim Young, B Company's Acting 2IC, who Laughlin had left at the ford to act as a guide for incoming companies. All but A Company were over the ford to safety, and B Company was in a final blocking position. O'Dowd radioed Bob Murdoch and asked him how he was going. When Murdoch replied that he was in contact with a Chinese force, O'Dowd ordered him to 'break contact and get down here fast'.[36]

Jim Young and O'Dowd waited very anxiously, standing in ice-cold water at the ford. Eventually, Brumfield's platoon came off the hill where O'Dowd was expecting them. They told him the rest of A Company was behind them. After an anxious wait, the remainder of A Company arrived at the ford from ninety degrees in the wrong direction.[37] Later, O'Dowd found out that in the dark at a fork in the track running down the ridgeline, Bob Murdoch, moving at the head of the A Company column, took the wrong path. When Brumfield arrived at the fork and saw no one in front, he chose the right track and arrived at the ford ahead of Murdoch's group. As it turned out, Murdoch's mistake became a tactical godsend.

While O'Dowd was waiting for A Company, the Canadians, aware of the Australian withdrawal route, began firing a 50-calibre machine gun in what O'Dowd thought was his direction. He ordered it stopped, but the Canadians insisted they were engaging the enemy. O'Dowd told them to cease fire, later learning that when Murdoch took the wrong track and couldn't find the ford or the guides, he made a sharp left turn. The Chinese following him thought the Australians had taken a direct route into the river and jumped in after them. These were the silhouetted figures the Canadians were firing at. Essentially, they were engaging the Chinese force following A Company and ensuring them of a clean break.

Norm Gravener remembered Bruce Ferguson and Alf Argent welcoming everyone passing through the 3 RAR checkpoint at the ford, 'like lost brothers' ... 'We were rather dishevelled – rather black from all the fire – very tired and, I might add, very relieved'.[38] The forward companies moved to their new positions in the safety of the Middlesex position, untroubled by enemy fire. They could hear the sounds of an intense battle across the valley as the Chinese attempted to dislodge the Canadians from their positions on Hill 677.

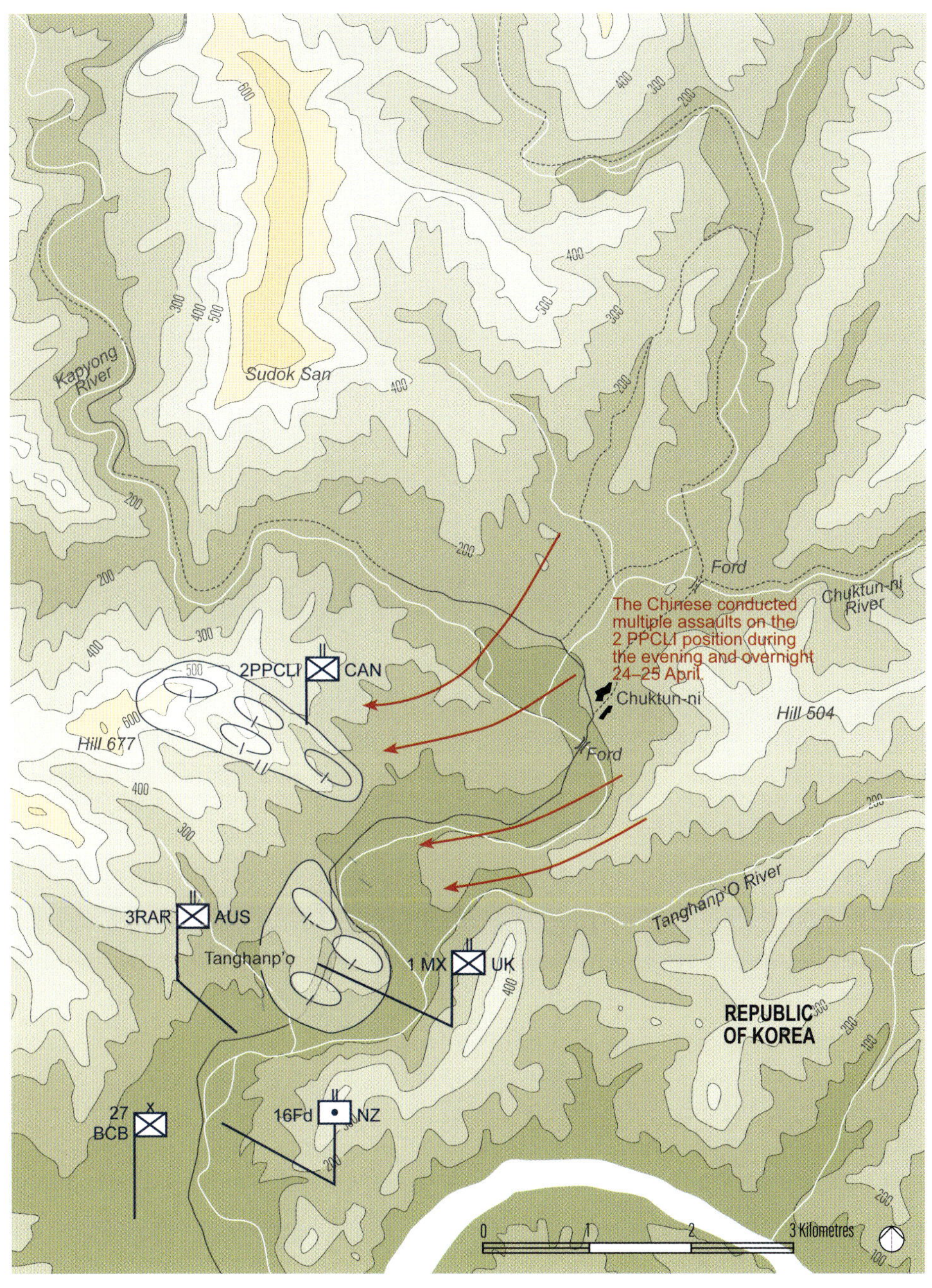

Map 8. 27 BCB positions at 2100hrs, 24 April 1951 (based on a trace provided by MAJ J. Gerke, DSO in 1952)

The forward companies' safe withdrawal to the security of the Middlesex position concluded 3 RAR's participation in the Battle of Kapyong. During the night and into the next day, the Chinese launched several major assaults against the Canadians in what was their last effort to advance on Seoul down the Kapyong Valley. Kenneth Koch and his tank company were again hard at work on the valley floor, supporting the Canadians and disrupting the Chinese advance along the valley floor.[39]

The forty-eight hours of respite provided by the Australian and Canadian infantry battalions, with the support of the US tank company, took the pressure off the 6th ROK Division's withdrawal to the south and allowed time for UN forces to consolidate a new defensive line.[40]

The US 5th Cavalry Regiment arrived and launched an unsuccessful and costly counterattack towards Chuktun-ni on 26 April, after 27 BCB withdrew. Fortunately, the Chinese were exhausted and unable to push through to Seoul when UN forces held the line further south. After several weeks of fighting, the UN advanced north again and reclaimed the Kapyong Valley.[41]

Summation

At Chuktun-ni, on 23–24 April, 3 RAR fought off a series of determined Chinese attacks overnight and the next day: first B Company, then A Company, and finally D Company. They fought from scrapes or sheltered behind mounds of stones. During lulls, they removed their dead and wounded, and soldiers moved from rear to forward positions to wait for the next assault, each man aware that his chances of survival should he suffer a serious wound were slight. Each was ready to meet his fate. The men at BHQ also had to repel attacks from Chinese infiltrators. Everyone knew they were cut off, with a slim chance of withdrawing. In such circumstances, any panic or decline in morale would have been disastrous. Officers and other ranks kept their composure.

This professional composure continued for the overnight withdrawal on 24–25 April. 3 RAR's withdrawal – carrying all casualties from D Company's defence of the Hill 504 summit, and after sustaining more from a napalm attack – without suffering further casualties in the darkness, with Chinese forces chasing them, was masterful. The credit for this feat goes to Ben O'Dowd, who took on his commanding officer's responsibilities after a night of hard fighting and witnessing half of his company becoming either killed or wounded. His orders were clear and followed the principle of achieving a clean break.

Firepower assists with achieving a clean break. After a delay in the execution of a fire plan and the absence of forward observers, O'Dowd took his chances and ordered the first move. Norm Gravener called in artillery to cover the withdrawal and protect his company before and during the Chinese assaults, especially after sustaining casualties from a napalm attack. He was crucial for achieving his company's clean break and targeting the Chinese pursuit of withdrawing companies with accurate artillery fire.

Clean breaks ultimately depend on personal battle discipline. The urge to run and distance oneself from danger is instinctive. 3 RAR's officers and soldiers were confident that their tactics were sound and took up their blocking positions quietly and efficiently to await the pursuing enemy. They were confident about each other's discipline. They fought and held the ground until ordered to pull back and withdraw calmly under covering fire. It was never a case of 'every man for himself'. Diggers protected their mates. Sections covered other sections. Platoons supported other platoons. Each company held and protected the others as they moved back.

CHAPTER 8

CONCLUSION

WHAT SHOULD THE AUSTRALIAN ARMY make of the performance of 3 RAR in Korea from September 1950 until its triumph on 23–24 April during the Battle of Kapyong? Why did these twenty-four hours of intense combat and danger during a long campaign become so consequential, and the subject of so much commemoration and admiration? Jeff Grey, a respected Australian Korean War historian, answered the second part of this question when he concluded that 3 RAR and 2 PPCLI, with the aid of 27 BCB's New Zealand gun regiment and a company of US tanks, had 'fought an entire enemy division to a standstill'.[1] The Canadian and Australian Official Histories support Grey's assessment, concluding that the battle had a direct bearing on saving Seoul from being retaken by the Chinese.[2] The citation award for the US Distinguished Unit Citation (redesignated a Presidential Unit Citation in 1966) confirms, 'Toward the close of the second day, the 25th of April, the enemy breakthrough had been stopped. The seriousness of the breakthrough on the central front had been changed from defeat to victory by the gallant stand of these heroic and courageous soldiers'.[3]

The framework for discussing contemporary lessons from 3 RAR's performance from the Apple Orchard to Kapyong is that collective human performance depends on selection, training and management. Within military training and management are the processes of binding, bonding and building groups under pressure to develop individual and collective knowledge, skills and attitudes for mission accomplishment under the physical and mental stress of battle. In 1950–51, these factors and processes laid the foundations for 3 RAR's success in a demanding climate, characterised by austere living conditions, against an enemy whose numbers, fieldcraft and aggression offset comparative deficits in firepower.

They all apply to the Army's success in 21st-century battlespaces. There were unique circumstances that existed in the late 1940s and early 1950s that are not replicable in the 21st century. Still, they should continue to guide contemporary selection, training and management, as well as the binding, bonding and building processes that prepare the Army's combat arms units for warfare.

The availability of battle-hardened officers, NCOs and soldiers who had fought in the Second World War enabled the Army to select personnel for service in Korea who were ready for combat, obviating the need for lengthy training. 3 RAR had a core of personnel in Japan who possessed the skills, knowledge and attitudes necessary for combat. K Force reinforcements from Australia added hundreds more individuals with these attributes.

The challenge was to bind, bond and build these experienced individuals with a group of younger, inexperienced volunteers into fighting sections, platoons and companies, to comprise a fighting battalion. There was no lack of time pressure and urgency in Japan to train hard to bind newly formed sub-units under newly appointed leaders. No one knew how long the government would give them to prepare, especially when warned for immediate movement in August, even before K Force reinforcements had arrived.

3 RAR relied on traditional weapons training at ranges, infantry minor tactics exercises and long, challenging route marches, to bond teams together and harden legs and core muscles for what lay ahead. There was no time to build proficiency in sub-unit and unit tactics for attack and defence before deployment to Korea. Fortunately, initial operations under Charlie Green's impressive leadership made up for the lack of pre-deployment mission rehearsal to bond teams in shared adversity and build collective skills with repeated tactical drills and episodes of close-quarter combat. Using the sporting analogy, Green built a champion team from a team of champions.

The lesson for the Army is that recruitment and subsequent personnel management, especially for combat arms units, must focus on the same individual attributes that enabled 3 RAR's success. Technology might change, but the brutality and stress of close combat on the ground stay the same. The Army's individual and collective peacetime training systems must produce individuals and groups with the skills and knowledge, as well as the attitudinal aggression and resilience, to prosecute and withstand the pressures of combat operations, as 3 RAR did more than seven decades ago. Mindful of the 'ready-made' residual skills of Second World War veterans who bolstered 3 RAR in 1950, the Army must invest in retaining trained and experienced personnel after discharge under a part-time refresher training regime to ensure there is a surge capacity of experienced personnel to mobilise the force-in-being for short-notice deployment and immediate employment on combat operations.

The brief period of Green's command, and the debacle at Pakchon, confirmed the importance of the personality and competence of commanding officers for success. Green's careful planning and clear orders, combined with O'Dowd's execution of operations, resulted in 3 RAR's successful completion of offensive and defensive tasks under British command from September until early November 1951. Green's replacement verified that the competence of company commanders will not overcome a battalion commander's incompetence.

Returning to the selection imperative for human performance, the Army decided to replace Green with Walsh, who had been assessed as unsuitable for commanding a battalion on operations. Ferguson, a proven sub-unit commander and Military Cross recipient, who was well known to the battalion, was the logical interim replacement until a lieutenant colonel from Japan or Australia could be selected and flown in. Unfortunately, the fate of 3 RAR on operations was not prioritised over the preferences of possessive generals to retain Tom Daly and Frank Hassett in Australia as principal staff officers. Both would subsequently command with distinction in Korea. With hindsight, either one of them was needed in November 1951 to take command of 3 RAR as its members were recovering from the death of their commanding officer, angry about the catastrophe of Pakchon and coping with heavy casualties in two rifle companies.

Ben O'Dowd and Norm Gravener were the right individuals to bond and rebuild a demoralised A Company and a mauled but unbowed D Company over the coming months, before the Battle of Kapyong tested 3 RAR in a defensive battle once again. Both A and D companies held their ground under pressure and withdrew with disciplined composure, despite A Company suffering 50 per cent casualties and D Company having to endure a napalm attack just before breaking contact after several hours of repelling multiple Chinese assaults.

The compromise was that 3 RAR did not have a Battle 2IC [operations officer] at BHQ to execute operations after Pakchon. Captain Len Eyles, the Adjutant, who graduated from Duntroon in 1947, did not have O'Dowd's experience, and there is no evidence from interviews with 3 RAR veterans that he, or any other officer, directed day-to-day operations or executed tactical plans on Ferguson's behalf when the battalion or a sub-unit was in a fight.

The selection lesson for the Army is not to allow peacetime priorities to trump appointing competent and proven commanding officers to command on challenging overseas operations. The training lesson is to ensure that commanding officers receive optimal political, cultural and tactical training for commanding in unfamiliar overseas theatres of operation. Fortunately, Green and Ferguson had experienced combat against an Asian enemy during the final years of the Pacific war, after two years of fighting in the Mediterranean theatre of operations. They were 'ready-made' for Korea. These prerequisites will most likely not apply to battalion commanders deploying overseas in the 21st century.

The management lesson is to train and deploy national commanders and headquarters in support of deployed Australian units. Bruce Ferguson wrote that he felt intense additional pressure being the officer solely responsible for 3 RAR's safety and performance. The number of times that the Australians found themselves isolated 'up front' in advance, attack and defence from September 1950 until April 1951 suggests a preference for brigade commanders to employ 3 RAR for some of the heaviest fighting. This suggestion is impossible to prove, and foreign commanders should be free to prefer Australians for their fighting qualities. Still, this lesson from Korea reaffirms the contemporary practice of deploying national headquarters to monitor and support Australian forces deployed under foreign command.

The combat operations before and during the Battle of Kapyong reaffirmed the golden rules of combined arms warfare. Green masterfully coordinated air, artillery, mortar and medium machine-gun support during offensive and defensive operations, in collaboration with assigned forward air controllers and artillery forward observers. Sherman tanks were assigned to forward companies for the advance in September and October, and for the battles of the Broken Bridge and Chonju. For unknown reasons, this relationship did not exist for the defence of the Kapyong Valley in April, leaving the Australians to negotiate with tank commanders, not direct them in accordance with the local commanding officer's tactics and priorities. Fortunately, Koch and his tank platoon commanders were amenable to Australian requests for support, and provided timely support without request. The management lesson from Kapyong is that commanding officers should have tanks under operational control for mutual support and the effective application of armoured firepower, protection and manoeuvre.

Before the Pakchon debacle in early November, 3 RAR's performance had been exemplary under Green. Subsequently, Ferguson commanded operations competently over the winter of 1950–51, relying on company commanders to achieve sub-unit level tasks. Unlike Green or Walsh, he did not command a battalion-level attack or defensive operation. Nonetheless, he had Green's example to inform him about what to do. Significantly, he had not witnessed Green commanding a battalion fighting withdrawal.

Based on available evidence, and differing accounts written after the Official History was published, it is reasonable to ask, 'Who actually commanded 3 RAR's participation in the Battle of Kapyong?' Brigadier Ivan 'Lou' Brumfield, one of O'Dowd's platoon commanders at Kapyong, eulogised in 2012 that O'Dowd was 'a father of the Regiment' and, during the Battle of Kapyong, commanded 3 RAR 'from the first enemy onset to the end of a terrific, well-planned but hotly contested fighting withdrawal'. He opined that, 'There were many heroes in this battle, but in the minds of the soldiers, there was no doubt that O'Dowd had fought the battle and brought the battalion to safe haven'.[4] Is he correct, or is Brumfield just repeating soldiers' gossip and offering fulsome adulation at O'Dowd's funeral?

Ferguson issued orders on 23 April and assigned terrain to his company commanders in a battalion defensive layout. Following his brigade commander's orders, he set up his headquarters in a location that made it challenging to command the defensive battle that unfolded that night. A and B companies fought individually overnight on 23–24 April. The Chinese troubled the BHQ but did not trouble the C and D companies. The only orders Ferguson issued overnight were to direct his Adjutant Len Eyles to withdraw BHQ after first light.

Ferguson spent several hours at the Middlesex position between 1.30am and 4.30am, conferring with Brigadier Burke during that time. It is not known why he did not confer with Burke using the British signals detachment located in his headquarters, whose sole mission was to maintain communications between 3 RAR and 27 BCB headquarters. Burke authorised him to prepare to withdraw the forward companies after consolidating B Company behind A and D companies on Hill 504. He also agreed to assign a Middlesex company to protect BHQ's withdrawal by securing high ground overlooking the BHQ location and its withdrawal route.

Ferguson's activities after ordering Darcy Laughlin to withdraw B Company and consolidate with the other companies on Hill 504 on 24 April resembled those of 3 RAR's 2IC rather than its commanding officer. Displaying both personal courage and compassion, Ferguson went forward on tanks with a resupply of ammunition and made two trips evacuating A Company's casualties. He discussed the coming twenty-four hours with O'Dowd, after ordering him to meet him where the tanks were unloading ammunition and taking on casualties on the valley floor. He did not walk up to O'Dowd's position to assess A Company's circumstances or encourage those who had survived a night's combat and witnessed the death and wounding of comrades.

Ferguson continued to fulfil the Battalion 2IC role for the withdrawal. He did not come forward with his tactical headquarters to direct the companies along the withdrawal route, or coordinate fire support to assist them in achieving a clean break. He met the companies as they came through the battalion checkpoint on the ford, after presumably arranging water, food, ammunition and medical support at their new locations near the Middlesex position.

For the withdrawal of the forward companies on 24–25 April, there is no doubt that O'Dowd played a role beyond his rank and appointment. Ferguson claimed to be a student of Charlie Green. However, it is unlikely that Green would have delegated the withdrawal of the rifle companies to a company commander, whose primary responsibility was to withdraw his own company intact. Arguably, after deciding not to command the withdrawal from a forward position, Ferguson might have selected his Second AIF comrade Darcy Laughlin to command the withdrawal, rather than O'Dowd, who had lost half of his company's fighting strength overnight in savage close combat. He appeared to respect O'Dowd's professional abilities and trusted his judgement. Whether Green would have commanded the withdrawal is speculation after the fact. Still, O'Dowd emulated Green's inspirational leadership and sound tactical orthodoxy for conducting a fighting withdrawal, ably assisted by Norm Gravener's mastery of calling in artillery fire.

Before discussing how the credit for commanding 3 RAR during the Battle of Kapyong went to Ferguson, without recognition for O'Dowd or Gravener, it is illustrative to review the fate of the Glosters, who had been mauled during a night and day of close combat and, like 3 RAR's forward companies, were isolated on a hill behind enemy lines. The purpose is to reinforce lessons, not to make critical comparisons, when the challenges faced by 27 BCB and 29 BCB were similar but not exact.

The postponement of reinforcement obligated 27 BCB and 29 BCB commanders to extricate isolated forward battalions. 3 RAR withdrew back to the main 27 BCB position overnight on 24–25 April, and then 27 BCB withdrew further south on 26 April after the Canadians held the line overnight on 24–25 April and the next day, before the US 5th Cavalry Regiment counterattacked. 29 BCB's withdrawal of the Glosters before the brigade's withdrawal went differently.

This brief description is included to show how things can go wrong if risks are taken with the principles of defence and withdrawal. 29 BCB were stretched like 27 BCB to cover their allocated area but had to sacrifice high ground early in the battle when the Glosters sustained heavy casualties on the first night, and more during the next twenty-four hours. The lesson is that taking risks with a defensive layout, and not achieving mutual support within and between units in all-round defence, can compound when attackers outnumber defenders and inflict heavy casualties, and high ground is conceded early.

The 29 BCB Brigade Commander, Brodie, spoke to Carne, the Glosters' CO, at 6.10am on 25 April, after the Glosters had endured another night of close combat. Carne responded that 'he would break away when a sufficient number of the enemy had been destroyed or driven back'.[5] He hoped to achieve a clean break with the application of firepower in the same way as Gravener and the 16th Regiment's fire plan, which combined smoke and HE rounds, had achieved a clean break for 3 RAR's forward companies.

Carne did not issue formal orders for a phased withdrawal. His final order, passed from Brodie down the line, was for the battalion to split up with every man to 'make his own way back'.[6] Gloster Hill was abandoned in minutes.[7] Able-bodied soldiers and walking wounded departed in groups. The Glosters had no option but to leave their wounded behind with their RMO, a medical sergeant and the battalion's chaplain.[8] 'The broad mass moving south-east through the valley immediately below Hill 235 [Gloster Hill] was halted by Chinese fire', wrote Farrar-Hockley. 'The great majority were captured at once; others were taken [prisoner] over the next few days.'[9] The Glosters lost 622 men through death, injury or being taken prisoner. Just forty of them made it to blocking positions further south.[10]

The remainder of 29 BCB withdrew under Chinese fire in what Hastings described as 'one long ambush'.[11] Fortunately, Centurion tank fire covered the withdrawal, and HQ 29 BCB and the Fusiliers, the Ulsters and the Belgians, made it out. 29 BCB's survivors reached safety behind the US 25th Regimental Combat Team's blocking positions.[12] The brigade had sustained 1091 casualties at the Battle of the Imjin River, more than half from the Glosters. Hastings wrote, '29 Brigade's battle is unlikely to find a place in any manual of military instruction, except as an example of how not to hold a difficult position'.[13] The fate of the Glosters was sealed when they had lost their cohesion to the point where their brigade commander could not support them, their commanding officer had no orders to give them, and there were too few able-bodied officers, NCOs and soldiers left to execute them if he had.

The credit?

Now to a discussion of giving credit where credit is due. The resistance of A and B companies overnight on 23–24 April, and D Company's defence of Hill 504 and achievement of a clean break, carrying its wounded, to become the last company to withdraw overnight on 24–25 April, testify to the grit of three company commanders of A, B and D companies,

their platoon commanders, section commanders and soldiers. It was an extraordinary tactical feat. O'Dowd and Gravener deserved credit. O'Dowd would have none of it, crediting success to the quality of 3 RAR's sections, the building blocks of infantry battalions. He said later that all reinforcements were ex-AIF men, making it challenging to select section commanders from such an experienced group of NCOs. All were in Korea, in

General James Van Fleet, Commander, US 8th Army, inspects members of 3 RAR while bestowing the Presidential Unit Citation to recognise the unit's action at Kapyong, Korea, 4 December 1952. (AWM 083857)

Major Jack Gerke of 3 RAR receives the Presidential Unit Citation emblem from General James Van Fleet, Commander, US 8th Army. Korea, 4 December 1952. (PHOTOGRAPHER: PHILLIP HOBSON, AWM HOBJ2713)

O'Dowd's words, 'for the sheer hell of fighting'.[14] In his summation, 'The diggers won the Battle of Kapyong ... there was nothing the officers could do. It was a matter of whether the diggers had the guts to go on with it or not. And they did'.[15] This assessment is only partially correct. It does not properly attribute the credit to himself and his fellow officers and the NCOs who led those diggers on the front line under fire.

Effective officers and NCOs were crucial to 3 RAR's performance at Kapyong. They made important decisions under the most testing and dangerous of circumstances, set an example of coolness under fire, maintained cohesion within their units, held their ground during attacks and withdrawal, and, when it was time to break from battle, brought their companies out safely, leaving no one behind. Still, their efforts would have amounted to little unless they led competent soldiers, imbued with self-confidence, courage and grit. That soldiers possessed these qualities was due in significant measure to the quality of their leaders over the previous months.

A gong gone wrong?

A week after the Battle of Kapyong, Lieutenant General Horace Robertson, the Australian Commander of BCOF, visited 3 RAR in a rear area. He was aware of the battle's strategic significance and took pride in the Australians' courageous performance. He pinned a Distinguished Service Order (DSO) medal on Bruce Ferguson's chest. Ironically, this medal had been sent to Robertson in anticipation of his presenting it to Charles Green on completion of his 12-month command period.[16] David Butler, who accompanied Robertson as his Aide de Camp, had carried the medal in his pocket. He commented to the author in 1992 that once the DSO was pinned to Ferguson's chest, the true story of 3 RAR's participation in the Battle of Kapyong could not be told. Alf Argent wrote 3 RAR's unit diary during the period covered in this book, often days after the events. It is unlikely he would have questioned Ferguson's interpretation of events at Kapyong. Bruce Ferguson donated his Korean War notebook to the Australian War Memorial, but there are no mentions of O'Dowd and no record of his withdrawal orders at Kapyong.[17]

Extracts of Ferguson's DSO citation confirm Butler's observation and testify to the initial success of a false narrative. The DSO citation promulgated in the London and Commonwealth of Australia gazettes less than a month after the battle reads in part:

> *... throughout the next day [24 April], when the full brunt of the Chinese attack fell upon his Battalion, he [Ferguson] remained master of the situation. He paid frequent visits to his forward Companies in a borrowed tank and inspired them to repel every effort to dislodge them and organised himself [sic] several telling counter attacks ... Late in the afternoon of 24 April, Lieutenant Colonel Ferguson was ordered to withdraw his Battalion to fresh positions. This movement was organised and conducted with such great skill by Lieutenant Colonel Ferguson that, although in contact with the enemy, it was effected with no casualties*

suffered at all ... Throughout the whole action, Lieutenant Colonel Ferguson displayed outstanding leadership.[18]

The errors in his DSO citation might have been overlooked if Ferguson had been generous enough to ensure others received their due credit when he directed either Alf Argent or Len Eyles to draft honours and awards citations and recommendations for him to review, sign and send up the chain of command in the weeks after the battle. Ferguson submitted recommendations for Lieutenant Len Montgomerie to receive a Military Cross for leadership of the attack on the Honeycomb and a stout defence against attacks on B Company overnight on 23–24 April. He also recommended his Adjutant, Captain Len Eyles, and Lieutenant Phil Bennett, the Mortar Platoon Commander, for a Mention in Despatches for courage under fire at Kapyong. The author could not find any record of him recommending any other 3 RAR officer for an award. The absence of any recommendation for an award to Ben O'Dowd and his silence or faint praise during interviews about O'Dowd's contribution over the coming decades testify to Ferguson's protection of his reputation at O'Dowd's expense.

Further exposition of the personal preferences and animosities, professional jealousies and careerism that worked against telling the truth about 3 RAR's participation in the Battle of Kapyong is unnecessary here. The Notes on Sources explain how the Army's and Official History's accounts evolved and were later corrected. This volume honours the battle's 75th Anniversary in 2026 with a truthful account. Hopefully, it affords those who fought there the recognition they earned and deserve. The lesson for the Army is to appoint historians to write operational histories soon after the events, when participants are available for interviews and records can be cross-checked with their recollections.

Ben O'Dowd did not die unrecognised. On Kapyong Day in April 1993, after the publication of the author's monograph on the Battle of Kapyong in 1992 acknowledged O'Dowd's role, the Chief of the General Staff (CGS), Lieutenant General John Grey, presented, through the Land Commander, Major General Peter Arnison, a CGS Commendation in front of 3 RAR on parade at Holsworthy military base. It read in part:

I commend you for continuing leadership and selfless devotion to duty and the leadership you displayed from 1951 into the 1990s ... [and for being] an outstanding commander whose actions were crucial for the success of the rearguard action of the 3rd Battalion.[19]

Ben O'Dowd died of pneumonia on 29 February 2012, aged 94, leaving his wife Marie, nine children – Patricia, Bernard, Cate, Brigid, Martin, Gabriel, Imelda, Rachel and Rebecca – eighteen grandchildren and four great-grandchildren. Several retired general officers attended his funeral. The Chief of the Army, Lieutenant General David Morrison, sent Brigadier John Frewen, Chief of Staff of Headquarters Forces Command and former 3 RAR company commander, to convey his and the Army's condolences to

THE KAPYONG BATTLEFIELD

ENDNOTES

CHAPTER 1

1 Horner and Bou (eds), *Duty First*, p. 1.

2 Ibid, p. 6.

3 Ibid, p. 8.

4 Ibid, p. 9.

5 Ibid, p. 44.

6 Ibid, Korea, Malayan Emergency, Malaysia (Konfrontasi and Butterworth Air Force base), Vietnam, Somalia, East Timor (Timor-Leste), Solomon Islands, Iraq and Afghanistan.

7 Ibid, pp. 48–9.

8 Argent, 'A Battalion Prepares for War', pp. 17–18.

9 O'Neill, *Australia in the Korean War*, Vol. 1, p. 37.

10 Ibid, pp. 36–7.

11 Ibid, p. 37.

12 Cumings, *The Korean War*, p. 11.

13 Ibid, p. 12.

14 O'Neill, *Australia in the Korean War*, Vol. 1.

15 Ibid, pp. 53–4.

16 Ibid, p. 34.

17 Ibid, pp. 63–4.

18 Ibid, pp. 37–8.

19 Ibid, p. 55.

20 O'Neill, *Australia in the Korean War*, Vol. 2, p. 8.

21 Ibid, pp. 8–9.

22 O'Neill, *Australia in the Korean War*, Vol. 1, p. 76.

23 Ibid.

24 Argent, 'A Battalion Prepares for War', pp. 19–20.

25 Ibid, pp. 80–1.

26 O'Neill, *Australia in the Korean War*, Vol. 2, p. 18

27 Beard, correspondence, 22 June 1992.

28 Gallaway, *Last Call of the Bugle*, pp. 13–14

29 O'Dowd, 'The Battle of Kapyong', p. 4.

30 Salmon, *Scorched Earth, Black Snow*, p. 56.

31 O'Dowd, 'The Battle of Kapyong', p. 92.

32 Ibid, p. 16. Salmon, *Scorched Earth, Black Snow*, p. 57.

33 O'Dowd, 'The Battle of Kapyong', p. 4.

34 Argent, 'A Battalion Prepares for War', p. 21.

35 O'Neill, *Australia in the Korean War*, Vol. 2, p. 17.

36 Daly, correspondence with Jack Gallaway.

37 O'Neill, *Australia in the Korean War*, Vol. 2, p.18.

38 Walsh, recorded testimony for Jack Gallaway, undated.

39 O'Neill, *Australia in the Korean War*, Vol. 2, pp. 17–18.

40 Ibid.

41 Dicker, 'My Korean Adventure, 1950'.

42 Horner and Bou, (eds), *Duty First*, p. 57.

43 Cumings, *The Korean War*, pp. 21–25.

[44] O'Neill, *Australia in the Korean War*, Vol. 2, p. 33. For a description of this battle, see Robert O'Neill, 'The Chongchon River', in Noble Frankland and Christopher Dowling, *Decisive Battles of the Twentieth Century*, Sidgwick and Jackson, London, 1976, pp. 289–303.

CHAPTER 2

[1] 27 BCB War Diary, October 1951, sheet 12.

[2] Ibid, sheet 15 and 3 RAR War Diary, entries 17–20 October 1951.

[3] 27 BCB War Diary, October 1951, sheet 20.

[4] O'Neill, *Australia in the Korean War*, Vol. 2, p. 34, 18 October, sweep through village of Samgapo (Enemy: five KIA and three POW without loss), pp. 35–7, 22 October, battle of the Apple Orchard (Enemy: 150 KIA, 239 POW, Australians: seven WIA), pp. 41–2, 25–26 October battle of the Broken Bridge (Enemy: over 100 KIA, 275 POW, Australians: eight KIA, twenty-two WIA), pp. 46–7, 28–9 October, battle at Chongju (Enemy: over 150 KIA, Australians: nine KIA and thirty WIA), pp. 50–1, on 30 October Lieutenant Colonel Green mortally wounded and died undergoing surgery on 1 November 1950.

[5] O'Dowd, interview with the author.

[6] Ibid.

[7] 3 RAR War Diary, entry 22 October 1951 and 27 BCB War Diary, October 1951, sheet 17.

[8] 27 BCB War Diary, October 1950, Appendix N.

[9] Horner and Bou (eds), *Duty First*, pp. 162–3.

[10] 3 RAR War Diary, entry 25 October 1951 and 27 BCB War Diary, October 1951, sheet 21.

[11] Ibid, entries 25–26 October and ibid, sheet 23.

[12] 3 RAR War Diary, entry 26 October 1951.

[13] 27 BCB War Diary, October 1951, sheet 23.

[14] Ibid, sheets 22–4 and 3 RAR War Diary, entry 26 October 1951.

[15] 3 RAR War Diary, entry 26 October 1951.

[16] 27 BCB War Diary, sheet 25.

[17] 3 RAR War Diary, entries 29–30 October 1951.

[18] Gallaway, *The Last Call of the Bugle*, pp. 91–2.

[19] 3 RAR War Diary, entries 29–30 October 1951.

[20] 27 BCB War Diary, October 1951, sheet 26–7 and 3 RAR War Diary, entries 29–30 October 1951.

[21] 27 BCB War Diary, October 1951, sheet 27–8.

[22] Ibid.

[23] 27 BCB War Diary, October 1951, sheet 28.

[24] 3 RAR War Diary, entry 30 October 1951.

[25] 3 RAR War Diary, entry 30 October 1951, entry 31 October 1951.

[26] Gallaway, *The Last Call of the Bugle*, p. 104.

[27] Walsh, recorded testimony for Jack Gallaway.

[28] Butler, Argent and Shelton, *The Fight Leaders*, p. 41

[29] Green, O, *The Name's still Charlie*, Chapter 9.

[30] Butler, Argent and Shelton, *The Fight Leaders*, p. 52.

[31] Ibid, p. 56.

[32] Argent, 'A Battalion Prepares for War', p. 21

[33] Ibid, p. 70.

[34] Andrew Salmon, *Scorched Earth, Black Snow*, p. 246.

[35] Ibid.

[36] O'Neill, *Australia in the Korean War*, Vol. 2, p. 53.

[37] Ibid.

[38] Ibid.

[39] Ibid.

40 3 RAR War Diary, entries 2 and 3 November 1951.

41 Gallaway, *The Last Call of the Bugle*, p. 109.

42 27 BCB War Diary, entry 2 November 1950, sheet 1.

43 O'Neill, *Australia in the Korean War*, Vol. 2, p. 56

44 Ibid, p. 61.

45 27 BCB War Diary, entry 4 November 1950, sheet 2.

46 Gallaway, *The Last Call of the Bugle*, p. 111.

47 Walsh, recorded testimony prepared for Jack Gallaway.

48 O'Neill, *Australia in the Korean War*, Vol. 2, p. 61.

49 27 BCB War Diary, entry 5 November 1950, Sheet 3 and O'Neill, *Australia in the Korean War*, Vol. 2, p. 62.

50 Salmon, *Scorched Earth, Black Snow*, p. 252.

51 Gallaway, *The Last Call of the Bugle*, p. 113.

52 The account of this attack is based on O'Dowd, *In Valiant Company*, pp. 18–19 that draws on Wilson, D, Brigadier, 'Attack at Pakchon', *Duty First*, Journal of the Royal Australian Regiment, Vol. 2, No. 5, Spring 1997 and Salmon, *Scorched Earth, Black Snow*.

53 O'Dowd, *In Valiant Company*, p. 18. Salmon, *Scorched Earth, Black Snow*, p. 252.

54 Salmon, *Scorched Earth, Black Snow*, p. 252.

55 O'Dowd, *In Valiant Company*, p. 19 and Salmon, *Scorched Earth, Black Snow*, p. 256.

56 O'Dowd, *In Valiant Company*, p. 19, Salmon, *Scorched Earth, Black Snow*, p. 256–8, Hall, correspondence with Jack Gallaway and O'Neill, *Australia in the Korean War*, Vol. 2, p. 62.

57 Charlesworth, correspondence with Jack Gallaway.

58 Hall, correspondence with Jack Gallaway.

59 O'Neill, *Australia in the Korean War*, Vol. 2, p. 62.

60 3 RAR War Diary, entry 5 November 1950, O'Dowd, *In Valiant Company*, p. 19 and Gallaway, *The Last Call of the Bugle*, p. 114.

61 Quoted from an unreferenced source in Salmon, *Scorched Earth, Black Snow*, p. 258.

62 Gallaway, *The Last Call of the Bugle*, p. 114.

63 Salmon, *Scorched Earth, Black Snow*, p. 258.

64 Ibid.

65 Gallaway, *The Last Call of the Bugle*, p. 114.

66 O'Dowd, *In Valiant Company*, p. 19. In 2003, Eric Larson's sister, Ruth, established the Lieutenant Eric Larson Memorial Travelling Scholarship at the Royal Military College Duntroon, to be awarded to broaden a young Australian Regular Army officer's education through travel overseas to visit sites of Australian battlefields and other places of historic military importance. The scholarship was awarded annually to an RMC graduate who, when a member of the Corps of Staff Cadets, was a determined and competent all-round performer throughout the RMC course, and who is judged to have strong potential to be a successful platoon commander or the equivalent in a combat arm of the Australian Regular Army. The Duntroon Society Newsletter, 'Commandant's Letter, Lieutenant Eric Larson Memorial Travelling Scholarship', 2/2003, Canberra, October 2003.

67 Gallaway, *The Last Call of the Bugle*, p. 115.

68 Walsh, recorded testimony prepared for Jack Gallaway.

69 Ibid.

70 O'Neill, *Australia in the Korean War*, Vol. 2, p. 62.

71 Walsh, recorded testimony prepared for Jack Gallaway.

72 Ibid.

73 Charlesworth, correspondence with Jack Gallaway.

74 Charlesworth, correspondence with Jack Gallaway.

75 Gallaway, *The Last Call of the Bugle*, p. 117.

76 Ibid.

77 O'Dowd, *In Valiant Company*, p. 21.

[78] Hall, correspondence with Jack Gallaway.

[79] O'Neill, *Australia in the Korean War*, Vol. 2, p. 63.

[80] Walsh, recorded testimony prepared for Jack Gallaway.

[81] O'Dowd, *In Valiant Company*, p. 21.

[82] Ibid, pp. 21–2.

[83] Quoted in Gallaway, *The Last Call of the Bugle*, p. 121.

[84] O'Dowd, *In Valiant Company*, p. 22.

[85] Walsh, recorded testimony prepared for Jack Gallaway.

[86] O'Dowd, *In Valiant Company*, pp. 22–3.

[87] Gallaway, *The Last Call of the Bugle*, p. 118.

[88] Ibid.

[89] Ibid, p. 120.

[90] Ibid, p. 118.

[91] Charlesworth, correspondence with Jack Gallaway.

[92] Gallaway, *The Last Call of the Bugle*, p. 118.

[93] Charlesworth, correspondence with Jack Gallaway.

[94] Ibid.

[95] Gallaway, *The Last Call of the Bugle,* p. 115.

[96] Hall, correspondence with Jack Gallaway.

[97] Charlesworth, correspondence with Jack Gallaway.

[98] Ibid.

[99] O'Dowd, *In Valiant Company*, p. 23.

[100] Ibid, p. 22.

[101] Ibid.

[102] O'Neill, *Australia in the Korean War*, Vol. 2, p. 63.

[103] Ibid.

[104] O'Dowd, *In Valiant Company*, p. 23.

[105] Hall, correspondence with Jack Gallaway.

[106] Ibid.

[107] Ibid.

[108] Charlesworth, correspondence with Jack Gallaway.

[109] Hall, correspondence with Jack Gallaway.

[110] Gallaway, *The Last Call of the Bugle*, pp.124–5.

[111] O'Neill, *Australia in the Korean War*, Vol. 2, p. 63.

[112] Australian casualty figures based on Gallaway, *The Last Call of the Bugle*, p. 125 and O'Neill, *Australia in the Korean War*, Vol. 2, p. 63 and Walsh, recorded testimony prepared for Jack Gallaway.

[113] Walsh, recorded testimony prepared for Jack Gallaway.

[114] Ibid.

[115] Gallaway, *The Last Call of the Bugle*, pp. 125–6.

[116] Ferguson, interview transcript by Kit Denton.

[117] O'Dowd, *In Valiant Company*, p. 37.

[118] Ibid.

[119] See Bob Breen, 'The Battle of Maryang San: 3rd Battalion, The Royal Australian Regiment, Korea, 2–8 October 1951', Headquarters Training Command, Sydney, 1992.

CHAPTER 3

[1] Beard, correspondence with the author.

[2] Ibid.

[3] A. Argent, 'Ferguson, Ian Bruce (1917–88)', *Australian Dictionary of Biography*, National Centre of Biography, Australian National University, 2007, https://adb.anu.edu.au/biography/ferguson-ian-bruce-12484 , accessed 13 February 2022, first published in *Australian Dictionary of Biography*, Volume 17, Melbourne University Press, 2007.

[4] O'Neill, *Australia in the Korean War*, Vol. 2, pp. 107–20.

[5] Ibid, pp. 120–1.

[6] Ibid.

[7] Ibid, p. 122.

[8] Ibid, p. 123.

[9] Ibid, p. 125.

[10] Ibid, p. 127.

[11] Ibid.

[12] Beard, correspondence with the author.

[13] AWM 85/4 3 Battalion, Royal Australian Regiment, entry 13 April 1951.

[14] Ibid.

[15] Headquarters 27 Infantry Brigade January–April 1951, sheet 4, April 1951.

[16] O'Neill, *Australia in the Korean War*, Vol. 2, p. 127.

[17] Headquarters 27 Infantry Brigade January–April 1951, sheet 5 and 6, April 1951.

[18] Ibid and O'Neill, *Australia in the Korean War*, Vol. 2, p. 127.

[19] Headquarters 27 Infantry Brigade January–April 1951, sheet 7, April 1951.

[20] 3 RAR War Diary entry, 14 April 1951 and O'Dowd, *In Valiant Company*, p. 146.

[21] Headquarters 27 Infantry Brigade January–April 1951, sheet 5 and 6, April 1951.

[22] O'Dowd, *In Valiant Company*, p. 146.

[23] O'Dowd, interview by the author and O'Dowd, *In Valiant Company*, p. 144, and 3 RAR Unit Diary, April 1951.

[24] Headquarters 27 Infantry Brigade January–April 1951, sheet 7, April 1951.

[25] O'Dowd, interview by the author and O'Dowd, *In Valiant Company*, p. 146, and O'Dowd, *In Valiant Company*, p.147.

[26] O'Dowd, *In Valiant Company*, p. 32.

[27] Ibid.

[28] O'Neill, *Australia in the Korean War*, Vol. 2, pp. 129–30.

[29] O'Dowd, *In Valiant Company*, p. 146.

[30] Bartlett, *With the Australians*, p. 91.

CHAPTER 4

[1] Ferguson, interview transcript.

[2] O'Dowd, interview by the author.

[3] O'Neill, *Australia in the Korean War*, Vol. 2, p. 131.

[4] Ibid, p. 132.

[5] Ibid.

[6] O'Dowd, correspondence with J Gallaway.

[7] O'Dowd, interview by the author.

[8] Farrar-Hockley, *The British Part of the Korean War*, Vol. II, p. 111.

[9] Ibid.

[10] Ibid, p.113.

[11] O'Neill, *Australia in the Korean War*, Vol. 2, p. 132.

[12] Hastings, *The Korean War*, p. 301.

[13] O'Neill, *Australia in the Korean War*, Vol. 2, p. 132 and Farrar-Hockley, *The British Part of the Korean War,* Vol. II, pp. 113–15.

[14] Hastings, *The Korean War*, p. 304.

[15] O'Neill, *Australia in the Korean War*, Vol. 2, p. 134.

[16] Farrar-Hockley, *The British Part of the Korean War*, Vol. II, p. 116.

[17] Farrar-Hockley, *The British Part of the Korean War*, Vol. II, p. 119.

[18] Hastings, *The Korean War*, p. 307.

[19] O'Neill, *Australia in the Korean War*, Vol. 2, pp. 132–3.

[20] O'Neill, *Australia in the Korean War*, Vol. 2, p. 133.

[21] Farrar-Hockley, *The British Part of the Korean War*, Vol. II, p. 118.

[22] Ibid, p. 120.

[23] Ibid, p. 122.

[24] Hastings, *The Korean War,* p. 314.

[25] Ibid, p. 134. O'Neill locates the 6th ROK Division 10–12 kilometres further north of where 27 BCB had handed over their defensive positions.

[26] Ibid. The book relies on Robert O'Neill's account of actions of the 6th ROK Division and 16th RNZA Regiment on 22–3 April 1951.

[27] Bartlett, *With the Australians*, p. 91 and O'Neill, *Australia in the Korean War*, Vol. 2, p.136.

[28] Ferguson, draft manuscript.

[29] Argent, correspondence with the author.

[30] O'Dowd, interview by the author.

[31] Beard, correspondence with author.

[32] Farrar-Hockley, *The British Part of the Korean War*, Vol. II, p. 117.

[33] Hastings, *The Korean War*, pp. 309–10.

[34] Ibid.

[35] Bartlett, *With the Australians*, pp. 91–2.

[36] 3 RAR War Diary entry, 23 April 1951.

[37] Ferguson, interview transcript.

[38] Ibid

[39] Ibid.

[40] Bartlett, *With the Australians*, p. 91.

[41] Raymond Norman Parry interviewed by Brad Manera, 4 February 2002 (AWM S02786).

[42] Ibid, interviewed by John Bannister, 5 January – 2 February 2005 (AWM S03749).

[43] Ibid, interviewed by John Bannister, 5 January – 2 February 2005 (AWM S03749).

[44] Ibid, interviewed by Brad Manera, 4 February 2002 (AWM S02786).

[45] 'Mentioned in Dispatches: Exploit with Commando Unit', *The West Australian* (Perth), 5 June 1943, p. 2.

[46] Saunders, Reginald, interview by Peter Read, typescript S520, Australian War Memorial, 1989, https://www.awm.gov.au/collection/C87890 accessed 26 September 2022.

[47] Lachlan Grant, 'The Fighting Gunditjmara', 3 July 2021, AWM website, https://www.awm.gov.au/articles/blog/the-fighting-gunditjmara

[48] Ibid, Tape 1, p. 4.

[49] Saunders, interview by Peter Read, Tape 1, transcript, p. 18.

[50] Ibid, Tape 2, transcript, p. 36.

[51] Ibid, Tape 3, transcript, p. 48.

[52] Ibid, Tape 3, transcript, p. 50.

[53] Australian War Memorial, 'Captain Reginald Walter 'Reg' Saunders', AWM website, https://www.awm.gov.au/collection/P11081121 accessed 2 October 2022.

[54] O'Dowd, interview by the author.

[55] Gravener, interview by the author.

[56] Ferguson, draft manuscript.

[57] Gerke, correspondence with Joe Vezgoff.

[58] Saunders, interview with Kit Denton.

[59] Ferguson, draft manuscript.

[60] Ferguson, interview transcript by Kit Denton.

[61] O'Neill, *Australia in the Korean War*, Vol. 2, p.138.

[62] Battalion Headquarters was comprised of fifty-two personnel (twenty signallers, three drivers, RSM and Regimental Police (five), Intelligence section and snipers (eight), RMO RAP staff and chaplains (eight), artillery and mortar fire control parties (six) CO and batman (two), Argent, correspondence with the author, 26 June 1992.

[63] Anon, 3rd Battalion, the Royal Australian Regiment, Personnel and Weapons available for Defence of BHQ.

[64] Argent, correspondence with the author, 26 June 1992.

[65] Bennett, correspondence with Jack Gallaway.

[66] Argent, correspondence with the author.

[67] Evans, correspondence with Jack Gallaway.

[68] Gallaway, correspondence with the author.

[69] Bennett, correspondence with Jack Gallaway.

[70] Gerke, correspondence with Joe Vezgoff.

[71] O'Neill, *Australia in the Korean War*, Vol. 2, p. 140.

[72] Ibid, p. 138.

[73] Brown, interview by the author.

[74] O'Dowd, interview by the author.

[75] Long, interview by the author.

[76] Bartlett, *With the Australians*, p. 93.

[77] Koch, correspondence with RF Stuart and O'Neill, *Australia in the Korean War*, Vol. 2, p. 138.

[78] Argent, 'Verbal Orders Issued Mon 23 Apr 51 by CO 3 RAR, at 1030hrs'.

[79] O'Dowd, interview by the author.

[80] Ibid, p. 137.

[81] O'Neill, *Australia in the Korean War*, Vol. 2, pp. 137–8.

CHAPTER 5

[1] Bartlett, *With the Australians*, p. 92.

[2] Ibid, pp. 92–3.

[3] O'Dowd, interview by the author.

[4] O'Dowd, interview by the author.

[5] O'Dowd, interview by the author.

[6] Bartlett, *With the Australians*, p. 94

[7] From, interview by the author.

[8] The author derived these views from interviews with Kapyong veterans in 1992 and subsequently in conversations at reunions.

[9] Ibid.

[10] Ibid, p. 58.

[11] Ibid, p. 85.

[12] Knowles, 'A Rifleman's View', p. 2.

[13] O'Neill, *Australia in the Korean War*, Vol. 2, pp. 144–5.

[14] Beard, correspondence with the author, 22 June 1992.

[15] Ferguson, interview transcript by Kit Denton.

[16] Gallaway, correspondence with Ben O'Dowd.

[17] Beeck, interview by Jack Gallaway.

[18] Ferguson, interview transcript by Kit Denton.

19 O'Dowd, *In Valiant Company*, p. 164

20 Laughlin, 'B Coy Report – Battle of Kapyong 23–24 Apr 51'.

21 O'Dowd, *In Valiant Company*, p. 165.

22 16th Field Regiment, RNZA, Commander's Diary entry, 23 April 1951.

23 Headquarters 27 Infantry Brigade January–April 1951, sheet 9, 23 April 1951

24 Gallaway, *The Last Call of the Bugle*, p. 295, specifies that LT Fielding died with his signaller Gunner Kemp. O'Dowd, *In Valiant Company*, p. 164, specifies LT Dennis Fielden was killed and one of his radio operators, probably Kemp, was killed and another, Gunner Mulligan, wounded.

25 O'Neill, *Australia in the Korean War*, Vol. 2, p. 145.

26 Koch, correspondence with RF Stuart.

27 O'Neill, *Australia in the Korean War*, Vol. 2, p. 141.

28 Miller, correspondence with RF Stuart, 6 December 1978.

29 Kealy, interview by the author.

30 O'Dowd, *In Valiant Company*, pp. 166–7.

31 Harris, interview by the author.

32 O'Dowd, *In Valiant Company*, p. 168.

33 Ibid.

34 Ibid.

35 Bombell, interview by Jack Gallaway.

36 Laughlin, 'B Coy Report – Battle of Kapyong 23–24 Apr 51'.

37 Headquarters 27 Infantry Brigade January–April 1951, sheet 9, 24 April 1951.

38 O'Dowd, interview by the author and Gravener, interview by the author.

39 Gallaway, correspondence with Ben O'Dowd.

40 Ferguson, interview by Kit Denton.

41 Eyles, L, telephone conversation with the author, 1992.

42 Argent, conversation with the author, 1992.

43 Gallaway, *The Last Call of the Bugle*, p. 253.

44 Argent, correspondence with the author, 26 June 1992.

45 Bartlett, *With the Australians*, p. 95.

46 Gallaway, correspondence with Mrs Taylor (Pte Goldsmith's widow).

47 Bennett, correspondence with Jack Gallaway.

48 O'Neill, *Australia in the Korean War*, Vol. 2, p. 144.

49 From, correspondence with Jack Gallaway and Evans, correspondence with Jack Gallaway.

50 Ferguson, interview by Kit Denton.

51 Headquarters 27 Infantry Brigade January–April 1951, sheet 9, 24 April 1951.

52 Beeck, interview by J Gallaway.

53 Argent, correspondence with author, 26 June 1992.

54 Spicer, correspondence with J. Stuart, 14 April 1992.

55 'Barry Reed, chairman of Austin Reed who brought dynamism and flared trousers,' obituary, *The Telegraph* (London), 5 November 2020, online edition.

56 Ibid.

57 Ibid.

58 Ibid.

59 Laughlin DP, 'B Coy Report – Battle of Kapyong 23–24 Apr 51'.

60 O'Dowd, interview by the author.

61 Ibid.

62 Ibid.

63 Hastings, *The Korean War*, p. 312.

CHAPTER 6

1 Beard, correspondence with Jack Gallaway.

2 Ferguson, draft manuscript and interview by Kit Denton expressing the same reasoning.

3 The 27 BCB Diary confirms communications from '3 RAR', probably from Ferguson using the Middlesex rear-link radio, 'at 0140 hours the CO of 3 RAR came up on the 1 MX [Middlesex] rear link set and gave a situation report'. 27 BCB Commander's Diary, sheet 9, 24 April 1951.

4 O'Neill, *Australia in the Korean War*, Vol. 2, pp. 145–6.

5 O'Dowd and Gravener, interviews by the author.

6 O'Neill, *Australia in the Korean War*, Vol. 2, p. 146.

7 Bennett, correspondence with Jack Gallaway, 14 May 1992.

8 Gerke. 'Battle of Kapyong – 23–24 Apr 51 – 3 BN RAR' and Gerke, correspondence with Joe Vezgoff.

9 O'Neill, *Australia in the Korean War*, Vol. 2, p. 148.

10 Gerke, correspondence with Joe Vezgoff.

11 Koch, correspondence with RF Stuart.

12 O'Neill, *Australia in the Korean War*, Vol. 2, p. 542.

13 Parker, correspondence with Jack Gallaway.

14 Ibid.

15 Ibid.

16 O'Neill, *Australia in the Korean War*, Vol. 2, p. 542.

17 Ibid, p. 544.

18 PJ Greville, 'Madden, Horace William (Slim) (1924–51)', *Australian Dictionary of Biography*, Vol. 15 (Melbourne University Press, 2000).

19 Ibid.

20 O'Dowd, interview by the author.

21 Ibid.

22 Harris, interview by the author and O'Dowd, *In Valiant Company*, p. 169.

23 Harris, interview by the author.

24 O'Dowd, interview by the author.

25 Long, interview by the author.

26 Ibid, pp. 170–1.

27 O'Dowd, interview by the author and O'Dowd, *In Valiant Company*, p. 173.

28 Ibid.

29 3 RAR Diary entry 24 April.

30 Laughlin, 'B Coy Report – Battle of Kapyong 23–24 Apr 51'.

31 Hatfield, interview by the author.

32 Saunders, interview by Kit Denton.

33 Miller, correspondence with RF Stuart.

34 O'Neill, *Australia in the Korean War*, Vol. 2, 149.

35 Ferguson, interview by Kit Denton.

36 Beard, correspondence with Jack Gallaway and O'Neill, *Australia in the Korean War*, Vol. 2, p. 151.

37 Ibid.

38 O'Dowd, *In Valiant Company*, p. 175.

39 Ibid, p. 176.

40 Ibid, p. 174.

41 Laughlin, 'B Coy Report – Battle of Kapyong 23–24 Apr 51'.

42 McGregor, telephone interview by the author.

43 Ibid.

[44] Ibid.

[45] Ibid.

[46] Ibid.

[47] O'Neill, *Australia in the Korean War*, Vol. 2, p. 149.

[48] McGregor, telephone interview by the author.

[49] Connelly, interview by the author.

[50] O'Neill, *Australia in the Korean War*, Vol. 2, p. 149.

[51] Long, interview by the author.

[52] Connelly, interview by the author.

[53] McGregor, telephone interview by the author.

[54] Laughlin, 'B Coy Report – Battle of Kapyong 23–24 Apr 51'.

[55] O'Neill, *Australia in the Korean War*, Vol. 2, pp. 149–50.

[56] Ferguson, draft manuscript.

[57] Miller, correspondence with RF Stuart.

[58] Argent, correspondence with Gallaway.

[59] Ibid.

[60] Gravener, interview by the author.

[61] O'Neill, *Australia in the Korean War*, Vol. 2, p. 151.

[62] Gravener, interview by the author.

[63] Gravener, 'D Coy in the Battle of Kapyong'.

[64] Ibid.

[65] Ibid.

[66] MacKenzie, interview by the author.

[67] Gravener, interview by the author.

[68] O'Neill, *Australia in the Korean War*, Vol. 2, p. 151, and Gravener, interview by the author.

[69] Gravener, interview by the author.

[70] O'Neill, *Australia in the Korean War*, Vol. 2, p. 152.

[71] Ibid.

[72] Ronald 'Ron' Dunque, Australians at War Film Archive, 10 May 2004 (UNSW, no.1987).

[73] Ibid.

[74] Ibid.

[75] Ibid.

[76] Ian R Finlayson, 'Rowlinson, William Josiah (1920–98)', *Australian Dictionary of Biography* (2024), accessed 8 October 2025 < https://adb.anu.edu.au/biography/rowlinson-william-josiah-33291/text41542>

[77] Ferguson, interview by Kit Denton (1986), Ferguson, draft manuscript, Ferguson, interview by Jeffery Grey (1986), and Ferguson, 'The Battle of Kapyong 23–24 Apr 51'.

[78] Billy C Mossman, *Ebb and Flow, November 1950 – July 1951*, United States Army in the Korean War Series, US Army Center of Military History, Washington DC, 1990, pp. 466–70.

[79] Farrar-Hockley, *The British Part of the Korean War*, Vol. II, pp. 126–7.

[80] Ibid, p. 127.

[81] Ibid, p. 128.

[82] Ibid, p. 130.

CHAPTER 7

[1] O'Neill, *Australia in the Korean War*, Vol. 2, p. 150.

[2] Ibid.

[3] Ferguson, interview by Kit Denton (1986), Ferguson, draft manuscript, Ferguson, interview by Jeffery Grey (1986), and Ferguson, 'The Battle of Kapyong 23–24 Apr 51'.

4 O'Dowd, interview by the author, Gravener, interview by the author and Saunders, interview by Kit Denton.

5 O'Dowd, interview by the author.

6 Gravener, interview by the author.

7 Saunders, interview by Kit Denton.

8 Argent, correspondence with Jack Gallaway.

9 Headquarters 27 Infantry Brigade January–April 1951, sheet 9, 24 April 1951.

10 Gerke, 'Battle of Kapyong – 23–24 Apr 51 – 3 BN RAR'.

11 O'Dowd, interview by the author.

12 O'Dowd, *In Valiant Company*, p. 179.

13 Headquarters 27 Infantry Brigade January–April 1951, sheet 10, 24 April 1951.

14 3 RAR Unit Diary, 24 April 1951.

15 O'Dowd, 'Kapyong from the Inside'.

16 Harris, interview by the author.

17 Ibid.

18 Gravener, interview by the author.

19 Ibid.

20 O'Neill, *Australia in the Korean War*, Vol. 2, p. 153.

21 MacKenzie, interview by the author.

22 3 RAR Unit Diary, 24 April 1951.

23 Dunque, interview by the author.

24 Conversations by the author with several Kapyong veterans.

25 Ibid, pp. 153–54.

26 Breen, *The Battle of Maryang San*, p. 25.

27 O'Dowd, interview by the author and O'Dowd, *In Valiant Company*, pp. 180–1.

28 Servos, interview by the author.

29 Knowles, interview by the author.

30 Ibid.

31 Ibid.

32 Ibid.

33 O'Dowd, interview by the author.

34 Gravener, interview by the author.

35 O'Dowd, interview by the author.

36 Ibid.

37 Ibid.

38 Gravener, interview by the author.

39 O'Neill, *Australia in the Korean War*, Vol. 2, p. 151.

40 Ibid, p. 161.

41 Ibid, p. 161.

CHAPTER 8

1 Jeffery Grey, *The Commonwealth armies and the Korean War: an alliance study*, Manchester University Press, 1988, p. 193.

2 O'Neill, *Australia in the Korean War*, Vol. 2, pp. 159–60, Herbert Fairlie Wood, *Strange Battleground: The Official History of the Canadian Army in Korea,* National Ministry for Defence, Ottawa, pp. 89–90.

3 Australian War Memorial, United States Presidential Unit Citation: 3rd Battalion, the Royal Australian Regiment, https://www.awm.gov.au/articles/encyclopedia/pow/korea/3rar_citation.

4 Obituary – Ben O'Dowd by Brigadier IRW Brumfield CBE DSO. Eulogy can be found on the RAR Association website rarnational.org.au Obituary – Ben O'Dowd https://rarnational.org.au/obituary-ben-odowd/

[5] Farrar-Hockley, *The British Part of the Korean War*, Vol. II, pp. 130–1.

[6] Ibid, p. 131.

[7] Hastings, *The Korean War*, p. 316.

[8] Farrar-Hockley, *The British Part of the Korean War*, Vol. II, p. 131.

[9] Ibid, p. 132.

[10] Farrar-Hockley, *The British Part of the Korean War*, Vol. II, pp. 135–36.

[11] Hastings, *The Korean War*, p. 316.

[12] Ibid, pp. 316–17.

[13] Ibid, p. 324.

[14] O'Dowd, interview by the author.

[15] O'Dowd, interview by the author.

[16] O'Neill, *Australia in the Korean War*, Vol. 2, p. 159.

[17] AWM C90022, Ferguson, Ian Bruce (Lieutenant Colonel) File 315 749/032/003 and 3DRL/6313 https://www.awm.gov.au/collection/C90022

[18] *The London Gazette*, 22 May 1951, p. 2817. Pos. 1 – promulgation of the DSO to LT-Col I.B. Ferguson (3 RAR) and *Commonwealth of Australia Gazette*, 22 June 1951. P. 1555, pos. 3

[19] Quoted verbatim in Rory Steele, Ben O'Dowd, *Hero of Kapyong*, Hesperian Press, Carlisle, WA, 2019, p. 169.

BIBLIOGRAPHY

COMMANDERS' DIARIES

27th British Commonwealth Brigade War Diary, 1–30 April 1951, 3 RAR Museum.

16 Field Regiment, Royal New Zealand Artillery War Diary, 1–30 April 1951, 3 RAR Museum.

3 RAR War Diary, 1–30 April 1951, 3 RAR Museum.

ARCHIVAL RECORDS – AUSTRALIAN WAR MEMORIAL

3DRL/6313, Ferguson, Ian Bruce (Lieutenant Colonel), private record, 1950–51.

AWM114, 665/7/1, Reports and comments on the Battle of Kapyong, 23–24 April 1951.

AWM192, 201, Box 193, Honours and Awards, post 1939–45 War (incl Korea): K–Z.

AWM192, 308, Box 18, Honours and Awards, post 1939–45 War (incl Korea): A–J.

AWM373, WO281/1232, Headquarters 27 Infantry Brigade, September–December 1950, Korean War Diaries.

AWM373, WO281/1233, Headquarters 27 Infantry Brigade, January – April 1951, Korean War Diaries.

AWM388, Papers of Colonel RJ (Bob) Breen, Army Operations Analyst, Land Headquarters, 1992–2002.

AWM85, Australian Army Unit War Diaries, Korea.

PR00466, Green, Charles Hercules (Lieutenant Colonel); Olwyn Green, private record, 1941–94.

PR01276, Dicker, MC 'Snow', 'My Korean adventure – 1950'.

PR83/154, Knowles, Patrick James (Lance Corporal), private record, c. 1980.

PR89/055, O'Dowd, Bernard Shelley (Lieutenant Colonel), private record, 1988, 1991.

RC11577.1293, Map of Kisan-Ni, Korea, US Army Map Service, 1945.

RC11577.1298, Map of Kap'yong, Korea, US Army Map Service, 1951.

OFFICIAL HISTORIES

Farrar-Hockley, Anthony. *An Honourable Discharge*. Vol. 2 of *The British Part of the Korean War*. HMSO Books, London, 1995.

Mossman, Billy C. *Ebb and Flow, November 1950 – July 1951*. United States Army in the Korean War Series, US Army Center of Military History, Washington DC, 1990.

O'Neill, Robert. *Strategy and Diplomacy*. Vol. 1 of *Australia in the Korean War, 1950–53*. Australian War Memorial and the Australian Publishing Service, Canberra, 1981.

——. *Combat Operations*. Vol. 2 of *Australia in the Korean War, 1950–53*. Australian War Memorial and the Australian Publishing Service, Canberra, 1985.

Wood, Herbert Fairlie. *Strange Battleground: Official History of the Canadian Army in Korea*. National Ministry for Defence, Ottawa, 1966.

BOOKS

Atkinson, James J. *The Kapyong Battalion*. NSW Military Historical Society, Sydney, 1977.

Bartlett, Norman. *With the Australians in Korea*. Australian War Memorial, Canberra, 1954.

Breen, Bob. *The Battle of Kapyong, 3rd Battalion, The Royal Australian Regiment (3 RAR), Korea, 23–24 April 1951*. Training Command, Georges Heights, 1992.

——. *The Battle of Maryang San, 3rd Battalion, The Royal Australian Regiment (3 RAR), Korea 2–8 October 1951*. (2nd ed), Training Command, Georges Heights, 1994.

Butler, DM, Argent, A and Shelton JJ. *The Fight Leaders: A study of Australian battlefield leadership: Green, Ferguson and Hassett, 3 RAR*. Australian Military History Publications, Loftus NSW, 2002.

Cumings, Bruce. *The Korean War: A history*. Modern Library Chronicles, No. 32, 2010.

Dear, ICB and MRD Foot (eds). *The Oxford Companion of World War II*. Online 2003, PBI.

Forbes, C. *The Korean War: Australia in the giant's playground*. Pan Macmillan, Sydney, 2000.

Gallaway, J. *The Last Call of the Bugle*. University of Queensland Press, Brisbane, 1994.

Gordon, H. *The Embarrassing Australian: the story of an Aboriginal Warrior*. Landsdowne Press, Melbourne, 1962.

Green, O. *The Name's Still Charlie*. University of Queensland Press, 1993.

Grey, J. *The Commonwealth Armies and the Korean War: An alliance study.* Manchester University Press, Manchester, 1988.

Hastings, M. *The Korean War.* Michael Joseph Publications, 1987.

——. *The Korean War.* Pan Military Classics, October 1988.

——. *The Korean War: An epic conflict.* 2020.

Horner, DM (ed). *Duty First: The Royal Australian Regiment in war and peace.* Allen and Unwin, Sydney, 1990.

—— and Jean Bou (eds). *Duty First: The history of the Royal Australian Regiment.* Allen and Unwin, Sydney, 2008.

——. *SAS: Phantoms of War: A history of the Australian Special Air Service.* Updated edition of *SAS: Phantoms of the Jungle*, Allen and Unwin, Sydney, 2009.

Odgers, G. *Remembering Korea: Australians in the war of 1950–1953.* Lansdowne Publishing, Naremburn, NSW, 2000.

O'Dowd, BS. *In Valiant Company.* University of Queensland Press, 2000.

Salmon, Andrew. *To the Last Round: The epic British stand on the Imjin River, 1951.* Aurum Press, London, 2009.

——. *Scorched Earth, Black Snow: Britain and Australia in the Korean War, 1950.* Aurum Press, London, 2011.

DOCUMENTARIES

Film Victoria. 'Heroes of the Forgotten War: The Battle of Kapyong', 2011.

Royal Military College, Duntroon. 'The Battle of Kapyong, Korea 23–24 April 1951'. Canberra, 1992.

JOURNAL ARTICLES

Argent, A. 'A Battalion Prepares for War'. *Australian Infantry*, 1972.

——. 'When Hopes were Dupes'. *Australian Infantry*, 1972.

——. 'Ferguson, Ian Bruce (1917–88)'. *Australian Dictionary of Biography*, National Centre of Biography, Australian National University, published first in hardcopy *Australian Dictionary of Biography*, Vol. 17, Melbourne University Press, Melbourne, 2007.

Editorial staff. 'Tanks in Defence in Korea – A detailed analysis of tank operations in Korea by the Chief of the Armoured Sect IX Corps'. *Australian Army Journal,* No. 31, December 1951.

——. 'The Battle of Kapyong'. *Australian Army Journal*, No. 59, April 1954.

Grant, Lachlan. 'The Fighting Gunditjmara', in 'Defending Country: Indigenous Service'. *Wartime,* Issue 76, Spring 2016.

Hopton, LI. 'Maintenance of the Australian Infantry Battalion in Korea'. *Australian Army Journal,* No. 25, June 1951.

O'Dowd, BS. 'The Battle of Kapyong: From the Inside'. *Duty First,* Winter 1990.

——. 'The Australian Battle of Kapyong: From the inside'. *Duty First*, Vol. 1, No. 4, 1992, pp. 41–51.

——. 'Charlie Green's Battle: The First 35 Days'. *Royal United Service Institute Bulletin*, No. 4, December 1999, pp. 13–20.

O'Neill, R. 'The Chongchon River'. Noble Frankland and Christopher Dowling, *Decisive Battles of the Twentieth Century*, Sidgwick and Jackson, London, 1976, pp. 289–303.

Pickett, GB. 'Tanks in Korea – A detailed analysis of tank operations in Korea by the Chief of the Armoured Sect IX Corps'. *Australian Army Journal*, No. 22, March 1951.

TRANSCRIPTS AND INTERVIEW NOTES

Ferguson, Lieutenant Colonel IB. Interview by Dr Jeffery Grey, 27 March 1984 (transcript). 3 RAR Museum.

——. Interview by Kit Denton, 1986 (transcript). 3 RAR Museum.

Laughlin, Darcy. 'B Coy Report – Battle of Kapyong 23–24 Apr 51'. 1992. 3 RAR Museum.

RECORDING

Walsh, Lieutenant Colonel FS. Recorded testimony for Jack Gallaway. 3 RAR Museum.

INTERVIEWS

Allon, Private J, and Geour, Private J, (Argylls). Telephone interview by Jack Gallaway. 3 RAR Museum.

Bandy, Sergeant RA. Interview by Bill Bunbury, undated. AWM S01903.

Beeck, Lance Corporal L. Interview by Jack Gallaway. 3 RAR Museum.

Bombell, Private S. Interview by the author, Canberra, 1992. AWM 388.
Boshamer, Lance Corporal C. Interview by Jack Gallaway. 3 RAR Museum.
Brown, Corporal W. Interview by Jack Gallaway. 3 RAR Museum.
Brown, Private GW. Interview by the author, Canberra, 1992. AWM 388.
Brumfield, Lieutenant IRW. Interview by the author, Canberra, 1992. AWM 388.
Connelly, Private SF. Interview by the author, Canberra, 1992. AWM 388.
______. Interview by Jack Gallaway. 3 RAR Museum.
Deed, Corporal R. Interview by Jack Gallaway. 3 RAR Museum.
Dunque, Private RE. Interview by the author, Canberra, 1992. AWM 388.
Evans, Lieutenant C. Interview by Jack Gallaway. 3 RAR Museum.
Ferguson, Lieutenant Colonel IB. Interview by Kit Denton, 1986. 3 RAR Museum.
Findlay, Temporary Sergeant R. Interview by the author, Canberra, 1992. AWM 388.
Fraser, Private G. Interview by Jack Gallaway. 3 RAR Museum.
From, Sergeant F. Interview by Jack Gallaway. 3 RAR Museum.
Gravener, Captain WN. Interview by the author, Canberra, 1992. AWM 388.
Harris, Sergeant GD. Interview by the author, Canberra, 1992. AWM 388.
——. Interview by Jack Gallaway. 3 RAR Museum.
Hatfield, Private KJ. Interview by the author, Canberra, 1992. AWM 388.
——. Interview by Jack Gallaway. 3 RAR Museum.
Holford, Lance Corporal JE. Interview by the author, Canberra, 1992. AWM 388.
Hollis, Private T. Interview by Jack Gallaway. 3 RAR Museum.
Jones, Sergeant J. Telephone interview by Jack Gallaway. 3 RAR Museum.
Kealy, Corporal C. Interview by Jack Gallaway. 3 RAR Museum.
Langdon, Private K. Interview by the author, Canberra, 1992. AWM 388.
Lawther, Private B. Interview by Jack Gallaway. 3 RAR Museum.
Learmonth, Private M. Interview by Jack Gallaway. 3 RAR Museum.
Lincoln, Private S. Interview by Jack Gallaway. 3 RAR Museum.
Long, Temporary Sergeant T. Interview by the author, Canberra, 1992. AWM 388.
McKenzie, Corporal RM. Interview by the author, Canberra, 1992. AWM 388.
O'Dowd, Lieutenant Colonel BS. AWM F04842.
Osbaldiston Private O. Interview by Jack Gallaway. 3 RAR Museum.
Portner, Private J. Interview by Jack Gallaway. 3 RAR Museum.
Rapley, Corporal R. Interview by Jack Gallaway. 3 RAR Museum.
Ryan, Captain MW. Interview by Jack Gallaway. 3 RAR Museum.
Saunders, Captain R. Interview by Kit Denton. 3 RAR Museum.
——. Interview by P Read. Typescript S520, Australian War Memorial, 1989.
Servos Private M. Interview by the author, Canberra, 1992. AWM 388.
Shields, Private JR. Interview by the author, Canberra, 1992. AWM 388.
Tampling, Temporary Sergeant NW. Interview by the author, Canberra, 1992. AWM 388.
Thorley, Private M. Interview by Jack Gallaway. 3 RAR Museum.

CORRESPONDENCE (3 RAR MUSEUM)

Beard, Captain DD. Correspondence with Kit Denton, 28 January 1987.
——. Correspondence with the author, 22 June 1992.
Bennett, Captain PH. Correspondence with Jack Gallaway, 14 May 1992.
——. Correspondence with Jack Gallaway, 2 June 1992.
Brain, H Herbert. Correspondence with the author, 20 January 2005 – 2 May 2006. AWM390, 1/8/36.

Charlesworth, Lieutenant N. Correspondence with Jack Gallaway, December 1992.

Connelly, Private SF. Correspondence with author, 5 March 1992.

Daly, Lieutenant Colonel TJ. Correspondence with Jack Gallaway, 1 July 1992.

Evans, Sergeant CB. Correspondence with Jack Gallaway, 14 June 1992.

Gallaway, Sergeant J. Correspondence with author, 23 May 1992.

———. Correspondence with KJ Hatfield, 27 February 1992.

———. Correspondence with Mrs Taylor (widow of Lance Corporal Bernie Goldsmith, KIA Kapyong), 13 February 1992.

———. Correspondence with Sir Phillip Bennett, 18 May 1992.

———. Correspondence with Sir Phillip Bennett, 27 April 1992.

———. Correspondence with William Keys, 15 February 1992.

Gerke, Major J. Correspondence with Joe Vezgoff, 10 July 1992.

Hall, Major CC. Correspondence with Jack Gallaway, 9 August 1992.

Hatfield, Corporal KJ. Correspondence with author, 29 February 1992.

———. Correspondence with Jack Gallaway, 25 February 1992.

Hayes, Private T. Correspondence with author, 26 February 1992.

Keys, Lieutenant W. Correspondence with Jack Gallaway, 10 February 1992.

Knowles, Private PJ. Correspondence with author, 20 February 1992.

Koch, Lieutenant KW (A Company, 72d Tank Battalion). Correspondence with RF Stuart, 12 October 1978.

McKenzie, Corporal RM. Correspondence with the author.

Mannett Lieutenant DJ. Correspondence with Jack Gallaway, 27 February 1992.

Miller, Lieutenant WD. Correspondence with RF Stuart, 6 December 1978 and 20 February 1979.

O'Dowd, Major BS, Correspondence with Jack Gallaway, 12 and 19 February, 11 March, 12 May, 22 June, 21 July, 3 and 24 August 1992.

———. Correspondence with the author, 13 and 26 February and 25 May 1992.

Shelton, Major J. Correspondence with Jack Gallaway, 12 August 1992.

Spicer, Private H, 1st Battalion, The Middlesex Regiment. Correspondence with editor. 3 RAR Association Journal, 14 April 1992.

Thorley, Private DFA. Correspondence with the author, February 1992.

Vezgoff, Temporary Corporal J. Correspondence with J Gallaway, undated.

———, Correspondence with the author, 21 January 1992.

Winter, Private FP. Correspondence with the author, undated.

OFFICIAL MILITARY SOURCE

The Nautical Almanac, Abridged for the Use of Seamen for the Year 1951. His Majesty's Stationery Office, London, 1950.

ARTICLES, ESSAYS AND PRESENTATION TRANSCRIPTS

Anon. 'A Coy 3 Bn RAR Battle of Kapyong'. Undated, (probably 1952). Note: Similar handwriting to Reg Saunders.

Anon. 'History of the 1st Battalion, 72d Armor'. US Archives, National Records Office, Suitland Maryland.

Chief of Army Field Forces. 'Tanks Above Kapyong'. *Combat Information Training Bulletin*, No. 2, 14 Mar 52 (US).

Ferguson IB, CO 3 RAR. 'The Battle of Kapyong 23–24 Apr 51'. (Note: Account written in 1953 after receiving Gerke's account and map traces).

Gerke, Captain (Temporary Major) J, OC HQ Coy. 'Battle of Kapyong: 23–24 Apr 51–3 BN RAR.' (Account written in 1952 and further notes attached in August 1953).

Gravener, WN. 'D Coy in the Battle of Kapyong'. Typed statement, undated, (probably 1952).

Laughlin DP. 'B Coy Report – Battle of Kapyong 23–24 Apr 51'. Undated, circa 1952.

McIntyre, Darryl. 'Saunders, Reginald Walter (Reg) (1920–90)'. *Australian Dictionary of Biography*, National Centre of Biography, Australian National University, published first in hardcopy 2012, Vol. 18; *Australian Dictionary of Biography*, Melbourne University Press, accessed online 24 April 2022.

O'Dowd, BS. 'The Battle of Kapyong: From the Inside'. Presentation to Brisbane United Service Institute, February 1991.

Saunders, RW. 'Report on the Battle of Kapyong C Coy 3 RAR 23–24 April 1951'. Handwritten statement, undated, circa 1952.

Stone, James R. 'The Battle of Kapyong'. No other reference information available, (probably an account by a Canadian author, published in Canada).

INDEX

A

B

D

H

I

J

K

L

M

N

O

V

W

Y